THE CHILD AS NATURAL PHENOMENOLOGIST

Northwestern University
Studies in Phenomenology
and
Existential Philosophy

Founding Editor †James M. Edie

General Editor Anthony J. Steinbock

Associate Editor John McCumber

THE CHILD AS NATURAL PHENOMENOLOGIST

Primal and Primary Experience in Merleau-Ponty's Psychology

Talia Welsh

Northwestern University Press
Evanston, Illinois

Northwestern University Press
www.nupress.northwestern.edu

Copyright © 2013 by Northwestern University Press. Published 2013. All rights reserved.

Printed in the United States of America

10 9 8 7 6 5 4 3 2 1

Library of Congress Cataloging-in-Publication Data

Welsh, Talia.
 The child as natural phenomenologist: primal and primary experience in Merleau-Ponty's psychology / Talia Welsh.
 p. cm. — (Northwestern University studies in phenomenology and existential philosophy)
 Includes bibliographical references and index.
 ISBN 978-0-8101-2880-4 (pbk. : alk. paper) — ISBN 978-0-8101-2881-1 (cloth : alk. paper)
 1. Merleau-Ponty, Maurice, 1908–1961. Psychologie et pédagogie de l'enfant. 2. Child Psychology. 3. Phenomenological psychology. I. Title. II. Series: Northwestern University studies in phenomenology and existential philosophy.
 BF721.W364 2013
 155.4—dc23
2012030084

⊚ The paper used in this publication meets the minimum requirements of the American National Standard for Information Sciences—Permanence of Paper for Printed Library Materials, ANSI Z39.48–1992.

For J. E. L.

Contents

	Preface	xi
	List of Abbreviations	xxiii
1	Early Work in Child Psychology	3
2	Phenomenology, Gestalt Theory, and Psychoanalysis	22
3	Syncretic Sociability and the Birth of the Self	45
4	Contemporary Research in Psychology and Phenomenology	72
5	Exploration and Learning	106
6	Culture, Development, and Gender	125
	Conclusion: An Incomparable Childhood	147
	Works Cited	153
	Index	161

Preface: A Philosopher Who Is Willing to Observe

Flannery O'Connor wrote, "The fact is that anybody who has survived his childhood has enough information about life to last him the rest of his days" (1969, 84). To begin a book asserting the relevance of childhood for our understanding of the human condition seems trite. Of course, childhood greatly shapes our adult experience of the world. One's situation at birth—genetic make-up, family, class, cultural milieu—initiates a history that one is compelled to continue. Rebellions will always be rebellions against the past; even if we define ourselves by rejecting the past, rebellions are inescapable. In adult life, childhood is present not only because it constitutes, for better or for worse, who we are, but also because we bring it forth in our interpersonal life. Our relationships are permeated by discussions about our own childhoods. We bond with new friendships comparing past humorous and sad stories. We relive our past with our own children, wondering if we should raise them differently than we were raised, wondering how much influence our behavior will have on them.

It is not just in our everyday life that we see a wealth of interest in childhood. The academic study of child psychology is so diverse and so specialized that no one person could hope to master the wealth of peer-reviewed articles and texts which concern themselves with the child. Yet, although childhood is evidently critical to our self-understanding, can we really speak meaningfully about the child's *experience*? I can only access my childhood self through memories of often questionable veracity. Since so much of how I view my childhood changes as my adult life transforms, it seems impossible to pronounce the truth of what my life was like when I was two, five, or ten years old. Any academic study of childhood would appear to be completely shut out from the child's experience. How can we say what the child, especially the preverbal or minimally verbal child, feels, thinks, desires, and knows?

This book approaches the child's experience through Maurice Merleau-Ponty's interdisciplinary work on child psychology. It acknowledges the difficulty of accessing the world of the child but encourages us to pursue a phenomenological approach to overcome these challenges and to resist objectifying the child. In so doing it finds that an examination of childhood sheds illuminative light on the nature of adult embodied experience. Our embodied existence is not a limitation to a scientific account of the human condition; it is its ground. In a 1948 radio address, Merleau-Ponty explains, "We can no longer flatter ourselves with the idea that, in science, the exercise of a pure and unsituated intellect can allow us to gain access to an object free of all human traces, just as God would see it" (2004, 44–45). The fact that we must begin with something as ambiguous and hard to quantify as "experience" should not strike us as unscientific but instead should cause us to avoid unquestioned faith in scientific "objectivity."

Our embodied experience has never been so well researched. Neurology, genetics, psychology, and psychiatry criticize our philosophical forefathers who so erroneously thought that the questions of the intellect were independent from questions of the all-too-human concerns of the physical-psychical being.* We know that our psychological and physical development conditions our later adult responses. As research in genetics has made us revisit and question assumptions regarding our freedom, the examination of our development calls into question if we can examine solely the adult to know the nature of motivation, character, freedom, and intersubjectivity. A study of human development helps outline the manifold influences that shape human experience, from the importance of physiology and psychology to culture, language, and the environment. To avoid the challenges that arise in any investigation of the child's experience, one could assume that the relevant aspects of it will reappear in the adult. Yet, while certainly the child lives on within the adult, the approach that addresses only adult experience fails to understand *how* the child lives on in the adult. A phenomenology—an exploration of the world of the child—is needed.

Merleau-Ponty's texts are rich with psychological, sociological, and anthropological references. His approach is strongly interdisciplinary and eclectic in his discussion of child experience, human development, social and cultural determination, and the role of scientific investigation. Such a diverse mixture of sources allows Merleau-Ponty to consider how cultural influences mark both childhood experience as well as our investigation of it. Psychology itself is not immune from cultural over-

---

* Three popular examples of this contemporary wave of texts wishing to dismantle dualist tendencies are Steven Pinker's *The Blank Slate* (2002), Antonio Damasio's *Descartes' Error: Emotion, Reason, and the Human Brain* (1994), and Richard Dawkins's *The Selfish Gene* (1976). A more phenomenologically orientated version of this trend can be found in Shaun Gallagher's *How the Body Shapes the Mind* (2005).

PREFACE

determination. Through describing his critique of cognitive psychology and his praise for Gestalt theory and psychoanalysis, this book addresses how Merleau-Ponty's work argues for the critical phenomenological importance of our earliest experiences. Because these experiences form the primordial, prehistorical ground upon which our later conscious, adult life is built, early life remains relevant both to our epistemology and our psychology.

Merleau-Ponty's phenomenological and psychological work is difficult to summarize given that he stands at the intersection of two traditions: phenomenology and postmodernism. One can portray Merleau-Ponty as the inheritor of Edmund Husserl's legacy. If we focus on his magnum opus, the *Phenomenology of Perception* (1945), we trace an original and fruitful investigation into the nature of perception. Merleau-Ponty extends Husserlian phenomenology by declaring that the phenomenological reduction is always incomplete. His innovative interdisciplinary approach utilizes various experimental studies and psychological theories. Whether Merleau-Ponty is conceived of as the continuation, via Husserl, of the Cartesian-Kantian tradition or as creating a serious alternative conception of phenomenology, this interpretative thread emphasizes his phenomenological leanings. Another branch of interpretation views Merleau-Ponty as the forefather of postmodernism, situating his posthumous masterpiece *The Visible and the Invisible* (1968), at the center. Merleau-Ponty's evocative notion of "flesh," his disintegration of the boundary between mind and body, as well as between body and world, clearly places him beyond the epistemological concerns of traditional phenomenology.

While his work has been inspirational for interdisciplinary research in embodiment theory, phenomenology, and the cognitive sciences, one aspect of his work that has received comparatively little attention in the secondary source literature is Merleau-Ponty's psychology of child development. After the explosion of work in psychology and psychoanalysis in the first half of the twentieth century, few thinkers today disagree with the importance of childhood for individual development. It is widely accepted that early childhood is decisively formative for the construction of an individual's subjectivity, and that traumas, injuries, or abuse in early childhood are generally more correlated with pathological behavior than traumas in subsequent adult life. However, does childhood experience have any larger philosophical significance? Given that the majority of the reception of Merleau-Ponty's work has been based on his philosophical texts, his psychology has been taken up only insofar as it provides examples for his main phenomenological theses about intersubjectivity and our embodied condition.

This book takes up Merleau-Ponty's child psychology to provide a concise account of his understanding of child development to expand current research and to illustrate why Merleau-Ponty's psychology is in itself a compelling and unique account of the human condition. To make the book accessible to those new to Merleau-Ponty as well as scholars from psychology, I have endeavored to write with a minimum of terminological jargon. *Child Psychology and Pedagogy: The Sorbonne Lectures 1949–1952* (2001; Eng. trans. 2010) is the main reference upon which this book draws. These lectures of Merleau-Ponty's are extensive—459 pages in English. They are a fertile and compelling mix of experimental work, field research, and theory. In any given lecture, Merleau-Ponty cites, analyzes, and critiques upward of twenty psychologists, anthropologists, neurologists, literary figures, and philosophers. The work of these figures is at times explained in great detail and at times passed over only with a surname. I have refrained from examining every reference Merleau-Ponty makes and focused on those that are most relevant to clarifying his own theory. When it helped elucidate a particular theme, I have cited some contemporary research. This text is the first book-length work on Merleau-Ponty's child psychology, and I anticipate that many of the fertile references in past and contemporary work will be later explored.

I focus on a central interpretation of Merleau-Ponty's child psychology: the concept that the child's experience is organized, socially interactive, and unique. Merleau-Ponty tries to balance work in anthropology and sociology with work in psychology and philosophy. In the former, research demonstrates the cultural locatedness of our conflicts between adults and children, our styles of upbringing, and our theories of childhood, whereas the latter tends to universalize the human experience to understand its basic nature. Merleau-Ponty illustrates how the child's experience is organized through his attention to Gestalt theory and experimental research. The idea of the child's experience as inherently socially interactive underlies the long history of intersubjective experience that precedes the more abstract intellectual forms that we find in classical psychological and philosophical accounts. The child is not internally preoccupied but engaged with the world as well as with other people. Children are active participants in their interpretations of the world not passive receivers of cultural information. And finally, the idea that childhood is unique highlights the critical part of Merleau-Ponty's charge to psychology that it must avoid reducing childhood in its attempts to understand childhood as the precursor to adult experience. Children are not minimal adults but beings with their own unique styles of interaction and understanding.

PREFACE

While Merleau-Ponty discusses child experience at various points through his work, the most extensive look at child psychology is in the lectures in child psychology and pedagogy at the Sorbonne. Merleau-Ponty published the *Phenomenology of Perception* in 1945. A few years later, in 1947, he published *Humanism and Terror*, and in 1948 *Sense and Non-Sense*. The following year, Merleau-Ponty joined the faculty of the Institute of Psychology at the Sorbonne where he lectured on developmental psychology and pedagogy until being appointed chair of philosophy at the Collège de France in 1952. He remained at the Collège de France until his early death in 1961. Jean Piaget would later have a position at the Sorbonne in child psychology, a figure whom Merleau-Ponty spent a good portion of the lectures criticizing. The position at the Sorbonne was not one where Merleau-Ponty was free to lecture on any topic he chose, as he was in his position at the Collège de France.* Rather, he was preparing psychology and pedagogy students for a battery of comprehensive exams.

Although other copies of lecture notes exist, the most authoritative and comprehensive version of student notes, approved by Merleau-Ponty himself, was compiled and appeared in the *Bulletin de psychologie* (formerly *Bulletin du groupe d'études de psychologie de l'université de Paris*) every few weeks from 1949 to 1952. In 1964 the *Bulletin de psychologie* gathered the notes and published them in full as *Merleau-Ponty à la Sorbonne: Résumé de ses cours établi par des étudiants et approuvé par lui-même*. This text was later acquired by Verdier, which came out with *Psychologie et pédagogie de l'enfant: Cours de Sorbonne 1949–1952* in 2001. The English translation of the entirety of these notes appeared in 2010 as *Child Psychology and Pedagogy: The Sorbonne Lectures 1949–1952*.

Complete English editions of the first and last lectures have previously appeared as *Consciousness and the Acquisition of Language* (1979) translated by Hugh J. Silverman and *The Experience of Others* (1982–83) translated by Fred Evans and Hugh J. Silverman. In addition, the text *The Primacy of Perception* contains two lectures: "The Child's Relations with Others" (1964a), translated by William Cobb, and "Phenomenology and the Sciences of Man" (1964c), translated by John Wild. The reader will note substantial differences between the lectures in *The Primacy of Perception* and those published in the 2010 *Child Psychology and Pedagogy: The Sorbonne Lectures 1949–1952* as "The Child's Relations with Others" and "Human Sciences and Phenomenology." Cobb and Wild based their translations on material provided by the Centre de Documentation Universitaire and not the material that appeared in the post-1964 French editions.

---

* A translation of Merleau-Ponty's course notes at the Collège de France can be found in Robert Vallier's 2003 translation: *Nature: Course Notes from the Collège de France*.

Even given the nature of his position at the Sorbonne as placing constraints on his lecture material, the lectures are relevant today for a number of reasons. First, they extend our scholarship on Merleau-Ponty and on postwar French psychology and philosophy. We find that Merleau-Ponty was the first to introduce a number of theorists to a French academic audience in these lecture notes. For instance, he was the first to discuss Jacques Lacan's family complexes theory as well as to lecture extensively on Melanie Klein. Merleau-Ponty also presents a unique reading of developmental psychology. Finally, Merleau-Ponty sketches a truly interdisciplinary study of philosophy, experimental psychology, field research, and clinical work. Merleau-Ponty truly engages with nonphilosophical work instead of searching for experiments that already support his theses. The French psychoanalyst Jean Laplanche praises Merleau-Ponty on just this account:

> My second digression is intended to point out how much we can learn from Merleau-Ponty's lecture notes [the Sorbonne lectures]. A philosopher who is willing to observe! A philosopher who is interested in clinical observation, in very concrete experiments involving children, and in the observations of an anthropologist. (1989, 92)

Given the rise of contemporary research in philosophy and the human sciences, Merleau-Ponty's lectures present an early method to emulate. Ever the phenomenologist, Merleau-Ponty engages with psychological work in a manner rarely reproduced since the Sorbonne lectures.

Psychological, anthropological, and historical approaches are integral because they address the subject's cognitive and physical development, as well as the nature of the subject's "interworldly" situation. In this light, the importance of developmental accounts of the subject provided by psychological studies is clear. Since our human condition is a historical and embodied condition, the origin of that condition—childhood—must be addressed. In particular, Merleau-Ponty is drawn toward positive accounts of childhood. Instead of imagining the child as an internally preoccupied being, Merleau-Ponty expands upon accounts where the child's behavior is a result of her immersion and connection to the world. The child's behavior is not simply caused by a set of chaotic internal impulses that are later mastered by the adult; she engages with the social environment. Admittedly, the child's engagement is not the self-conscious participation that we see in adult behavior, but it is the limit of our imagination to thereby conclude that the child's responses must be mere physiological reflexes or instinctual impulses.

Indebted to psychoanalytic theories of child development and Gestalt theory's concept of background experience, Merleau-Ponty focuses less on how pathology originates in childhood traumas and more on how childhood experience reveals an original meaningful experience that provides the grounding for adult experience and hence our continued investment in this often comparatively short period of our lives. In our everyday experience, we might assume that the child's understanding and organization of her experience is meaningful insofar as it approximates our own. Merleau-Ponty strives to appreciate the child on her own terms. He argues that the child's organization has its own forms that are, at times, even more engaged with direct experience than our more sophisticated ones. While he embraces the value of psychological, anthropological, and sociological research, Merleau-Ponty is critical of attempts to overgeneralize human development. One can see certain conflicts as universal (adult-child, male-female), but not the content or shape of those conflicts. His interest in contemporary experimental research leads us to examine some of his claims in light of the significant amount of research in early childhood development and work in gender studies since 1952. One finds that some of his claims need to be revised, in particular his idea that young infants cannot visually perceive, but I maintain that the Merleau-Ponty of the Sorbonne lectures would have remained current with trends in research and likely would have revised his own theories in line with contemporary phenomenologically motivated thought.

The Child as Natural Phenomenologist

The first chapter, "Early Work in Child Psychology," explores Merleau-Ponty's psychology prior to his position at the Sorbonne. Although the two texts relevant for a discussion of psychology, *The Structure of Behavior* and the *Phenomenology of Perception*, are not primarily concerned with early experience, they do lay out a vision of the child's experience that will remain largely consistent throughout his work. For Merleau-Ponty, the use of psychology is not meant to affirm its validity or worth over and above philosophy, but to indicate that if philosophy is serious in taking up the real, concrete, historical situation of humankind, it must begin with the living, situated subject. On this front, a properly conceived psychology and phenomenology converge. In these works, Merleau-Ponty develops the theory that we can understand child perception and behavior as both primary and primal in our everyday experience. Contrary to some accounts in scientific psychology, Merleau-Ponty views the child's world as organized and meaningful even if it is not structured the same as the adult's. This model works against the theory that the child lives in a state of affective and sensorial confusion. Merleau-Ponty also presents the initial lines of discussion about the nature of early social relations and the idea that without the child's unreflective sense of community with others we would be hard-pressed to explain the genesis of intersubjectivity.

Chapter 2, "Phenomenology, Gestalt Theory, and Psychoanalysis," begins the in-depth discussion of *Child Psychology and Pedagogy*. Merleau-Ponty works through the relationship between phenomenology and psychology and asserts that they can and should be interconnected enterprises to the same question of existence. Merleau-Ponty adopts an existentialist reading of the goals of phenomenology. While he acknowledges that Husserl's texts are split on this matter, he argues not only that psychology is capable of being parallel to phenomenology when properly executed, but also that phenomenology needs to remain in contact with empirical facts. A good psychologist would need to be careful to address the conditions of experience through detailed examinations of particular cases instead of assuming objectivity is discovered in a large study of many cases. In the latter, we are hard-pressed to justify our interpretations of these studies without acknowledging the way in which our own situation shapes the very nature of our inquiry. But likewise, the philosopher must be open to the observations and research of the human sciences because without such research she will find it difficult to fully describe the human condition. It is the human condition from which even the most abstract of philosophies finds its origin. Gestalt theory's notion of a background to our perceptual experience is co-opted into Merleau-Ponty's understanding of the child as living in a structured world. The child's world is primal, but that is not to say that it is chaotic and disorganized. While our adult experience leads us to consider child experience as more minimal and less developed than our own, Merleau-Ponty's view of the child suggests that she has a significantly different, not reduced, experience. Psychoanalysis is another main influence on Merleau-Ponty's theory of childhood. He redevelops the Freudian unconscious with the idea of ambivalence. Merleau-Ponty argues that ambivalence better captures how what influences us is not due to what is hidden from us, such as a deep unconscious, but instead what is on the very surface of our experience makes it difficult to objectify experience. We find pathology results not from secret drives but from incompatible structures of experience. In this chapter, we see that Merleau-Ponty revises these three theories from their more canonical forms and finds them compatible tools to help bring the child's world and human development to light.

Chapter 3, "Syncretic Sociability and the Birth of the Self," explores the thesis that our earliest life is social and shared, but not subjective. We witness intersubjective behavior in the infant; the infant is responsive and engaged. Instead of viewing this as evidence of a proto-self and other-awareness, Merleau-Ponty discusses the concept of a syncretic, transitive experience. This syncretic sociability fills out the concept of a background experience as explored in previous chapters. Instead of considering intersubjectivity as first requiring subjective awareness, this theory argues that social awareness precedes and underlies our sense of self-awareness. To explain the rise of self-awareness, Merleau-Ponty works with Henri Wallon and Jacques Lacan's theories regarding the mirror stage. The mirror stage initiates the child into understanding that her body is located somewhere and is an object for others. It initiates the child into being able to represent herself as one thing among many. Merleau-Ponty reiterates the importance of this stage, which brings the child out of her original, syncretic experience. In addition, he adds an important dimension to discussions about early self-awareness: the mirror stage is first and foremost about the *other's* mirror image. The infant first pays attention to the image of the parent in the mirror and then compares her image with this parental image. The mirror stage helps us learn about the comparative roles mediated by the two images—parent and child—and is not solely about individual self-recognition and consciousness. Merleau-Ponty describes the development of an ego as fragile and unstable due to the disjunction in experience the mirror image introduces and demands. The infant is caught between the image in the mirror—a unified, located body—and her primal expansive embodied condition. Original, primal experience does not encounter the world as a circumscribed, spatially localized body. The mirror stage causes a rift that can never be totally overcome between the "new" subjective life—a subject among other subjects—and the original syncretic life. The mirror stage confirms that syncretic sociability is never completely overcome by the advent of self-awareness.

Chapter 4, "Contemporary Research in Psychology and Phenomenology," asks if we need to revise Merleau-Ponty's conclusions about our early experience given contemporary research. Extensive research in early infant life has shown that the infant is not visually unaware and unable to imitate the other, but actually quite capable of controlling some gestures. This has led a number of researchers to propose that a primary intersubjectivity in infants exists and thus we come to the world with a primal sense of self- and other-awareness. First, we discuss the experimental research that is cited in claims of primary intersubjectivity—studies regarding neonatal and early imitation. These studies show that infants are capable of imitating facial gestures and we have good reason to suppose this is not an innate-releasing mechanism. The second section of the chapter explores a common interpretation of this research—that intersubjectivity is governed by a theory of mind. Theory of mind accounts argue that to explain imitation, we must assume that basic intersubjective behavior is based in the ability to "theorize" about the other's mental states. The third section explores experimental work that complicates a simple reading of neonatal imitation and two contemporary phenomenological writers—Shaun Gallagher and Beata Stawarska. Their texts present contemporary cases of interdisciplinary work in developmental psychology and phenomenology. Gallagher's interaction theory provides a better understanding of the nature of both human and infant intersubjectivity and a more fruitful way to connect studies on neonatal imitation with other developmental research. Stawarska's dialogical phenomenology exposes how our attention to studies of early infant imitation need to stress the "I-you" pre-linguistic communication in caregiver-infant interaction instead of a theory of minds or a phenomenology of subjectivity. While it still remains important to emphasize the uniqueness of early experience, Merleau-Ponty looks for a more social and less solipsistic description of development. I argue he would have likely followed such phenomenological interpretations of early infant experience given his strong interest in contemporary empirical research, but he still would have wished to preserve the concept of syncretic sociability to explain some aspects of our interactive social life that are not fully captured by intersubjective accounts.

Chapter 5, "Exploration and Learning," studies two examples of the child's perception and understanding of the world: drawing and explanations of magic tricks. In these examples, we see that children are naturally engaged with experience and will provide reasonable explanations for surprising phenomena if they are allowed to express themselves freely. Merleau-Ponty contradicts Jean Piaget's claim that the child is a natural metaphysician by portraying children more as natural phenomenologists. Merleau-Ponty lectures that researchers are often blind to their own metaphysical assumptions and assume that the fact the child does not share in them reveals that the child is less attentive to her perception. In Merleau-Ponty's view, the child has a natural engagement with her experience, one that the adult has latently. Merleau-Ponty is especially interested in providing a description of childhood experience that identifies it as coherent and rooted in the world. He contrasts this with theories which argue that children are prone to create fantasy worlds or have difficulty making sense of their perceptions. Hence, creative expres-

PREFACE

sion in children and adults can often be best understood as appealing to this more original form of experience, rather than toward fantastical mental creations. This chapter also explores Merleau-Ponty's estimation that the child's perception, and fundamentally our own, is synesthetic and that a closer examination of the child's perception is illuminating for our general philosophical conceptions about experience.

The last chapter, "Culture, Development, and Gender," addresses how Merleau-Ponty incorporates the influence of sociocultural norms and the path of physical development in his theory. The discussion of gender is particularly interesting when considering the intersection of biology and culture. Two examples in his work are explored: menstruation and pregnancy. The example of menstruation highlights how Merleau-Ponty does not think physical maturation equals psychological maturation. Psychological maturation can precede physical transformations or alternatively lag behind physical development. In addition, Merleau-Ponty discusses, with reference to Simone de Beauvoir, that in societies where women have few opportunities, such transformations can remain a source of ambivalence throughout the woman's life. The case of pregnancy explores how we cannot understand the development of the child without considering the mother's situation. We find that the mother's experience mirrors some of the language of syncretic sociability spoken of previously. Pregnancy is a prime example of the difficulty of understanding our experience in subject-centered terms. In conclusion, I address contemporary feminist scholarship on Merleau-Ponty and pregnant embodiment. Contemporary research discusses in greater depth the way in which pregnant experience challenges our understanding of a gender-neutral phenomenology, as well as drawing attention to the need to consider development before birth as well as after.

This text is designed to introduce Merleau-Ponty's child psychology and its philosophical implications to those in the social sciences who are interested in knowing more about what a phenomenological approach might contribute to theories of development and for those coming from philosophy interested in Merleau-Ponty's interdisciplinary work. Merleau-Ponty does not offer a comprehensive theory of development. The lack of a comprehensive system makes his psychology more open to revision based on ongoing research. This text connects Merleau-Ponty's discussion of the late 1940s and early 1950s with contemporary work demonstrating the living relevance of his discussion of child psychology. His reflections on the intersection of theory and praxis and his attention to particular examples do provide us with a style of interdisciplinary engagement that is desirable to emulate.

Merleau-Ponty affirms that the historically primary—our childhood experience—remains primal in our adult experience. The child is a natural phenomenologist in her intimate engagement with others and the world. Since the fracture between primordial and self-conscious experience is never resolved, adult experience is shot through with traces of nascent life. Any understanding of the human condition requires understanding the child's experience.

Abbreviations

Texts by Merleau-Ponty

CPP   *Child Psychology and Pedagogy: The Sorbonne Lectures 1949–1952.* Translated by Talia Welsh. Evanston, Ill.: Northwestern University Press, 2010. Originally published as *Psychologie et pedagogie de l'enfant: Cours de Sorbonne 1949–1952.* Paris: Verdier, 2001.

PP   *Phenomenology of Perception.* Translated by Colin Smith. London: Routledge, 1996. Originally published as *Phénoménologie de la perception.* Paris: Gallimard, 1945.

SB   *The Structure of Behavior.* Translated by Alden L. Fisher. Pittsburgh: Duquesne University Press, 1983. Originally published as *La Structure du comportement.* Paris: Presses Universitaires de France, 1942.

THE CHILD AS NATURAL PHENOMENOLOGIST

1

Early Work in Child Psychology

Merleau-Ponty's philosophical commitments make it difficult to easily situate him. He evidently is committed to Edmund Husserl and Martin Heidegger's work, but takes up a range of political inquiries and empirical research in the human sciences that are largely absent in their canonical philosophical texts. It is his inclusiveness that makes him a valuable source for a broad range of contemporary thinkers both in and outside of traditional philosophy. But this inclusiveness makes it difficult to view his works as producing a philosophical system. Or, to use phenomenological terms, it is difficult to perform a phenomenological reduction on Merleau-Ponty and to isolate the essential features of his philosophy. To eliminate the broad sweep of his interests eliminates Merleau-Ponty. This book addresses one area of focus often passed over in secondary source literature on Merleau-Ponty—his child psychology.

Merleau-Ponty's first published book, *The Structure of Behavior* (1942), has within it the beginnings of many of the authors and themes that would occupy him, at least in part, for the rest of his career: Gestalt theory, phenomenology, the connection between the sciences and philosophy, and the role of perceptual experience. Merleau-Ponty works to negotiate a meaningful way to see the connections between various disciplines—biology, psychology, philosophy—without falling into reductive and exclusionary practices and theories. In his second book, his magnum opus, the *Phenomenology of Perception* (1945), Merleau-Ponty continues his interest in empirical research, but more thoroughly criticizes the way in which our lived experience is ignored in philosophies that consider the body as nothing but a kind of transmission machine of data to consciousness. Instead, a careful investigation into experience, importantly perception, reveals that the nature of experience is itself the philosophical ground upon which all other theories, scientific or not, must find their footing.

Neither of these texts is primarily occupied with the child's experience or with child psychology. However, we do find some insights within them that tie both to Merleau-Ponty's larger philosophical interests and to his later discussion of child psychology in the Sorbonne lectures, which is the main focus of this book. This overview of Merleau-Ponty's discussion of the nature and relevance of the child's experience prior to his tenure as a professor of child psychology and pedagogy at the Sorbonne helps to position his discussion of child psychology. In this chapter, we find that the child's behavior indicates a structured, meaningful experience as our primary and primal connection to the world and others. Although Merleau-Ponty makes significant modifications upon this initial rough outline of the child's experience, his subsequent research remains largely sympathetic to these initial forays into the philosophy and psychology of early life.

Consciousness and Action

An astounding wealth of research in the fields of evolution, genetics, psychology, and physiology has sharply changed our view away from seeing the animal as a mechanical beast and the human as a rational agent ensouled within a brute physical body. Studies of animal behavior have become more nuanced, and as we understand the human animal better, we have also learned that animals are far more emotional, intelligent, and social than we previously thought. One trend in this post-Darwinian age is the knowledge not only that animals are our forefathers, but also that our early life is more akin to the social and communicative life of animals. Merleau-Ponty's early writings affirm the intelligent and responsive life of the animal, but assert that human life is, from infancy, unique in its mode of experiencing self and others.

The passages in *The Structure of Behavior* that do consider our earliest experience of life are notable for their clear rejection of the theory that early human experience is akin to animal life. Merleau-Ponty understands animal existence as intelligent and responsive. In his extensive consideration of nonhuman life in *The Structure of Behavior*, Merleau-Ponty contentiously avoids reducing the animal to merely an instinctual machine. Additionally, he argues against overvaluing the intellectual in humankind. Nonetheless, he does view human life as having unique characteristics that make our experience fundamentally different than that of animals. In this description, Merleau-Ponty begins to develop his own understanding of our experience and distinguishes himself from some of his contemporaries.

The question of the uniqueness of human consciousness was a part of a collection of debates that embroiled the beginning of the twentieth century in France. The division between science and philosophy had grown, forcing psychologists to claim their allegiance. Influential scientists and mathematicians such as Henri Poincaré (1854–1912) and Pierre Duhem (1861–1916) advocated for science as an independent study. In *Science and Method,* Poincaré argues for the objectivity of scientific investigation (1952, 16–20). For Poincaré, scientific truth does not necessarily stand upon a philosophical conception of truth. At the same time, strong components of spiritualism and idealism sought to undermine any claims science would make about its independence from the intellect. Philosophy itself was dominated by critical neo-Kantian philosophers, such as Léon Brunschvicg (1869–1944). Brunschvicg (1922) did not consider science the enemy of philosophy and admitted that exterior facts did intrude upon interior mental states, but he maintained the supremacy of philosophy on questions of validity and truth.

A philosopher who inspired much of twentieth-century French philosophy, Henri Bergson (1859–1941), is well known for his attempts to liberate human perception from the confines of intellectual, critical philosophy by viewing human experience as not a matter of a reified intellect possessed only by humans, but rather as a natural extension of humankind's instinctual relationship with the world. Merleau-Ponty sympathizes with the move away from critical philosophy and scientific psychology, but he does not tie human experience (the "human order" in *The Structure of Behavior*) too closely to the life of the nonhuman animal (the "vital order"). Contrasting himself with Bergson, Merleau-Ponty indicates that the human order is not merely a response to the same problems of reality that animals face.

Bergson writes that intelligence and instinct distinguish human and animal experience. Yet, fundamentally animals and humans use instinct and intelligence for the same purpose. He writes, "*Instinct and intelligence therefore represent two divergent solutions, equally fitting, of one and the same problem*" (1944, 158, italics original). To Bergson, instinct and intelligence both attempt to solve how materials are directed toward various aims. Intelligence must build upon the instinctual ability to take up objects in the world. "But, on the other hand, intelligence has even more need of instinct than instinct has of intelligence; for the power to give shape to crude matter involves already a superior degree of organization, a degree to which the animal could not have risen, save on the wings of instinct" (157). Even though the human situation is unique, it still remains an evolution from the instinctual level. The relationship to the world for animals and humans is a matter of degree, not of fundamental difference.

Merleau-Ponty argues against such an understanding of human existence and human behavior for it fails to note anything uniquely human and thus fails to provide any true definition. Bergson understands human action as "always vital action, that by which the organism maintains itself in existence. In the act of human work, in the intelligent construction of instruments, he sees only another manner of attaining the ends which instinct pursues in its way" (*SB* 163). By not acknowledging the uniqueness of consciousness, Bergson fails, in the end, to understand what is *human*. Bergson mechanizes human action by ignoring the intentional motivation for our actions and thereby passes over conscious activity. Intelligence becomes a merely complicated conduit for instinctually motivated action.

Rather, the human order must be defined by *consciousness*—"In the final analysis, consciousness is defined by the possession of an object of thought or by transparence to itself; action is defined by a series of events external to each other. They are juxtaposed; they are not tied together" (*SB* 164). Bergson was right to point out that empirical psychologies often take perception to be something that is "immediately contemplative, as if the primary attitude of man were that of a spectator" (164). However, Bergson fails to explain how human behavior could be an extension of vital action. The key is that human behavior requires consciousness, and Bergson's vitalism does not provide an explanation for what it means to be a being endowed with consciousness. While Bergson is correct to remind us of the place of the living, contextual situation, the uniqueness of human mental life and its connection to behavior is erased.

A human act, such as speech, has no inherent meaning. The articulation of sound is not speech without a connection to the "aims of life" (*SB* 163). I speak to communicate, to create, or to express. To understand my act of speaking, you must not just appeal to material concerns (the sounds I make, my physiology), but you must also, at least implicitly, attend to the point of what I am saying (my aims). Without intuiting the intention behind my speech, it would merely be sounds signifying nothing. In addition, you must have an organizing consciousness yourself to identify which sounds are important to focus on and which are not. My action requires consciousness as does the understanding of my action. My consciousness is intimately connected to my acts, and my acts, in return, inform my consciousness. Merleau-Ponty names this a dialectic following G. W. F. Hegel. We must see how the mind comes to life in action, not how action takes place without the mind. A tendency of materialist analyses is to try to reduce acts to their apparently material and external attributes. Figuring out the why behind an act, the causal chain of any action, thus becomes a material matter and not a mental one. Merleau-Ponty charges Bergson with erring on this materialist side, where action becomes thoroughly material and thus motorized and mechanized.

Merleau-Ponty notes that Bergson's tendencies are grounded in a long-standing problem for philosophy and psychology—how to connect consciousness with behavior. Traditionally philosophy and psychology are unable to explain the connection between individual existence, such as revealed in perception, and the action of that individual. Philosophy acknowledges that somehow they are linked, but it does not provide a way to understand that connection (*SB* 164). Consciousness is defined as the possession of a thought that is transparent, immediately revealed to the thinker. Action is defined as a set of external events. But the question for us remains, how are the external events enacted in action tied to the internal self-transparency of thoughts? A traditional division of labor might be to assign the psychologist the task of analyzing the meaning of the actions and the philosopher the task of determining the meaning of the thoughts, but since we assume that one not only affects but also is constituted and shaped by the other, this is an unappealing prospect. The dialectical approach Merleau-Ponty prefers presents a clear call to provide a structure in which these two interact without reducing one to the other. Merleau-Ponty argues for a third way, where an examination of behavior shows us the living conception of consciousness.

Nascent Perception

Merleau-Ponty suggests that infant perception reveals an original structure of perception that will later ground the more complex interactions between thought and action. What is missing from previous accounts, including Bergson's, is the idea of structure as providing a bridge between thought and action. He discusses the concept of structure, borrowed and refined from Gestalt theory as "the joining of an idea and an existence which are indiscernible, the contingent arrangement by which materials begin to have meaning in our presence, intelligibility in the nascent state" (*SB* 206–7). In bodily action, the mind is not using the body to achieve its ends. Instead, in action the mind realizes itself. Only through action does my consciousness take up its presence in the world. Merleau-Ponty describes his work on structures of behavior as elucidating how a mind "*comes into the world*" (*SB* 209, italics original). Our first behaviors, the first perceptions and their realizations, will provide the original structure of this dialectical engagement.

In our first experience of the world, we already find the normative structuring capacity that later permits the acquisition of cultural and abstract thoughts and beliefs. Merleau-Ponty claims that perception is dialectical for both children and adults. Children cannot be assumed to be more determined by material forces since this merely pushes off the question of the mental into the future. Merleau-Ponty argues that even infant perception is part of the human order and thus dialectical. No matter how ambiguous we assume infant perception to be, when an infant reacts to the perception of the mother consistently, the infant has perceived the mother *abstracted* from the environment. The infant has neither merely received a collection of visual sense-data, nor has she simply reacted to a contextual situation:

> Nascent perception has the double character of being directed toward human intentions rather than toward objects of nature of the pure qualities (hot, cold, white, black) of which they are supports, and of grasping them as experienced realities rather than as true objects. The representation of the objects of nature and of their qualities, the consciousness of truth, belong to a higher dialectic; and we will have to make them appear in the primitive life of consciousness which we are trying for the moment to describe. It is a known fact that infantile perception attaches itself first of all to faces and gestures, in particular to those of the mother.* (*SB* 166)

There is no doubt that scientific discourse "belongs to a higher dialectic" than that of the infant. The problem for Merleau-Ponty is to demonstrate *how* the ability for symbolization arises from nascent perception. He doesn't want symbolization, language, and subsequent scientific, philosophical, and cultural discourses to be miraculous creations ex nihilo from our animal natures. Here, and in all subsequent work, Merleau-Ponty finds the roots of our most abstract and intellectual capacities within basic human experience.

We witness in the infant's behavior with her mother this original ability to form a sense of the mother's intentions and not, as in animal life, to merely engage with the situation. In the above quotation, we can see that by "perception" Merleau-Ponty does not mean merely the stimulation of our visual system. Rather, it is a perception *of* the mother: the mother who is desired when she is absent, who comforts, who feeds. Perception is first and foremost *normative*, not just a physical capacity to visually focus on certain discrete objects. The mother is always already imbued with significance. The infant has a nascent Gestalt when she perceives her. Thus, the child's relations with the mother are never simply a set of instinctual responses to a situation.

The infant's structuring of her world is based upon more than an

---

* Merleau-Ponty cites Milicent Shinn (1893).

increasing set of motor skills; she places *value* upon certain external objects. Of course, an animal certainly shows preference for "good" over "bad" objects, but it, in Merleau-Ponty's conception, lacks the ability to identify "good" objects independently from the contextual background. We can say that animals experience positive or negative *situations*, whereas only humans can experience good or bad things or people.

Human faces are not just part of a situation in the child's world. The mother's face is the basis for the child's perceptual constitution of the world. Following and responding to the mother's own gaze becomes a way in which to monitor and structure new experiences. The child will bury her face in the parent's neck or legs when faced with something unpleasant as the primary method in which to remove herself from a difficult encounter. Much more than a vehicle for comfort and food, the parent's body is the site from which the child will learn to interact with the larger social world. Perception is both dialectical, in that it is originally about the other person's gaze and face, and also primarily normative, in that perceptions are first and foremost organized around values.

To speak of perception is to speak of an organization of experience that is not reducible to sensations. We cannot explain where the cause of the "sensation" is that causes a toddler to shyly bury her head in her father's legs when a stranger says hello without going far beyond the givens of the external world. Instead of concluding that secondary—that is, cultural and linguistic—forms of human life overlay a natural, animalistic manner of being-in-the-world, Merleau-Ponty writes that within the primary, "natural" world of infants one already finds the roots of the secondary. The child directs her attention toward her mother; she misses the mother in the parent's absence and scans her surroundings for the mother's return. The mother's reactions to others will provide clues for how the infant should interact with them, thus providing the child with immediate access to the social and linguistic world.

Merleau-Ponty's interest in the roots of an original structuring of the world began at least a decade before the publication of *The Structure of Behavior* in 1942. In 1933, at the age of twenty-five, he applied for, and received, a fellowship from the Caisse Nationale des Sciences while working at a lycée in Beauvais (Silverman and Barry 1996, xiv). Merleau-Ponty proposed to study the nature of perception in a manner that used Gestalt psychology and neurology to criticize the "critical," neo-Kantian school of philosophy (Geraets 1971, 6). During the year that he was awarded money to pursue his research project, Merleau-Ponty not only studied Gestalt psychology, experimental psychology, and neurology, but also began a serious examination of both child psychology and Edmund Husserl's phenomenology.

In his second proposal for a continuation of funding (he was denied), Merleau-Ponty begins to unite Gestalt theory and phenomenology as necessary to complement physiology and neurology. The facts of our physical nature must be accounted for. We must address the rich meaning perception gives our experience and thereby our behavior. Gestalt psychology is cited not just for its notion of form (as it was in the first proposal), but also for its notion of *organization* providing a new paradigm with which to understand perception. Gestalt psychologists, with particular focus on Wolfgang Köhler (for example, in Köhler's *Mentality of Apes*, 1956, and his *Selected Papers*, 1971), emphasize that not only is a particular perception an organization of disparate sensory givens, but that the subject adjusts her behavior in Gestalt-like structures to adapt to changing environmental or physical conditions. Once a chimpanzee discovers that a stick can be used to obtain food, it spontaneously restructures its behavior accordingly. In Merleau-Ponty's own thought, the use of the terms "coordination" and "organization" are later replaced by the superior notion of structure. Gestalt psychology demonstrates, in its studies of child perception, that children do not simply have inferior perceptual capacities to those of adults; instead, they possess different *forms* of perceptual organization—"The child's perception is nonetheless already organized, but in its own fashion" (Merleau-Ponty 1996a, 82). Development occurs not only by addition of new information, but also by reorganization. This idea coheres with Merleau-Ponty's developing thesis that perception is not about intellectual functions that "add" themselves to sense-data.

We often take the child's lack of participation in our much more abstract symbolic systems as a mark of the child's introversion. For instance, we assume that the child's lack of comprehending our standards of truth and falsity is proof that we are objectively engaging with the external world and that the child is more caught up in her internal desires. Citing Piaget, Merleau-Ponty notes that children do have an "egocentric" notion of the world. But this is not to say that they are less engaged with the world:

> If one says, for example, that the child's perception of the world is "egocentric," this is true enough, in the sense that the world of the child ignores the simplest criteria of objectivity of the adult. But precisely to be unacquainted with adult objectivity is not to live in oneself, it is to practice an unmeasured objectivity; the notion of egocentricity should not be allowed to suggest the old idea of a consciousness enclosed in "its states." (Merleau-Ponty 1996a, 82)

EARLY WORK IN CHILD PSYCHOLOGY

Merleau-Ponty wants to ensure that child consciousness is not understood as more internally preoccupied than adult consciousness. As he will continue to underline for the rest of his career when speaking about child psychology, the child is engaged in her world.

Child perception becomes increasingly important in Merleau-Ponty's thought because it suggests a manner by which to critique critical (neo-Kantian) philosophy's assumptions about meaningful perceptions. Young children are capable of perceiving and behaving meaningfully: as Max Wertheimer (1925) writes in "Über Gestalttheorie," physical and psychological development do not reveal that children deal with part sensations and adults with whole sensations. Rather, comprehension of a "part" of an experience (for instance, an isolated spot of color, a single sound) is something only adults are capable of under specific instructions. Children first perceive "wholes." Merleau-Ponty adds that childhood perception precedes intellectual distinctions such as objective and subjective. The egocentrism of children simply reflects the fact that they behave directly on the basis of their sense-experience with no conception that sense-experience is something that one possesses. There is no "subjective" state for children, as opposed to an "objective" world, because sense-experience simply *is* this phenomenal whole of which Köhler and Wertheimer speak. Perception is not part of the child, nor does it reflect part of the world. For the child, there is nothing but perception, nothing other than perception. Therefore, the child senses no "lack," no deficiency in her perceptions.

The child's experience is not only structured and organized, but also foundational. Although developmental psychology is a field with significant divisions, we have largely achieved consensus in the theory that our earliest years of life are grounding for our later life, even though most of our lives are typically passed as physically mature adults. Our childhoods disproportionately mold our lives despite their relative brevity. Merleau-Ponty took great interest in a variety of developmental theories during his later tenure at the Sorbonne.

One lasting influence was that of Aron Gurwitsch. Merleau-Ponty attended Gurwitsch's lectures at the Sorbonne in the 1930s. Gurwitsch influenced Merleau-Ponty's integration of psychology and philosophy and likely drew his attention to certain famous cases, such as that of the brain-damaged patient Schneider and the work of a variety of Gestalt thinkers such as Adhémar Gelb (1887–1936) and the neurologist Kurt Goldstein (1878–1965). Dermot Moran notes that often Gurwitsch and Ernst Cassirer are neglected influences from whom Merleau-Ponty drew much of his Hegelian-Husserlian approach to psychology (2000, 411–12).

Merleau-Ponty also draws heavily upon psychoanalytic theory throughout his written and lectured material on child psychology. Many elements of Sigmund Freud's theory of childhood development support Merleau-Ponty's own analysis. Freud conceives of childhood development as integrally connected to adult experience. Instead of viewing the child as an incomplete, yet-to-be-formed adult, Freudian theory emphasizes that it is the child's experience that determines later adult experience. *The Structure of Behavior* affirms Freud's child psychology while also incorporating a strong critique of Freud's energetic model as being too linear in its causality. To view early experience as complete in itself, Merleau-Ponty avoids causal language that sees the child as an object solely controlled by libidinal forces. Nonetheless, Merleau-Ponty does want to incorporate the concept that the "child is the master of the man." Hence, we can see that in *The Structure of Behavior*, Merleau-Ponty argues that the same Freudian conclusions can be found through "another language," one that does not need the energetic model:

> Without calling into question the role which Freud assigns to the erotic infrastructure and to social regulations, what we should like to ask is whether the conflicts themselves of which he speaks and the psychological mechanisms which he has described—the formation of complexes, repression, regression, resistance, transfer, compensation and sublimation—really require the system of causal notions by which he interprets them and which transforms the discoveries of psychoanalysis into a metaphysical theory of human existence. For it is easy to see that causal thinking is not indispensable here and that one can use another language. (*SB* 177)

Recalling his former critiques of scientific psychology, Merleau-Ponty is wary of attempts to reduce behavior to a set of laws, whether internally or externally motivated. Freudian theory can be seen to make the subject a passive puppet in the hands of instinctual forces.

It is always important to note that what is usually (such as in the Standard Edition) translated as "instinct" in English is actually the German term *Trieb*, which is better translated as "drive." Instinct (*Instinkt*) for Freud is similar to the lay sense of the term: something both animals and humans possess, whereas *Trieb* is something uniquely human. The term for *Trieb* in French is *pulsion*. However, Merleau-Ponty addresses summaries of Freudian theory prior to his lectures in child psychology and pedagogy and not Freud's texts themselves. Merleau-Ponty's early critique of Freud is an appropriation of Georges Politzer's interpretation of psychoanalysis in the *Critique des fondements de la psychologie*, in which Politzer heavily admonishes Freud's theory of instinct (Politzer 1968; Geraets 1971, 73).

Politzer takes issue with any attempt to "naturalize" human behavior, any attempt to make it a causal response to certain innate instincts. He proposes a new concrete psychology that would achieve the long-held dream of psychology: the status of an independent science. Politzer writes, like Merleau-Ponty, that classical psychology is lacking in its intellectual model (Politzer 1968, 77–109). Yet, objective psychology (scientific psychology) also fails to become an independent science. Politzer declares that the behaviorism of John Watson (which Merleau-Ponty critiqued earlier in *The Structure of Behavior*) is the most consequent of all objective psychologies. Watson achieves a psychology that truly parallels a natural science and by implication absolutely and without conditions rejects an interior life. However, Politzer notes that behaviorism logically excludes psychology as a *distinct* study: it saves objectivity, but it loses interior life. In rejecting the relevance of our subjective, "interior" states, behaviorism is no longer a study of the psyche. Through its strict method, behaviorism successfully becomes objective, but it collapses into merely another empirical science. As such, behaviorism fails to capture the human element of human experience and thus misses the goal of any human psychology.

Psychoanalysis, on the other hand, does not lose its independence from other sciences, but it is unable to reconcile theory with concrete application. Politzer's conclusion is that a proper psychology would cease to be occupied with given perceptions and instead would concern itself with "*a conscious act of a more abstract structure than simple perception*" (Politzer 1968, 247, italics original). At first, Merleau-Ponty's own structural approach mirrors Politzer's critique of Freud. However, as *The Structure of Behavior* progresses, Merleau-Ponty's idea of perception becomes anything but simple and straightforward. Instead, he combines a Politzerian critique of Freud with a "dialectical" understanding of perception to argue that one finds structure *within* perception itself.

According to Merleau-Ponty, Freud claims that instincts "cause" behavior. Instincts are innate motors of activity that make the subject act, on occasion even against the subject's wishes. Merleau-Ponty goes to great lengths to argue that behavior cannot be understood as action caused by internal forces. Such a conception fails to integrate the subject as *interacting* with the world and makes the subject an automaton: "The complex is not like a thing which would subsist deep within us and produce its effects on the surface from time to time" (*SB* 178). Any behavior must be understood in the entirety of the subject's own consciousness and the dialectic between the subject and others.

Merleau-Ponty claims that to understand the psychological reasons behind human behavior, one must address the general structure the subject exhibits in her behavior. The subject has a certain structure (or, as he will later say, "style") of behavior. Abnormal and pathological behaviors reveal a restructuration, usually not a successful one, of the subject's behavior due to a psychological or physical injury. Because they focus on the accomplishment or non-accomplishment of isolated acts, many psychological models pass over the complex manner in which behavior reveals a manner of being-in-the-world. Pathological behavior does not just result in particular abnormal reactions. Rather, it affects a disturbance in an entire mode of being-in-the-world.

Influenced by the work of the Gestalt psychologist Kurt Goldstein and Politzer's work, Merleau-Ponty forms a developmental model of normal and abnormal structuration. Merleau-Ponty was influenced by Goldstein's critique of traditional Gestalt theory. Goldstein's more holistic psychology is best explicated in his 1934 book *Der Aufbau des Organismus,* which soon appeared in English as *The Organism* (1939, republished 1995). Therein Goldstein argues for an integrative approach to the organism that takes into account its physical nature, its environment, and its ability to adapt. Goldstein also argues for a mind-body unity, a theme that becomes increasingly important for Merleau-Ponty's conception of embodiment. Goldstein writes: "Neither of the two [mind and body] realms can be regarded a priori as dominating and determining the other, leaving to it, at best, a modifying influence. The mind must no more be regarded as the sole expression and the real nature of the living organism than the body" (Goldstein 1995, 263).

Normal structuration means a harmonious interaction, or dialectic, between the individual, naturally perceiving subject and the symbolic, intersubjective social order. Since the perceiving infant is always-already within this dialectic, she is always-already participating in a structure. However, structuration does not remain static for adults, and it certainly does not for infants. Childhood development is a progressive incorporation of new experiences into the symbolic order. Adult experience requires that new experiences be likewise integrated. Freudian theory is successful insofar as it lays out a framework in which to understand why the past must be successfully integrated into the present. When a break occurs between present and past experience (for example, when a traumatic memory causes disharmony with present experience), pathology ensues:

> Development should be considered, not as the fixation of a given force on outside objects which are also given, but as a progressive and discontinuous structuration (*Gestaltung, Neugestaltung*) of behavior (Goldstein

> 1995, 326). Normal structuration is one which reorganizes conduct in depth in such a way that infantile attitudes no longer have a place or meaning in the new attitude; it would result in perfectly integrated behavior, each moment of which would be internally linked with the whole. (*SB* 177–78)

Repression occurs when the integration of past experiences is so disharmonious that the subject is unable to unify it with present experience. Since it is impossible to remove oneself from one's situation, abnormality ensues.

As an aside, we might draw out the following example to illustrate what would differentiate this model of normal and abnormal behavior from a standard analysis of abnormality. Since the focus is upon behavior and not isolating particular pathological symptoms, we could envision two worlds wherein the same deaf individual would and would not be received as deficient. If the deaf person lived in a world where no stigma or limitations existed in the cultural milieu, no deficiency would exist in his behavior. In the world where deafness was coded as a serious liability, deficiencies would exist because his behavior as human, and thus symbolic, would be affected. This is not to disagree that being able to hear affords one certain possibilities, but so would being able to fly unassisted or being able to see through brick walls. Since I do not perceive those physical limitations as indicating infirmity, why deafness? It is because our culture has certain *standards* of normal and abnormal behavior. What Merleau-Ponty's model offers is a manner in which to focus on the activity of the individual as part of this human order, including its cultural norms.

Development

Merleau-Ponty argues that development is a progressive series of new structurations and that no single path of development exists. Depending upon the individual's personal experiences, physiology, and her environment, development will be unique. The concept of a necessary level of organization remains unchanged, but Merleau-Ponty has inserted a path that leads to understanding development's interplay with culture, history, and individual upbringing, thereby providing various manners in which to understand pathological behavior. Pathology might be the result of a physiological abnormality, but it also might be the result of unintegrated cultural impositions or experiences unique to the individual.

Yet, Merleau-Ponty's notion of harmonious development, through "a progressive and discontinuous structuration" that would result in "perfectly integrated behavior," does not lead one to assume that nascent perception is especially relevant at all (*SB* 177–78). Since adult life is usually longer than childhood, subjects progressively would replace the infantile states of perception with new experiences and childhood experiences would progressively become irrelevant. To justify the persistence of childhood, Merleau-Ponty links traumatic memories with childhood experience and suggests that when new experiences are threatening one's current order, one either learns to address the old trauma, or one returns to a childhood manner of structuration. Childhood perception is thus the ur-Gestalt of all perceptual experience.

Pathological behavior occurs when a traumatic experience leaves the individual incapable of integration. In reaction, consciousness returns to an earlier infantile state. As the first manner in which the infant perceives the world, the structure of childhood perception operates as a "last resort" for a troubled psyche. Traumatic memories struggle to find a harmonious place of integration within the structures of perception and thus continue to disturb the individual long after the experience occurred. In this sense, past experiences constitute present experiences: "For life, as for the mind, there is no past which is absolutely past; 'the moments which the mind seems to have behind it are also borne in its present depths'" (*SB* 207).* We can conclude that childhood traumas are much more disturbing than adult traumas because they have hindered an original harmonious structuration. Childhood traumas make the possibility of finding peace (even if the price of psychological comfort is pathology) challenging because the original structure is unstable. Therefore, infantile consciousness and infantile modes of structuration remain a type of original template upon which all subsequent experiences are laid. In the healthy individual, infantile structures of organizing the world lose their importance over time, but in the traumatized individual, infantile modes of structuring the world show their presence more forcefully given that they are constantly revisited.

While the *Phenomenology of Perception* is largely unconcerned with development or child psychology, Merleau-Ponty does occasionally appeal to childhood experience as revelatory for our understanding of perception's grounding role in all future scientific and philosophical inquiries. The moment of birth also provides a parallel to understanding how an individual transforms the situation; she does not just appear within a

---

* Here he paraphrases Hegel's 1853 *Vorlesungen über die Philosophie der Geschichte,* which appears in English as *Reason in History* (1953).

situation and is shaped by it; rather, the environment itself is transformed around not only the actuality of the child's birth, but also the anticipation and investments that go beyond the child's physical presence. Post-birth, the child's naive interactions with others are not read as simply immature, but as demonstrating how an intersubjective world is not just first initiated, but actually possible. Our earliest experiences with others demonstrate the non-intellectual, shared lifeworld and move Merleau-Ponty's thinking more away from the stage-theory of Piaget.

Later in the *Phenomenology of Perception,* Merleau-Ponty elegantly writes that "my first perception, along with the horizons which surrounded it, is an ever-present event, an unforgettable tradition; even as a thinking subject, I still am that first perception, the continuation of that same life inaugurated by it" (*PP* 407). In terms of *The Structure of Behavior,* the first mode of structuration is the beginning of not just an intellectual, cognitive capacity, but the beginning of meaningful lived experience. Merleau-Ponty continues his positive appraisal of the child's experience in the *Phenomenology of Perception,* but he appears less content with the idea that the introduction of a child into the symbolic community somehow initiates the perceived object's being now understood by the child. We could argue that it is only when we are incorporated into our system of signs that things achieve a meaningful existence. Prior to receiving these cultural significations, we exist in a floating, meaningless flux of experience. In other words, all meaning is carried within language. Without language, we cannot organize our sense-data meaningfully.

Speech complicates such a picture. In speaking, I do not just "tap into" a symbolic system like that of language, but I am creating the very embodiment of language. Speech is not a conduit for the child to access a preexisting transcendental world of thought; rather "speech, in the speaker, does not translate ready-made thought, but accomplishes it" (*PP* 178). If speech merely opened the door to ready-made thought, learning would be instantaneous or impossible. Two states would exist: the state of having access to thought and the state of being pre-linguistic. "The fact is that we have the power to understand over and above what we may have spontaneously thought" (ibid.). This conception of spoken language as a bodily, living experience that holds its own meaning rather than its meaning being "somewhere else" also entails that children are not excluded from the meaningfulness of speech. Children possess meanings that extend beyond our own, even when they are not masters of a particular language.

How we structure our early experience is admittedly pre-linguistic as well as prescientific. We haven't yet learned how to use the world of symbolized objects in language or, in the language of science, to achieve an objective stance from them. As children, we cannot abstract ourselves from our immediate situation; thus we appear egocentric, naive, and unsophisticated. We have not yet integrated the scientific understanding that separates our experience of something from the qualities of the thing itself. For instance, in dreaming, children don't assume that the dream in contrast to waking reality is not real. They haven't yet learned to assume their intimate experiences are "unreal" whereas extended matter is "real." "The child attributes his dreams, no less than his perceptions, to the world; he believes that the dream is enacted in his room, at the foot of his bed, the sole difference from perception being that the dream is visible to sleepers alone" (*PP* 343). Children simply haven't yet learned adult conventions of dividing the extended world into parts with laws that govern those parts and excluding our experiential states from this objective discussion.

Merleau-Ponty describes how in everyday perception, the child experiences a sense of absoluteness, a kind of perspective-free perception. The child appears egocentric because she does not understand there are points of view at all. When we call an adult egocentric, we assume she could be otherwise; she is being self-centered instead of other-centered. But children do not reject the other's point of view in favor of their own; they are unaware of their perspective. Merleau-Ponty writes how for the child "men are empty heads turned toward one single, self-evident world where everything takes place, even dreams, which are, he thinks, in his room, and even thinking, since it is not distinct from words" (*PP* 355). The child's egocentrism reflects her inability to consider that there is something other than this experience. Experience is not yet owned by an individual, it simply is. This leads the child to provide what we clearly consider nonmaterial states of being with a kind of material existence, including the gaze of the other: "Others are for him so many gazes which inspect things, and have an almost material existence, so much so that the child wonders how these gazes avoid being broken as they meet" (*PP* 355). There is a true naiveté in this childish way of seeing the world, and obviously many philosophical questions cannot be approached with the view that people have "empty heads." Nonetheless, Merleau-Ponty notes that in our drive to provide a scientific lens through which we see the world, to fully externalize and objectify the "outer" things (objects) and fully psychologize and internalize the "inner" things (thoughts, perceptions, emotions), we miss the truth of the child's unsophisticated view. We are not empty heads turned toward a self-evident world, nor are we isolated within our heads only able to peer out of our eyes and dissect what is before us.

The child's perspectiveless perspective is not simply an indication of a lack of mature intellectual ability. Instead, the idea that the world is and we are intimately immersed in it and not casual observers locked inside our minds is required for real intersubjective experience. If it were the case that I was firmly convinced that your perspective and mine could be radically different, so different that no amount of discussion or negotiation would make a bridge between them, then it would seem pointless to even try to interact. It would be equivalent to interacting with a bat, to use Thomas Nagel's (1974) famous example. Instead we first find ourselves sharing a common view and later are educated to divvy up our internal states as owned and external things as shared. The child's egocentric view is also paradoxically intersubjective in that the world setting is assumed for all. Piaget takes this as proof of the child's intellectual immaturity, but Merleau-Ponty notes that without this primary view it is hard to explain the naturalness of intersubjective life for children. "But, in reality, it must be the case that the child's outlook is in some way vindicated against the adult's and against Piaget, and that the unsophisticated way of thinking of our earliest years remains as an indispensable acquisition underlying that of maturity, if there is to be for the adult one single intersubjective world" (*PP* 355). Reversing the traditional notion that children are more isolated within their subjective experience and that objectivity frees us from such immaturity, Merleau-Ponty draws our attention to how children's perspectives are in certain respects more open to intersubjective life than closed.

In his famous discussion of perception, Merleau-Ponty writes that in adult experience, we find the continued presence of our earliest mode of experience. The child's belief that dreams are as real as waking states continues in adult hallucinations and even our normal imagination. We find in imagination and hallucination "our bewildering proximity [*voisinage vertigineux*] to the whole of being in syncretic experience" (*PP* 343). Merleau-Ponty continues to discuss how hallucinations are not discovered by insisting upon the apodictic certainty of perception. Perception always entails a place within a proximity to the imagined and the hallucinatory as well as to the nonperceived. Another solution would be to retain the "scientific" status of perception by discussing it as revealing the possible and the probable, hence distinguishing it again from hallucinations. Merleau-Ponty rejects this solution as well and insists that the "percept is and remains, despite all critical education, on the hither side of doubt and demonstration" (*PP* 344). We are educated to consider perceptions as real and illusions as false. But the more we investigate perception and how it operates within the horizon of world experience, we realize such real-unreal distinctions are always made after our embodied, living insertion into the world. We cannot establish the veracity of our experience of the world in general because it is the ground from which questions of real and unreal take their sense. "To ask oneself whether the world is real is to fail to understand what one is asking, since the world is not a sum of things which might always be called into question, but the inexhaustible reservoir from which things are drawn" (*PP* 344).

René Descartes (in *Meditations on First Philosophy*, first published in 1641) famously brings dreams into philosophy by posing the problem of dreaming. If I perceive a dream to be real, then how do I know when I am dreaming and when I am not? After all, any moment that feels like waking life could itself be a dream. We can see that a child might answer this dilemma by assuming that dreams are real, so the frustration Descartes feels is foreign. Descartes extends this worry to considering whether or not very basic existential beliefs are true—Does my house exist? Does the world exist? Do stars exist? Does any extended matter exist? Like Descartes, Merleau-Ponty thinks you cannot question the existence of everything. For Descartes the cogito must be doing the doubting, so it must exist at every moment of thought (one cannot doubt without proving the existence of oneself as a doubting thing). For Merleau-Ponty, it is the lifeworld, that setting of all experience, that cannot be doubted. Cartesian doubt appears meaningful, but Merleau-Ponty points out that such a radical doubt always occurs within the inexhaustible reservoir. What would it mean to consider the world as nonexistent? We can envision the things of the world disappearing, the earth itself not being there. We could imagine a view of a map of the solar system with the world deleted, or in addition, all the planets deleted, all the stars and galaxies erased into a world of blackness. But this is not the world of which Merleau-Ponty speaks. In perception, I am not just aware of the objects of the world, the composition of soil, and the stars in the sky; perception is also determined by the endless possibilities of this perception being negated and other ones coming forth. To use Gestalt theory language, the background is not just the aspect of perception that is not attended to, it is also the possibility of perception. If we imagine existing in this world of darkness with no visible bodies, no planets, and no stars, we are still somewhere, in this imagined darkness, with the reservoir of new possibilities that might come forth out of the nothingness.

Our tendency to identify the quantifiable thing with objectivity also tends to pass over the way in which things are connected and transform the place they inhabit. When the world draws upon its infinite reservoir and brings something into presence, everything else is shifted and modified by that possibility becoming an actuality. But unlike things which can disappear from the world, birth is characterized by its resistance to disappearance:

> The event of my birth has not passed completely away, it has not fallen into nothingness in the way that an event of the objective world does, for it committed a whole future, not as a cause determines its effect, but as a situation, once created, inevitably leads on to some outcome. There was henceforth a new "setting," the world received a fresh layer of meaning. In the home into which a child is born, all objects change their significance; they begin to await some as yet indeterminate treatment at his hands; another and different person is there, a new personal history, short or long, has just been initiated, another account has been opened. (*PP* 407)

My first experience is the opening of myself onto a world. I do not arrive fully formed with a set of instinctual impulses that will determine my existence, nor do I come as an empty slate waiting for my shape to be given. Rather, I arrive as a dynamic, living being constantly structuring and restructuring my environment.

In this chapter, we have seen the outline of Merleau-Ponty's description of our historically primary experience of the world and others. In addition, we have found that this historically primary experience is also primal in our adult lives. We will now turn to his lectures in child psychology and pedagogy to explore his characterization of the child, the child's relation with adults, and the child's interaction with the world. The following chapter will introduce the lectures by exploring the main theoretical influences on Merleau-Ponty's work: phenomenology, Gestalt theory, and psychoanalysis.

2

Phenomenology, Gestalt Theory, and Psychoanalysis

This chapter will discuss the relationship between philosophy and psychology in the Sorbonne lectures to provide an introduction into the manner in which three theories—phenomenology, Gestalt theory, and psychoanalysis—shape Merleau-Ponty's work. Merleau-Ponty argues for the relevance of phenomenological theory to experimental praxis and also the relevance of psychological and anthropological studies for a phenomenology of human experience. Merleau-Ponty draws a link between phenomenology's conception of a primal, prescientific experience, Gestalt theory's model of figure-background, and psychoanalysis's concept of the unconscious as intersecting and parallel studies of the tacit elements of lived experience. A mixture of these approaches is seen as the best way to understand the child, but moreover, the study of the child helps draw attention to the limitations in our thought about adult experience.

Phenomenology

The rise of interest in anthropological studies in the late nineteenth and early twentieth centuries helped dismantle traditional European monoculturalist ideologies. Alongside the developing understanding that radically different styles of social life were possible, comprehensive critiques of philosophical truth in Marxist, Nietzschean, and Freudian thought further alienated us from our belief in universal truths. In addition, the Darwinian revolution in the sciences indicated that an evolutionary explanation can be provided for everything from our motor skills to sexual desire.

In their radical forms, a completely evolutionary or economic-historical approach provides us with little entryway into the subjective individual experience. When behavior is explained as a result of the demand of genetic material to reproduce itself or the story of the individual's historical position in economic development, subjective individual experience is lost. If I am a pawn of my libidinal drives, my socioeconomic position, and my genetic make-up, then what relevance does my experience have? It appears epiphenomenal, an evolutionary curiosity, or a site where political oppression plays out.

Merleau-Ponty takes a compelling position in the Sorbonne lectures where he integrates empirical research with a phenomenological approach. Following and expanding upon his early thought about child experience in *The Structure of Behavior* and the *Phenomenology of Perception,* he embraces experimental psychology, neurology, and cultural anthropology. The child's experience is an ideal site from which to work through the complexity of how psychophysical maturation and culture shape development. In the child, we also find a spontaneous ability to respond, mold, and change. Thus, the individual retains her "individuality" and is not merely a biological and socially determined product.

In traditional philosophical accounts, children are often seen as not having sufficient freedom to mark themselves as distinct individuals from other children. Like animals, children do not yet possess sufficient capacity to be in control or responsible for their actions. But unlike animals, the destiny of children is to eventually become rational individuals and participate in the adult world of free and conscious interaction. Such accounts do provide grounds to not blame children for the sins of their parents, since children are deemed largely incapable of being any different than their biological fate and upbringing has destined them to be, but they fail to explain exactly how the uniqueness of adult experience emerges from the irrational commonness of childhood. Too often both cultural and scientific theories start with adult life and expect the relevant aspects of the child's experience to be only those that we find in some form in mature experience. Such an approach, as Merleau-Ponty argues in the 1949–1950 lecture "Structure and Conflicts in Child Consciousness," fails to capture the *positive* and *unique* aspects of the child's behavior (*CPP* 134). Psychology looks at how child behavior, speech for instance, has not yet achieved adult fluency. Seeing the child as needing to achieve adulthood overemphasizes what the child lacks rather than what the child possesses.

It is the child, Merleau-Ponty lectures, who "reveals a certain common ground of all human life out of which various cultural differences take form. In the child, all these possible formations are rediscovered in outline" (*CPP* 156). If we search only for the adult in the child, we pass over the idea that other possibilities exist for adult behavior. What is now the case can seem destined and impossible to change. To grasp the child's experience as both unique and spontaneous, we must avoid language that is blindly invested in adult meaning. Merleau-Ponty's discussion of child experience can in large part be seen as an attempt to find a path to express the child's experience as the *child's* experience and not merely as it relates to other philosophical and psychological investments we may have. Merleau-Ponty speaks extensively about how our adult investments, including our theoretical ones, often cause us to misunderstand the child. He lectures that our concepts make it impossible to capture the child's unique perspective and thus, if our project is to better understand adult experience, make it impossible to understand what influences our own adult behavior. "However, in child psychology, it is necessary to abstain from employing these adult concepts and even abstain from an adult vocabulary. To refrain from falsifying the child's thought, we must describe it in a new language that departs from the distinctions of adult language" (*CPP* 142).

A philosopher might suggest that the discussion of psychological states, human behavior, and development is all very interesting, but that it remains some species of anthropology and not philosophy. Merleau-Ponty sees psychology not only as a task intimately influenced by a careful descriptive method, but also as an endeavor parallel to philosophical inquiry. He addresses the nexus of psychology and philosophy primarily by referring to and considering Edmund Husserl's phenomenology. In his reading, Husserl's own theory led him to consider psychology and phenomenology as mutually engaged disciplines.

Merleau-Ponty lectures that the scientific turn in psychology—where psychology called into question its own unexamined assumptions about its method—was a watershed moment since it initiated a true self-examination. Psychology ceased to be merely an unreflective handmaiden to positivism and became a methodology that addressed its own presence. "All scientific methodology has evolved in this direction since 1900. Science no longer thinks of itself as the registration of facts, à la John Stuart Mill, but rather as a construction of concepts which permits the ordination and coordination of facts" (*CPP* 341). Psychology was thus able to remove itself from the debate between materialist and idealist poles of thought and to return to a careful examination of the body's relationship to mental states. "This revision of the relation of the objective and the subjective allows it to move beyond the alternating choices of objectivist empiricism and subjectivist introspectionism" (341). It might appear surprising to read such a championing of "scientific" methodology in psychology after parts of the *Phenomenology of Perception* lambast science. However, it is important to know that Merleau-Ponty's work in the *Phenomenology of Perception* critiques the unquestioned *faith* in science, the concept that one can simply go and "collect facts" as if facts were simply lying outside like pebbles waiting to be gathered and sorted. He praises the scientific methodology that takes into account the interpretive nature of its inquiry. If psychology becomes self-conscious, it can achieve the same rigor that constitutes a properly conceived phenomenology.

Merleau-Ponty highlights three key paradigm shifts that this new psychology has permitted. First is the revised understanding of the objective and subjective. A methodological approach that includes subjective criteria is needed since the "objective" is itself a subjective, human conception. Second, psychology reintegrated the living body, in particular the nervous system: "Psychology recognized that the investigation of the body, and the nervous system in particular, as a means of comprehending the mind (e.g., to explain language on the basis of linguistic functions) was a mystification" (*CPP* 341). Merleau-Ponty continues to note that this kind of "mystification" is a result of previous materialist ideals where one thought physiology alone could explain psychology. Instead psychology has found that one must understand physiology within the context of behavior, of action, rather than as a meaningful given without correspondence to a living, acting being. Third, psychology stopped privileging the general over the individual: "All objective understanding is not necessarily general understanding. There is no reason for science to devalue the understanding of the individual and the singular" (341). Psychology began to embark upon in-depth studies of individual cases and thereby, like phenomenology's careful descriptions, provided subtler understandings of the human condition.

At this point, the psychologist might intervene and question if this convergence between phenomenology and psychology would not remove the gains psychology made in its turn toward science and away from philosophy. Careful phenomenological descriptions are not easily subsumable to experiments or quantification. Indeed, we might even suggest such a psychology would lose its objectivity with such anthropomorphic descriptions. Merleau-Ponty argues that starting from the description of the human condition is inevitable. Attempting to rid psychology of its original human position does not make psychology more objective. "The ideal of objectivity is a chimera if it consists of a simple notation of external givens, because the external world is always grasped from a human situation" (*CPP* 345). We must turn to a study of lived experience in both psychology and phenomenology to understand the essential elements of the human situation. Only then will we be able to find a true psychology instead of introspectionism (which denies the relevance of the external situation) or objectivism (which denies the determining nature of our human condition).

Much more so today than in Merleau-Ponty's time, psychology hopes to become more objective by standardizing its method of inquiry and quantifying its results. The experiment that permits a statistical measurement of a broad range of individual cases provides more objective data than the detailed description of a particular case. The unquestioned assumption is that since a quantified result is less dependent upon the contingencies of the individual state, it is more open to the critical method that allows for real progress in the sciences. Additionally, we assume that more cases are more indicative of a general pattern of behavior. Instead of analyzing a few cases in depth, we survey many cases in a particular situation to have a real test of our hypothesis. Thus, the psychoanalytic method of analyzing a few persons in depth is far less telling than a large survey of a thousand persons.

Contradicting this trend in "scientific" psychology, Merleau-Ponty cites Kurt Goldstein, arguing that "the particular in-depth study, if it is an in-depth work, has as much, even more, value than a superficial study of numerous cases" (*CPP* 386). One of the concerns of scientific psychology is that an in-depth study of a particular case leaves us lost in the specificity of that case. We might outline this particular case well, but what does it possibly tell us about the *general* human condition? Merleau-Ponty acknowledges that psychology does want to provide a general account, but it mistakes what kind of generality is of most value:

> The concept of "generality" has two meanings: either the kind found when one examines a great number of cases (and thus, generality is much greater as the cases become more sketchy); or the generality that one obtains in returning to the core of the concrete phenomenon, in which case one is dealing with an "essential generality." Yet, most often psychologists employ a statistical generality: they find that three years is the "age of negativism" and compare all observations on the basis of this assertion. But then they can no longer explain anything; they simply give names to certain facts without explaining them. Psychology ought to tell us why such phenomena occur. (*CPP* 387)

An essential generality can be discovered only through in-depth studies. Statistical studies that simply refer to a generality derived from multiple cases give us a summary of incidents with no explanatory framework. To explain the *genesis* of phenomena, psychology must embrace, not deny, its interpretive method. While a wide survey of all children at the age of three might provide some information, it will only be comprehensible *within* an implicit or explicit theory of human development and the nature of the child. Merleau-Ponty worries that if we assume that we can move from statistical studies to a theory, we will reinforce our prejudicial tendency to assume that all past behaviors are merely precursors to our present behavior. We will exclude what is unique about childhood experience. As critiques of simple empiricism have pointed out, sense-data alone does not provide us with meaning. We have to unite our sensory experience with frameworks that provide such experience with sense. Likewise, statistical studies are akin to sheer sensory data without any analysis. Without an interpretative framework, we cannot assess their relevance. In-depth studies allow us to see human experience in its complexity and thus give us frameworks with which to make sense of scientific studies.

Merleau-Ponty argues that Husserl was aware of the intimate and parallel connection between psychology and phenomenology. Unlike Max Scheler and Martin Heidegger, who clearly drew a line between psychology and philosophy, Husserl understands the "secret connections" between the two: "Scheler and Heidegger both affirm the opposition of the ontological to the ontical and of philosophy to positive science. Husserl, on the contrary, indicates the secret connections between these two orders of research" (*CPP* 337). Merleau-Ponty believes Husserl to be, like himself, interested in eradicating the boundaries between philosophy and the sciences. "Husserl says that philosophy is 'humanity's civil servant'" (317).

Although Merleau-Ponty is critical in the Sorbonne lectures of various philosophical and scientific claims, he remains committed to the concept that all philosophical theories arise from the same world experience. For instance, a Cartesian dualist believes that the mind is a metaphysically distinct thing from the body. Minds, in this view, have no physical properties; they do not inhabit space and time as bodies do. Merleau-Ponty's *Phenomenology of Perception,* written a few years before the Sorbonne lectures, can be read as a long examination of why such a dualist view fundamentally misunderstands perception, knowledge, and our embodied status. One could conclude that if the theory—here dualism—fails, we should reject it and move onto more sophisticated theories. But Merleau-Ponty presents a view where any theory springs from the same world as any other theory, practice, or narrative does. In this sense, all theories, no matter how obscure or fabricated, contain within them some truth: the truth of their existential origin. There is a why behind every theory that speaks of the original connection or motivation from our lived experience. Dualism captures a truth about how we are not things-in-themselves, like a rock or a chair, but we are things-for-ourselves: we have conscious states that can appear as a kind of miraculous addition to our physical experience. Where does this consciousness arise from? Why don't other things appear to have it? As a therapist tries to work out the reasons behind a client's worldview and does not discredit it if it seems at face value false, so too can we find a truth behind every theory. Even the most fantastical beliefs are still beliefs that arise from our lifeworld.

The descriptive method in phenomenology does not begin with an assessment of the conclusions of a particular theory; rather it starts by elucidating through description the constitution of a theory. Phenomenology does not start by arguing that a certain philosophy or scientific approach is wrong; it suspends judgment about the rightness or wrongness of any theory and instead looks to find the universal human origin. Thus phenomenology applies itself to a particular aspect of our experience, such as perception, but also engages in a constant evaluation of the method and reasons for the exploration: the psychology or philosophy of perception as well.

Merleau-Ponty understands Husserl's project to have a similar openness to all experiences and all theories. Husserl presents us with a descriptive, self-critical search for origins. He argues that we need to suspend all conditioning, be it biological, psychological, or cultural, but he does not deny the existence or relevance of such conditioning. This inclusive approach depends on being open to the truths in theories even if we disagree with the conclusions. In addition, even an ideal theory will itself inevitably be rooted in lived experience and never quite able to capture a universal picture. Merleau-Ponty argues in the 1951–1952 lecture "Human Sciences and Phenomenology" that "even the philosopher descends into the flux of our experience; even the thought which pretends to dominate descends and takes its place in experience" (*CPP* 319). As he famously lectures in the preface to the *Phenomenology of Perception,* no complete reduction is possible. "The most important lesson which the reduction teaches us is the impossibility of a complete reduction" (*PP* xiv). In Merleau-Ponty's interpretation of Husserl, phenomenology understands itself as arising from the located, human condition of the phenomenologist.

In principle, both psychology and philosophy arise from this same original position; neither can take a privileged position outside of experience. The human experience that any science or philosophy is engaged with is not some abstract "state of nature," but an experience that takes place in a constantly changing historical, cultural, and social milieu. Merleau-Ponty claims that philosophy's compatibility with the human sciences is this common historical and experiential ground:

> Philosophy remains on the horizon of our thought as the limit of possible operations and is only validated in an open-ended historical process. Thus, philosophy is not the reaffirmation of ancient philosophical entities (e.g., eternal truths and the like), but rather the elaboration of an integral philosophy that is compatible with all research in the human sciences. (*CPP* 320)

He emphasizes that in addressing and describing the historical human condition, phenomenology does not relativize the claims of the human sciences, but actually provides them with a rigorous method by pulling them out of an ungrounded, ahistorical analysis. And it is phenomenology, Merleau-Ponty concludes, that best captures the nature of both experience and the study of experience in philosophy and the other sciences.

As Rudolf Bernet, Iso Kern, and Eduard Marbach note, Husserl's work post-1920 does claim to provide the conceptual foundations of psychology. Husserl's goal is the "ideal of *one*, universal science embracing all the positive sciences and resting upon an ultimate philosophical foundation" (Bernet, Kern, and Marbach 1999, 218). While psychology, as the study of mental events, is closely similar to many philosophical questions, it is not itself necessarily concerned with the manner in which it is connected to the other areas of knowledge. It is philosophy, or more precisely phenomenology, that provides the actual explanation for the sciences. Husserl is concerned with the fundamental ground of the sciences and how this ground is necessarily structured.

Nonetheless, there are places in Husserl's corpus where it seems difficult to understand the difference between philosophy and psychology. In his 1925 lectures published as *Phenomenological Psychology*, Husserl writes about the need to return to the prescientific experiential world. He writes that we need to find clarity when it comes to what gives any particular scientific inquiry "its essential unity, and how it branches off essentially, both internally and externally, on the basis of its first originary sources of sense" (1977, 39). It appears that since both psychology and philosophy would be exploring this prescientific lifeworld, would they not therefore be the same thing? Husserl emphasizes that psychology is a *"science of the most universal forms and laws of mental facts"* (39, italics original). For Merleau-Ponty, Husserl's own discussions indicate that to properly discover any psychological essence I am compelled to grasp its phenomenological significance. Phenomenology is not, and should not be, some kind of subjective introspection (which is Husserl's very worry about any kind of psychologism in phenomenology). However, this concern does not mean that psychology cannot become self-conscious of its naiveté and overcome it. For Merleau-Ponty, any investigation is capable of converging with phenomenology and becoming truly philosophical:

> Philosophy should discover the meaning of phenomena described by the scientist [*savant*]. The role of philosophy is to reconstitute the world that the physicist sees, but with the "fringe" that the scientist does not mention that is furnished by his contact with the qualitative world. This program remains valuable for us; there will be no difference between psychology and philosophy. Psychology is always an implicit, beginning

philosophy and philosophy has never finished its contact with facts. (*CPP* 7)

Every experience reveals our primary connection with the world, and inaccurate or misleading ideologies are as much a symptom of our condition as correct, fruitful theories. Our return again and again in philosophy and psychology to fundamental questions of human development, motivation, behavior, beliefs, and thoughts is indicative of this constant beginning. The facts of existence are not something philosophy avoids, but are required for its practice.

Husserl would agree that all sciences are connected in the unity that phenomenology exposes and that all experiences must be grounded upon a primordial, prescientific experience. Therefore any and all experiences, including the experience of building a science or formulating a theory, must arise from this common experience. However, for Husserl the project is to delineate the connections between the scientific world and the lifeworld and to explain the complexities of the constitution of the lifeworld. Merleau-Ponty acknowledges that his interpretation would likely not be well-received by Husserl, suggesting that Husserl thinks psychology operates without questioning the validity of common sense (*CPP* 322–23). Psychology, in Husserl's view, uses a naive view of the human subject and thus cannot be self-grounding. For Husserl, phenomenology is the geometry of psychology's physics; geometry can stand independently of physics, but not vice versa.

Yet the real distinction between Merleau-Ponty and Husserl's view on the connection between psychology and phenomenology does not seem to be so much the value of common sense, but rather what the difference would be between the work of a phenomenologist considering psychology versus a psychologist with a phenomenological method. For Husserl, a phenomenologist is working on a complex system of fundamental concepts and their connections that arise from the insight about the prescientific lifeworld that underlies all theory and practice, including scientific theory and practice. A psychologist would certainly have one of the closest studies to philosophy, but would not necessarily need to be concerned with all fundamental concepts and how they provide for the one science. Merleau-Ponty appears largely unconcerned in the Sorbonne lectures with a careful categorization of philosophy and the human sciences that arises from a strict method. Rather, his investigations are a constant return to describing the prescientific primordial experience that unifies all of the human condition while at the same time providing for its immense diversity. In this light, there is little difference between philosophy and psychology other than that they address the question of primordial experience through different lenses.

Gestalt Theory

The growing separation between the empirical sciences and philosophy in the twentieth century received significant attention from a variety of philosophers. Like Husserl and Merleau-Ponty, Bergson heavily critiqued scientism in psychology and philosophy. However, Merleau-Ponty champions Husserl's work while remaining largely critical of Bergson's, despite the fact it would appear that Bergson's theory of vitalism has strong ties to Merleau-Ponty's focus on embodiment. For Merleau-Ponty, Bergson's vitalism does not overcome the problems of scientism; rather, it forms an ill-conceived idealism that is an equally untenable antithesis. Despite the terminology of life, Bergson fails to accurately capture experience with a model where lived experience is relegated to an abstract concept. In Bergson, we lose the body's very physical nature—its skin, its sensations, its nervous and digestive systems. The body is not an object as a scientist might make it; yet, Bergson's vitalism flees the objectivity of the sciences by making the lived body a purified abstraction impossible to investigate or to connect to empirical research. "For psychologists, this notion of lived experience posited by Bergson is an inexpressible idea. Bergson himself, in explaining what he means by the lived experience by recourse to a rough theory of language as incantatory and metaphorical, provides them with ammunition for their arguments" (*CPP* 340). The solution will be to remain responsive and connected to actual empirical research without falling into a simple materialism. For Merleau-Ponty, Kurt Goldstein is an exemplar of the proper approach to embodiment: "We are, once again, presented with a good example of a nondeliberate convergence between experimental research and the demands of the phenomenological method" (*CPP* 361). Goldstein, as a neurologist, is not interested in denying the findings of science as being necessarily ontic and through and through contaminated by materialist dogma. But, at the same time, Goldstein doesn't begin with a preset definition of the physiological because this would greatly limit his investigations into neurology.

What does it mean to not limit the definition of the physiological? What could the physiological be but the nature of the physical body? It is precisely this prejudice that Merleau-Ponty thinks Goldstein rightly avoids. *Behavior* must be integrated into physiology; physiology cannot remain the analysis of the physical parts of the body. Only when examining the acting, living, and experiencing body will physiology as a study have coherence. The doctor who understands the body on the dissection table does not necessarily understand lived experience.

Goldstein is also praised for his focus on a complete phenomenology of individuals instead of working backwards from a symptom to the "cause." When one focuses upon the symptom in exclusion from the rest of the organism's life, one assumes that the symptom has a singular cause that would be similar in all subjects. This prejudice of "objective" psychology is highlighted in Goldstein's experiments where he explains how a particular pathology that has been caused by a brain injury cannot be explicated solely with recourse to the physiological location of that injury. Instead, it is about understanding *how* the patient restructures his world after an injury. Only then do we understand the ramifications of the injury as well as the pathology itself. For instance, aphasia cannot be understood without referring to damaged language patterns—that is, the behavior of the patient. Familiar for the readers of *The Structure of Behavior*, Merleau-Ponty argues that we must not leave behavior and search for the "real" as in a physical origin, but rather remain with the idea that an analysis of behavior is inherently needed for a physiological analysis.

Although Merleau-Ponty acknowledges the transformative effect of physical development and physical injury (or disease) upon the individual, he is also careful to acknowledge that our study of these transformations is itself always located in a particular time, place, and history and, therefore, is always a culturally determined study. Looking for a more dynamic and integrative approach to human development, Merleau-Ponty works against materialistic or intellectualist accounts in his Sorbonne lectures. For him, psychology is always a human endeavor and, as such, is always interpretative.

Standard Gestalt theory describes how our perception of a figure is always informed by a background. When I say that I am looking at a tree, what allows the tree to be a meaningful perception is not just an identification of the tree "as a tree," but also the visual and kinesthetic space in which the tree-perception occurs. Often in our discussions of perception, we ignore the implicit background elements that allow the figure, here a tree, to be a meaningful perception. When we perceive an optical illusion, we can see how perception is not simply a registering of the conscious object of perception. Take the common illusion of where one sees either a vase or two faces. Oddly enough, the visual givens are the same, but one's perception remains unstable, one vacillates between "seeing" the vase or "seeing" the two faces. If perception were just the registration of visual givens, optical illusions would appear impossible to explain. If the "faces" were completed with two bodies drawn onto them, the "vase" image would recede since a stable background for the image has now been provided. A background is normally not part of our explicit awareness, but it is very much at play in any perception.

In the Sorbonne lectures, Gestalt psychology is, as in the *Phenomenology of Perception* and *The Structure of Behavior*, a common source of inspiration for a positive account of the child's experience. Gestalt psychology presents a view where the child might indeed show immaturity in identifying and representing objects, but this does not mean the child's perception is somehow less organized than adult perception. Instead the child is more connected to the actual structuring of perception and is more aware of the background than the representational, figure-centered perception of adults. The concept of a background not only applies to particular static perceptions, but also includes our living, changing perceptual world. In Gestalt theory, a general, unthematic background underlies discrete and new experiences. Gestalt psychology teaches us that infantile perception is structured from the outset. The infant experiences a sensible world, not an incoherent set of random visual givens. Merleau-Ponty lectures, "all of this confirms the fact that the infant's experience does not begin as chaos, but as a *world already underway* [*un monde déjà*]" (*CPP* 148). If no background, or "world already underway," is present, then no figure-perception is possible. I cannot learn, I cannot encounter the new, I cannot develop, unless I already have a place in which to, at least provisionally, situate challenging and new experiences.

Merleau-Ponty distinguishes two ways of understanding perceptual intelligence: classical theories and Piaget's theory. The classical, neo-Kantian theory is to think that somehow judgment or intelligence adds itself onto brute physical givens. In such a conception, perception has no sense of its own. Not only does such a model fail to explain perception, but it provides no understanding of human development. How does one "learn" these appropriate judgments and to what sense-data should they be attached? Yet, Piaget does not separate himself enough from the classical tradition because this sensory-motor intelligence itself becomes a kind of Humean collection of sense-data: "For Piaget, sensorimotor intelligence is either an *association of ideas* or a *logical operation*" (*CPP* 152). Piaget includes a discussion of perception's role in intelligence and development, but he relegates it to a function of intelligence. His theory fails to capture how children experience a total world. Merleau-Ponty lectures that "as a result, all of his studies describe perception as an incomplete intelligence and not as a positive fact. In addition, Piaget lacks an understanding of something else which is crucial: the *world perceived* by the child" (ibid.).

Piaget's understanding of perception and intelligence will not allow for an explanation of *how* his various schemas work and, thus, how development occurs. If intelligence is required for objects to have permanence, then Piaget seems to be back in the classical dilemma. How does perception inform, teach, and challenge the intellect? Piaget rejects the Gestalt analysis that there is an order immanent in perception because he thinks that to accept this would be to conflate intelligence and perception. The alternative he doesn't consider is that the "intelligence" in perception is of a different kind than the intelligence in judgment and abstract thought.

What we need is a positive conception of the child's perception that doesn't return to old schemas wherein the child is perceived as the incomplete adult. Piaget is right to be critical of classical theories as well as of any species of Gestalt psychology that reduces intelligence to perception. Such a "solution" answers no questions about perception; rather, it adopts the opposite extreme. Instead, perception has to be given its own sense, a sense that provides a ground upon which the intelligent analysis of the world arises.

We need to return to the child's embodied experience to understand the meaning inherent within perception. Merleau-Ponty lectures that the totality of the child's experience includes her sense of embodiment. Hence, children have no understanding of their bodies as "bodies," for that would mean they had objectified their bodies. Instead, their experience is a unity: body, world, and perception are parts of a meaningful whole. A type of schema of being exists in the child, but not yet a world of discrete objects. It requires abstract intelligence to think of one's body as an object. To say that the child perceives the background is to say that the child experiences life as sensible and organized, but not as a composite of various objects and corresponding judgments about those objects. It is the primal base of changing, living experience that makes our later abstractions from the world possible.*

Good psychologists grasp "the totality of the child's becoming" (*CPP* 388). The child is in the state of "becoming" rather than "being" insofar as the child has not yet isolated her life from the world in general. In

---

* The other psychologist who deserves important mention but isn't either in the Gestalt psychology, Piagetean, or psychoanalytic school is Henri Wallon, whose theory will be discussed more extensively in chapters 3 and 5. Wallon (1879–1962) was one of the three most influential child psychologists of the twentieth century in France (along with Jean Piaget and Sigmund Freud). The lack of influence Wallon had on English-language psychology is likely due to the fact that few of his works have been translated. Wallon's (1963) child psychology highlights the child's natural behavior as having its own meaning. Piaget's psychology is seen to force the child within a preset developmental schema where adult experience is presumptively considered the fullest and most accurate connection with the external world. Speaking of Wallon's work, Merleau-Ponty lectures that "here we are no longer in the presence of an objectivist psychology, but rather of a psychology which examines the contents of behavior in order to *seize its sense*" (*CPP* 349, emphasis original). Wallon, like Kurt Goldstein, doesn't assume the same behavior must be based in the same internal sense. Hence, one might do a study where a number of children produce the same action, but unless one studies particular cases in depth, one cannot be sure that these actions have all arisen for the same reason.

perception, the child has not yet learned to invest the figure with its abstract representation, thus distancing it from its inherent place within a background context. As adults, we both gain and lose due to our social, cultural, and formal education. We become more adroit at representing what we perceive and in reducing what we perceive down to component parts. We are better able to vary our perspective and imagine ourselves as possible objects of variation. However, this ability to take the "figure" and abstract it from the "background" means we tend to devalue and ignore the relevance of the context of our experience.

Psychoanalysis

Merleau-Ponty argues throughout the Sorbonne lectures that child development must be understood as a dynamic process rather than a sequential achievement of various stages. Child development theory that desires to see child development in successive stages with successive capacities achieved, such as perceptual, motor, and cognitive skills, idealizes itself as more objective. Its faith in its scientific method comes from experiments which map whether or not children have acquired these various skills. However, for Merleau-Ponty, Gestalt theory and psychoanalysis far better understand the child's experience because these approaches understand the contextual, temporal, and personal aspects to child experience, whereas scientific psychology's investment in its "pseudo-objectivity" overdetermines the child prior to letting the child's behavior reveal its essential characteristics:

> Pseudo-objective thought lacks the constitutive truth of the child's life. The atomistic conception is impossible, since this mode of thought consists in statically cutting out [*découpage*] the child's development. However, if the child constitutes a moment in a dynamic totality, it is impossible to dissect [*découper*] infantile behavior. (*CPP* 382)

This section focuses on Merleau-Ponty's interpretation of psychoanalysis. Like his summarizing of Piaget, Merleau-Ponty's idea of Freud's work at times appears to be based in a very cursory knowledge of Freud's own texts. Sometimes Merleau-Ponty is aware of how far he diverges from psychoanalytic theory and at others he writes as if he is simply expressing the self-evident conclusion of psychoanalytic theory. For instance, Merleau-Ponty lectures that Freud thought there was an Electra complex, something Freud not only did not argue for, but also actually argued against (*CPP*

88). It was Carl Jung (1970) who advanced a theory of young girls' sexuality with this name. Merleau-Ponty's idea of a Freudian Electra complex might be due to the fact that many texts by Freud were not translated into French until the 1950s or later. While Merleau-Ponty read German, some of his mistakes in his reading of Freud might be due to some French Freudian theorists' interpretations of Freud due to the lack of translations and Merleau-Ponty relying heavily on secondary source accounts. I focus on providing a coherent account of Merleau-Ponty's thought on the importance of psychoanalysis and in so doing avoid discerning the authenticity of Merleau-Ponty's understanding of Freud's theory.

Merleau-Ponty argues that there are two general ways to understand the relevance of psychoanalytic theory: a broad and a narrow sense (*CPP* 72). A narrow sense of psychoanalysis's reach concerns itself with a strict interpretation of child sexual development and its subsequent impact on adult behavior such as explored in Freud's *Three Essays on the Theory of Sexuality* (1905). Narrow psychoanalytic interpretations focus on how the adult's behavior is constituted by earlier experiences and the progressive repression of childhood traumas. Freud accurately understands the importance of the individual child's family and situation; however, a narrow Freudian interpretation approaches scientific psychology's obsession with mapping out stages of child development. In so doing, it has a tendency to both interiorize and historicize behavior. For instance, a neurosis is a symptom of an early, unresolved conflict. To explain present behavior, one must reach into the past of the individual and find the *cause* of the present behavior.

While a narrow analysis of individual sexual and psychical development is critical in Freudian theory, Merleau-Ponty views the broad interpretation of psychoanalytic theory as more trenchant and relevant. There are two manners in which he takes up a broader psychoanalytic theory: one is to see it as a historical and cultural analysis, such as evidenced in Freud's *Totem and Taboo* (1913), *The Future of an Illusion* (1927), and *Civilization and Its Discontents* (1930), and the other is to argue against the narrow sense where the individual's behavior is "caused" by earlier events. The broad sense in Merleau-Ponty's estimation better understands how the individual also constitutes and participates in present behavior. He lectures that this dynamic and broader understanding of human behavior dominated the latter part of Freud's career and is seen in the existential psychoanalysis of Gaston Bachelard and Jean-Paul Sartre, the work on family complexes in Jacques Lacan's theory, and in Politzer's *Critique des fondements de la psychologie* (1968).

Psychoanalysis in the broad sense argues that the infantile traumas that determine adult behavior are constantly *relived* and *reinstituted* by the adult. Early traumas are not buried deep within an individual's psyche, somehow creating specific negative effects on the individual's adult behavior, but rather remain very much a living part of the adult's structure of behavior. Failing to accept and assimilate past traumas has as much to do with adult life as with the original childhood experience.

Merleau-Ponty's psychoanalysis emphasizes that the symptom is not something interior within the individual's psyche, but very much part of everyday life. What accounts for its "hidden" nature, one that often needs a therapist to uncover, is not its depth in the psyche, but its place on the very *surface* of experience. The language used in Gestalt theory's notion of background and in Husserl's concept of horizon is used in tandem with Freudian psychoanalysis. I am unaware of my pathology not because it is inaccessible, but because it is a nonthematic part of my everyday lived experience.

In his interpretation of psychoanalytic theory, Merleau-Ponty agrees with Politzer that there is no deep unconscious, but rather, "the notion of the unconscious is replaced by the notion of ambivalence" (*CPP* 73). Ambivalence better captures how an original symptom—say a dream—can never be recaptured by a latter interpretation, whether proffered by the analyst or the subject. I could only possibly provide an accurate representation of my dream if I could dream it while interpreting it. As I am always trying to capture a past state in my lived present, any meaning I suggest to explain a previous state will always come up short. Merleau-Ponty wants to allow the past to shape the present; but the present is dynamic and is not solely a product of the past. In Merleau-Ponty's developmental theory the past shapes the present insofar as the past has formed a style of life that is reinforced by the individual's actions. What is unconscious is what is paradoxical to the individual's current life. It is a past that isn't subsumable by the present.

For instance, a previous experience of strong affect toward the opposite-sex parent can continue to pervade the adult's relationship with that parent, parental figures, and other relationships. However, this affect is inconsistent with much of the rest of the subject's life, her developing connection with her parents, and her past and contemporary relationships. She feels strongly ambivalent about her desire and this transforms her behavior. The ambivalence, or unconscious, aspect is a kind of symptom of an inability to reconcile conflicting parts of her feelings into a harmonious whole. Since she cannot reconcile this affect to her present experiences, it remains hidden from conscious awareness even though it is very much present in her experience. The struggle to change a pathological behavior to a healthy mode of being stems from the difficulty of identifying and reintegrating the pathology. The struggle is not evidence, in Merleau-Ponty's view, of an unconscious motor to lived experience, but an ambivalence *within* lived experience.

Merleau-Ponty refuses to separate the psyche into sharply demarcated sections, such as conscious and unconscious states, due to his emphasis upon lived experience. Admittedly, experience is confused, ambivalent, and complex, but it is always present. A standard reading of the unconscious argues that certain mental states are inaccessible to the individual, hence their power and their mysteriousness. Such a theory draws a picture where the unconscious is not part of experience, but an inner cause of experience. Thus, the unconscious is not exactly present, as in an atmosphere or part of experience, but an internal engine that drives experience often due to the frustration of the individual ego's conscious awareness. Alternatively the unconscious might be portrayed as an inaccessible structure where internal and external givens are processed. In this structural reading, the unconscious is also absent from phenomenal awareness.

For Merleau-Ponty, the ambivalent unconscious is very much part of the individual's subjective, phenomenal experience even if it is difficult, if not impossible, to capture with conscious, representational language. It is akin to an element of the background of a perception. When I turn my attention toward the background, it ceases to be a background and becomes a figure which itself has an implicit background. Likewise, the ambivalent unconscious often slips past our conscious "gaze" since it isn't supported by our adult understanding. The unconscious doesn't control us or "play tricks" on us; rather, it subsists beneath all contemporary experience:

> It is not a question of an unconscious which plays tricks on us; the phenomenon of mystification maintains that all consciousness is a privileged consciousness; consciousness that privileges the "figure" and tends to forget the "ground," without it, consciousness has no meaning (Gestalt theory). We do not know the ground despite the fact we live it. We are for ourselves our own ground. (*CPP* 380)

Ambivalence captures how a former experience can still constitute a living one. How can I both know I shouldn't do something and yet find myself performing just that act? Why and how would I be "complicit" in a behavior that harms me? Any resistance to treatment is partially due to the subject being complicit in her behavior even if she isn't quite capable of grasping the motivations behind her pathology. It isn't an informed, conscious complicity. The initial moment doesn't reach out from the past and strangle the present; rather, the subject experiences the ambivalence the trauma causes. The notion of "ambivalence" instead of a deep unconscious better describes "all that is equivocal in certain behaviors, 'resistances' to treatment, in which the subject is partially complicit, attitudes of hate that are at the same time love, desires that express themselves as agony, and so forth" (*CPP* 73).

The final major concept that psychoanalysis in the broad sense overcomes is the idea that sexual drives are motors that push us to achieve genital sexuality. This narrow ideology argues that, "in other words, sexuality is all affective investment, implicated equally in the genital but which largely overflows this category" (*CPP* 73–74). A proper, broad psychoanalytic interpretation of sexuality is one where sexuality is tied to corporality in general, to body consciousness in general, and not just to parts of the body, that is, the oral, the anal, and the genital. If sexuality were limited to the genitals in healthy adult experience, we would expect to experience a world largely devoid of erotic and sexual coloring aside from genital sexual intercourse. As in the pansexualism of the child, sexuality colors adult life. Asserting that Freud understands sexuality to be context-dependent, Merleau-Ponty argues for an understanding of sexual development that has its roots in the broad historical, cultural, and embodied condition of the subject.

Following Lacan, Merleau-Ponty notes that we should avoid taking Freud's theory as a command to oversexualize the child. For the child, sexuality is not overt and lived in the way it is for the adult. The child experiences the sexual nature of life without having directed such sensations exclusively toward the genitals. If as asserted above, the child's world is one reminiscent of a Gestaltist background, sexuality would likewise not yet be objectified. This would not be to say that the child is not sexual, but merely that the child is not intentionally sexual.

One of the problems with Merleau-Ponty's holistic conception of early experience—where no deep unconscious drives motivate our behavior, where sexuality is part of a general mode of life—is that it is challenging to understand the motivation for development. If the child has a structured and meaningful experience of the world, it seems hard to understand human maturation. Why wouldn't we remain in the child's world?

Merleau-Ponty's mixture of psychoanalytic theories of development read within a Gestalt theory and phenomenological approach suggests that the child's embodied experience contains within it an anticipation, or pre-maturation, of future development. But this is not to say that all future states are contained within the child or that the child is fated to develop in a certain manner. Thus, while we can see some of the reasons for our development in our childhood, we must be careful not to think that the ultimate experience was present in its same form in childhood. For instance, take sexuality. One could say in a narrow psychoanalytic theory of development that a sexual tension, for example, the standard Oedipus complex, is caused by a childhood event. Thus, if a man has unconscious desire for his mother, then he must have also had this desire as a child and subsequently repressed that desire. But Merleau-Ponty disagrees with such an assessment, pointing out that as Lacan notes, it doesn't make sense to assume that an adult's understanding of sexual desire and a child's are the same, even if they appear to have similar objects or occur within the same individual. All the same, somehow the child's affective experience toward the mother must be connected to the adult's.

Merleau-Ponty follows Lacan by conceiving of development as a kind of anticipation where the child has precocious experiences for which she is not quite prepared. One could think here of the sexual play of young children where it is wrong to say that their playing mommy and daddy is due to a desire for genital intercourse, but also wrong to suggest that there is no connection between the play of young children and later sexual life:

> According to Freud, the Oedipus complex is the situation created by an incestuous attachment to the parent of the opposite sex. Lacan objects by claiming it is not possible to conceive of a sexual attachment in children as young as four to seven years, where the child's sexuality does not correspond to any precise experience. For Lacan, no feeling exists that exactly corresponds to the adult's feeling. Rather, a kind of anticipation exists that, as we often find in the course of child development, abruptly pulls the child to a psychological level quite advanced for his age. (*CPP* 87–88)

Lacan takes a broad view in that he does not link the child's sexuality to any precise experience. We cannot codify what experiences cause development or alternatively what physical changes cause psychological and sexual development. Children anticipate future development in their games and behavior, and this is best shown in the strangely adult behavior that occurs at times in children that are otherwise fairly immature. Children might display an intellectual precociousness at a young age, appearing wise and oddly mature, and then recommence playing with Legos and crying at the sight of a dog. This profundity isn't simply random; it demonstrates that children have traces of anticipation of future stages, perhaps even ones that will never come to pass.

Bodily change also spurs development as it transforms the child's life and requires a reorganization of one's attitudes, behaviors, and understanding. But Freud's genius was to recognize that development cannot be reduced solely down to a registration of physical changes. *"Freud was one of the first to take the child seriously;* not by showing an explanation for bodily functions, but that these bodily functions take place in a psychic dynamism . . . Freud wants to return the child to the current of existence where the body is the vehicle" (*CPP* 280, italics original). We cannot remain in the child's world because we cannot remain children. Any bodily development implies change. But at the same time, we recognize that physical development does not simply cause psychological development. One has to be "ready" for the physical change or alternatively one can be ready prior to a physical change. Children can be mature or immature for their physical age in comparison with their peers.

In puberty, we witness children playing with sexually precocious heterosexuality. At the same time, such a sea change in responsibility and subsequent ambivalence about one's transforming body leads children to display infantile tendencies. There is a strong hesitation to reach the next stage of development as well as a desire to return to a previous one: "At the same time, we find *anticipation* and *regression* to infancy. During this period, a constant ambiguity exists: a desire for and a fear of adult life, a persistent need for protection and simultaneously the will to do without it" (*CPP* 403). Such developments are not merely representative of the child restructuring her world around physical development. The desire and fear of adult life is colored by what kind of adult life is expected of the child.

For example, take the case of female puberty, which will be discussed further in chapter 6. The mother's own ambivalent feelings about the girl's puberty will create a cyclical shared loop. At the beginning of menstruation it is false to say that without question the girl is now a "woman." Merleau-Ponty lectures that she must integrate new physical developments into her existence. "The appearance of menstruation is by no means the same thing as puberty. Once menstruation has begun, everything still remains to be done: the integration of the elements into a whole" (*CPP* 405). On the mother's side, she both wants her child to grow up as well as desires her daughter to remain a child. The mother herself has a division between anticipating future life and wanting to return to the past. Healthy, true maturation is when one does manage to surpass prior states but still preserves them, integrates them into the new, but retains an openness to inevitable future change. Physical development alone is never sufficient for true development. As the subject is partially complicit in preserving a pathological behavior, the subject is also required to participate in development. Development is not a mindless drive which pushes the subject; the subject must take up and live the new body and find how to live in the social world.

One obvious way to highlight what healthy embodiment might be is to differentiate it from unhealthy, pathological experience. Merleau-Ponty argues, as he does for the child, that the pathological subject must too have a mode of structuring her environment. It cannot be that pathology presents us merely with anomalies that we need not explain; or, alternatively, that the pathological case is useful only in how it displays what happens when normal experience is disrupted. Instead, Merleau-Ponty argues that pathological cases must be interpreted in a similar fashion to a normally developing child. The mentally ill are not exceptions to the rules that define the healthy. The pseudo-objective thought that sees child development as the sequential acquisition of cognitive and physical stages also tends to want to exclude the pathological since such behavior refuses to conform to laboratory-style experimentation:

> Another aspect of this "general prejudice" is the exclusion of pathological cases. This is a prescientific mode of thought which separates the sick from the healthy human. We commonly say, "It is an exceptional situation" and "The exception confirms the rule." But this notion of "exception" is a contradiction, since, on the contrary, the exception invalidates the rule. In fact, these "slogans" show our prejudice in thinking that there is a "general science." Once generality is obtained, one gathers up all the results pell-mell and produces reports on "the unique child of Vienna in 1928." (*CPP* 388)

If I want to describe the positive and unique characteristics of the child's experience, I have to be wary of generalizing. A generalization which lays out a path of proper and healthy development ignores the individual child's situation. More critically it approaches the child, or the mentally ill individual, from the effects they make on the world instead of grasping how these effects, these behaviors, are representative of a personal style of structuring the world.

The defining feature of the psychoanalytic conception of pathology—the complex—becomes not just the hallmark of pathological behavior but also of all behavior. Given the highly ambivalent, constantly modifying nature of our experiences, the complex forms stable structures around which we can organize our behavior. Referencing Lacan, Merleau-Ponty says that stereotypical attitudes that determine our relationships allow us freedom from the anonymity of our background life. "We must understand the notion of 'complex' not in the sense of an unhealthy formation, but, rather, as the key to all normal formation (there is no 'man without complexes')" (*CPP* 84). When I interact with others, I do so in a habitual set of roles that I have established. These roles are not necessarily more engaged in the contingencies of the external situation than the behaviors of the mentally ill. In fact, it might be that the healthy individual's behavior is more removed from the situation and it is this remove that makes it functional. "A complex is a stereotypical attitude regarding certain situations. In some way, the complex is the most stable element of behavior, being a collection of behavioral traits which are always reproduced in analogous situations" (84). The complex becomes unstable, or pathological, when it is incapable of changing because it arose from an early, infantile trauma.

This present book emphasizes a Merleau-Pontian approach where child experience is seen positively and, thereby, not reduced to a minimal version of adult experience. Merleau-Ponty also broadly included "pathological" consciousness as likewise demanding a positive description. As we often interpret children as incomplete adults, and thus fail to capture childhood experience, we likewise tend to see pathological experience as defective. Instead, Merleau-Ponty views it on a continuum that reveals common truths of consciousness. An implication of this view is to reinterpret delusions as having positive content. Although delusional behavior may be largely unstable and nonfunctional, Merleau-Ponty lectures that it still provides a structure around which the mentally ill organize their behavior. This time referring to Alain, Merleau-Ponty lectures that "the falsehoods of mentally disturbed individuals are not themselves deceiving; there is always something positive in their vision which serves to ground their actions" (*CPP* 177). Delusional patients do believe in the reality of their hallucinations, but they still are able to differentiate between a perception and a hallucination. If this were not the case, we could expect that few hallucinating patients could successfully negotiate a room. Rather, we find that they are able to see furniture, doors, and walls even if they might also see, but somehow in a different manner, other objects, things, and persons. It is more reflective of our prejudicial constitution of the perceived world to assume that the hallucinations of the mentally ill are "like" our perceptions but simply false, than to correctly understand they have their own sense. "We must reconstruct the symptomatology by posing questions to the organism that are more precise than those of common sense. Truth only arises from the moment that we reach the center of the personality" (*CPP* 388).

Merleau-Ponty's interpretation of the relationship of phenomenology, psychology, and psychoanalysis is integrative. Reluctant to see Gestalt theory, phenomenology, or psychoanalysis as entailing mutually exclusive methodologies or concepts, Merleau-Ponty draws them out as three sides to an essential insight about the ability of a descriptive developmental approach to the human condition. In his reading of Husserl's phenomenology and its connection to psychology, Merleau-Ponty emphasizes that primal experience underlies all life and all theory construction, instead of focusing on the grounding role Husserl had for phenomenology in relation to the sciences. In so doing, Merleau-Ponty does not see in principle why phenomenology and psychology could not be parallel in all respects even if much of psychology is dominated by an unreflective scientism. Primal experience is held as being similarly explored in Gestalt psychology's understanding of background. Conscious experience calls to our awareness the object, or figure, of perception and causes us to be unaware of the field, or background, in which that figure takes its meaning. The connection between psychology and phenomenology provides an increasing set of tools with which to explore how what is very much present in our experience can become obscure to us. The connection also suggests that while what we desire to represent, believe, explore, or invent can be constructed by social and cultural norms, there is a common background to all human life and thus a way in which a psychology (or phenomenology) can find some general truths without being trapped in relativism. Merleau-Ponty adds psychoanalysis as another theoretical and psychological method to explore this common background. Instead of primal experience or background, psychoanalysis gives us the idea of the unconscious. Merleau-Ponty, in tune with other existentialists, considers this concept too related to metaphors of hiddenness from lived experience and prefers the idea of ambivalence. Ambivalence can show how a conflict between the different stages of development with previous stages can result in disharmony. This could be found in pathological behavior but also would be part of normal development and normal adjustments to change. While such a characterization passes over key elements of standard psychoanalytic theory, it will permit Merleau-Ponty to integrate a wide array of experience into its reach, much as his broad reading of phenomenology in the Sorbonne lectures allows him to include experimental research in his phenomenology. In the next chapter, we will turn to the birth of the self as providing evidence for primal experience as being historically primary and also a residual background in mature life.

3

Syncretic Sociability and the Birth of the Self

The first chapter provided a historical introduction to Merleau-Ponty's work in child psychology by summarizing his pre-1949 comments on childhood. The second chapter introduced the Sorbonne lectures in child psychology and pedagogy by outlining the main theoretical influences of the lectures: phenomenology, Gestalt theory, and psychoanalysis. This chapter will address Merleau-Ponty's characterization of our earliest experiences.

In this chapter, we begin by looking at how Merleau-Ponty depicted early life. Merleau-Ponty describes initial human experiences as displaying a syncretic sociability where the infant does not distinguish between herself and others or between herself and the world. In contrast to thinkers who view the infant as enclosed within an interior world, Merleau-Ponty argues that primary experience is characterized by openness and lack of barriers. This syncretic sociability grounds our intersubjective later life, rather than any kind of cognitive understanding of the other. Given this discussion, Merleau-Ponty must address from where our sense of self and otherness springs. The second section of this chapter will address Merleau-Ponty's view of Henri Wallon and Jacques Lacan's mirror stage. The mirror stage initiates, but does not complete, the formation of a sense of self and other as two similar, but distinct, beings.

Syncretic Sociability

Merleau-Ponty's work suggests that early experience is defined by a continuum with life rather than by an innate sense of selfhood and otherness. We come to the world unable to distinguish ourselves from others. It might seem difficult to explain how we develop a sense of selfhood and a sense of the other from such an original state. For Merleau-Ponty, the question is more, how do we understand the genesis of intersubjectivity if we are isolated within a self-enclosed subjectivity from the beginning? In Husserl, we find the notion of "coupling" which Merleau-Ponty interprets as "I see the other's body and I sense in him the same intention that reciprocally animates my own body. We cannot perceive the other if we make a distinction between *ego* and other. On the contrary, this becomes possible if the psychogenesis begins in a state where the infant ignores differences" (*CPP* 247–48). Merleau-Ponty will contend that developmentally our initial state is one where a distinction between ego and other is not yet present and that this stage is the basis for intersubjective life. Merleau-Ponty's suggestive language implies that primary intersubjectivity is a shared experience.

There are two main parts of Merleau-Ponty's description of our life after the womb to around three to six months of age. First, the infant originally lacks a sense of her body as hers. She has no knowledge of her bodily limits, including what are sensations that arise from internal conditions and what are those that touch us from without. Second, given this lack of a sense of the location and limits of one's embodiment, the infant also draws no distinctions between herself and others.

During Merleau-Ponty's life, the dominant view, one that Merleau-Ponty shared with thinkers such as Freud, Piaget, and B. F. Skinner, was that the infant was unable to focus or direct her visual attention. From his observations of newborns, Piaget concludes that children under eight months old are incapable of imitation. For imitation to be possible, Piaget (1962) suggested that there must be a coordination of vision with the infant's body schema (19). Given that young infants were thought to be incapable of focusing or controlling their bodily movements, imitation could not occur until later. In these views of the earlier part of the twentieth century, the neonate and young infant was conceived to live in a world of a kind of "blooming, buzzing confusion" where internal and external, touch and vision, self and other are intermingled. Although as we will see in chapter 4, contemporary research has indicated that infants are much more aware and able to control their movements than previously thought, one can imagine why this was the dominant view given how a newborn appears to be unable to focus or control her movements. Without certain experimental controls being in place, newborns do not appear to be able to concentrate on an object visually or control their own movements.

Merleau-Ponty followed the view that infants had minimal visual perception and a weak body schema. In early life, consciousness of the body is at most fragmentary. Before three months, the "soldering" between external and internal bodily states has not taken place (*CPP* 248–49). For Merleau-Ponty, this process is physiological; an insufficient amount of neural development has occurred, and in particular, he argues that myelination (the process of acquiring a medullary sheath—the layer of myelin surrounding a medullated nerve fiber) begins to take place from three to six months. Focused attention to one's own body is found later; the child is only able to grasp one hand with another at around two months.

During this time, a sense of the body's extension, possibilities, and limits has not yet formed. Without the body as a type of enclosure for the self, no self-awareness can develop. Merleau-Ponty lectures that our first experiences are marked by a slow progression of a sense of the body: "I am little by little conscious that my body is closed around me" (*CPP* 248). As the infant matures, she will progressively acquire a better sense of her body and the ownership of mental states. Yet, her earliest life is not one of chaos but rather of a radically different structure than our own.

Merleau-Ponty writes that, due to the child's own lack of a strong identification with a "self," the child easily transfers her own intentions and bodily movements onto others and quickly takes on the other's intentions. Syncretic sociability is seen as a phase where the infant, due to an inability to organize her perceptual and tactile world, confuses herself with others. She has no subjectivity and hence no intersubjectivity, traditionally speaking. However, this does not mean that infants are internally preoccupied with no connection to others; rather they have a peculiar existence where internal and external sensations are commingled, including the other's intentions. This anonymous, asubjective life is social in that it is extended out toward others. Merleau-Ponty struggles to express a human intersubjectivity that does not rely upon discrete subjectivities. To speak of encountering the other as not merely a moving object, he deepens a conception of asubjective intersubjectivity and impersonal life. Yet, the accounts of infantile syncretic sociability, however suggestive, run the risk of being the stuff of poetry rather than philosophy or psychology.

Such an idea sounds paradoxical. The absence of subjectivity would seem to necessarily entail the absence of inter*subjectivity*. Much of lived experience is meaningless without the assumption that the other is another human subject just *like* oneself. Language, culture, our sense of being distinct, unique individuals are all grounded in the social world. My nonconscious faith that the other is another subject complete with her own assortment of beliefs, desires, and memories grounds my interactions with her. By the same token, I need the other to understand the value and degree of uniqueness of my own conceptions, acts, and desires. The very idea of "being an individual" can only take place against the relief of a shared social world from which I seek to individuate myself. Our very individuality depends upon this interpersonal world. To speak about myself as an individual, a subject, a woman, a philosopher, and a Canadian, I need to inhabit a world where such terms are meaningful.

Thus, I can inquire into what others are like and can debate the generality of certain traits, but I cannot doubt the other's subjective existence, for that would call into question my own.

Yet, when I examine this faith, I find myself stymied to explain its origins. Why do I feel this awareness of myself as a self and others as other selves? Perhaps my awareness of myself as "me," as a "self" is a product of my upbringing; perhaps I am conditioned to see the world in a certain way. I see that my expectations of relationships are strongly colored by my situation. Rochefoucauld's quotation on love—"There are people who would never have been in love, had they never heard love spoken of"—calls into question how much even our most cherished passions might be determined by our culture (1930, 136). We find variance in our expectations of romantic love and the place it holds in our choices across cultures. Thus, perhaps my relations with others and my sense of self in respect to others reveal more about my situation than something about the human condition in general.

However, explanations that suggest I am merely conditioned by the social world to make this assumption are unsatisfying. While I can see how my affective states toward others are molded by my upbringing and the society I find myself in, my basic intersubjective experience is qualitatively different. The sense that others are experiencing the world with me is much more primary. As much as traditions vary across cultures, a sense of a common shared world experience and human bonds remain universal. It is in this spirit that Merleau-Ponty seeks to discover the affective and original foundation for intersubjective acts and, thereby, for human social life. His solution is to claim that we can, and do, find within the infantile a true lack of difference between subject and other, a continuum that later constitutes adult relations.

Children have an inherent intersubjective bond with others that allows for our later, mature relations to develop. It is this primal connection to others that allows us to not be overwhelmed by our mature alienation from each other. He remains realistic about the relevance of physical and neural development to an understanding of the individual's constitution and maintains a traditional distinction between normal and abnormal development. However, development is not a linear slope toward adulthood where previous states would be jettisoned once self-conscious adulthood is achieved. William Wordsworth's line "the child is the father of the man" is very much prevalent in Merleau-Ponty's psychology. Thus, although all our experiences shape who we are and how we see ourselves and others, our childhoods are particularly influential in mental life when measured against the relative brevity of their temporal duration.

SYNCRETIC SOCIABILITY AND THE BIRTH OF THE SELF

Merleau-Ponty wants to rid psychology of the problem of constructing methods that explain development as always normative—that is, that normal maturity necessarily equates to an improved awareness of self and others. This Piagetean assumption skews research design because it fails to provide sufficient space for intelligent, but not adult, responses. Intelligence is only understood from the standard of the adult and thus uniquely childish responses are poorly interpreted. The value of such accounts is that they provide a history of how adult capacities arise. But the possible error is in assuming that all forms of childhood thought and object-manipulation are nascent forms of corresponding adult variants. With such a reading, one interprets childhood acts as inherently having an adult purpose. In other words, one argues that children merely lack the motor-coordination, learning, and neurological development to engage successfully in adult acts.

For example, child's play is seen as a kind of mimicry of adult behavior; on its own child's play has no significance. Merleau-Ponty strongly argues, in his Sorbonne lectures, that children's acts and behavior have their *own* logic and style of comportment. Even though children often express their acts in relation to adults—for example, "I am playing house like Mommy"—this is not a reflection that the child is truly exhibiting a reduced form of the acts of the mother, father, or another adult figure. Children do not directly imitate adult acts in order to *be* an adult. Rather, they have their own style of behavior based in the meanings they have given the world that are not all similar, nor are all nascent forms of adult meanings. (Merleau-Ponty's best examples of the difference between childhood and adult styles of behavior are taken up in his discussion of child interpretations of surprising phenomena and children's art which will be discussed in chapter 5.)

Merleau-Ponty finds that the infant likewise has a fluid boundary between self and other that finds its origins in this lack of body schema of our earliest post-womb life. "Individual consciousness only appears later, along with the objectification of one's own body, establishing a dividing wall between the other and me and the constitution of the other and of me as 'human beings' in a reciprocal relationship" (*CPP* 248). Intersubjectivity as two subjectivities is preceded by intersubjectivity as a communal experience. For example, Merleau-Ponty refers to the phenomenon of "contagion of cries" where infants spontaneously erupt in wails when one of them cries (249). This first stage of existence is called "a kind of precommunication, an anonymous collectivity . . . a kind of group existence" (248). This early stage is also called syncretic sociability wherein the ego "lives as well in others as in itself" (248). Wallon is paraphrased as describing syncretic sociability as being when "the child cannot limit himself to his own life" (253). What does it mean to argue that there is a state of "anonymous collectivity" where the ego has no, or few, boundaries between itself and others? Is this a kind of delusion on the part of the infant or actually supposed to be a description of intersubjectivity itself?

Merleau-Ponty does not restrict his descriptions of this transitive, syncretic stage to early infantile life. Instead, he continues to use the metaphors of a kind of adualism in his description of adult intersubjectivity. Merleau-Ponty's discussion of the infantile reveals his increasing interest in ideas that push the limits of a subject-centered phenomenology. His concept of syncretic sociability does not destroy the subject; it simply strengthens the claim that another kind of communicative life underlies conscious subjectivity. Merleau-Ponty links his notions of inborn innate processes with his understanding of a primitive anonymous existence. This anonymous existence is not just a period of the subject's early life; it is interwoven within everyday experience.

Merleau-Ponty started in *The Structure of Behavior* to emphasize that we need to understand behavior in global and organized terms. What changes is that a greater stress is placed upon the importance of childhood *experience*. Moreover, the variety of psychological and psychoanalytic studies increases tenfold from his pre-1945 work. In *The Structure of Behavior*, adult behavior and child behavior are described as different solutions to the same existential problem. Development is a consequence of new demands being leveled against the subject by physical or environmental changes. In the *Phenomenology of Perception*, and much more markedly in the Sorbonne lectures, childhood experiences overdetermine adult ones. Childhood experiences are more than just another style or structure in which to encounter the world. Instead, they are "a change in the structure of consciousness, the establishment of a new dimension of experience, the setting forth of an *a priori*" (*PP* 30). For this reason, childhood experience is both original and foundational for adult experience. This basic and early experience sets the ground, or the "*a priori*" as Merleau-Ponty says above, for more complex representational kinds of intersubjective life.

Instead of discovering ourselves firmly within a mind that possesses its own thoughts and understands its boundaries, we find at the base of our experience something that precedes such a centered subject formation: "It can be said that my organism, as a prepersonal cleaving to the general form of the world as an anonymous and general existence, plays, beneath my personal life, the part of an *inborn complex*. It is not some kind of inert thing; it too has something of the momentum of existence" (*PP* 84). Merleau-Ponty notes that this anonymous existence asserts its presence even in the midst of the strongest and most personal sentiments:

"While I am overcome by some grief and wholly given over to my distress, my eyes already stray in front of me, and are drawn, despite everything, to some shining object, and thereupon resume their autonomous existence" (84). He continues to note that my existence as subjective, conscious individuality is precarious and cannot be the ground upon which meaning in my life is built: "Personal existence is intermittent and when this tide turns and recedes, decision can henceforth endow my life with only artificially induced significance" (84).

Childhood's disproportionate significance enables one to understand how intersubjective relations are based in the formative years. To Merleau-Ponty, Piaget errs by considering normal development as ending in a mature, adult perspective free of infantile immaturity. He contradicts such a view and argues that, in fact, the child's asubjective perceptions are the basis for adult intersubjectivity:

> Piaget brings the child to a mature outlook as if the thoughts of the adult were self-sufficient and disposed of all contradictions. But, in reality, it must be the case that the child's outlook is in some way vindicated against the adult's and against Piaget, and that the unsophisticated thinking of our earliest years remains as an indispensable acquisition underlying that of maturity, if there is to be for the adult one intersubjective world. (*PP* 355)

Piaget's mistake is to assume that a new developmental stage completely overlays the previous one. For Piaget, when a conflict exists between two stages, the more "mature" outlook will eventually succeed. Merleau-Ponty counters such an assumption by pointing out that adult experience would be senseless without an overdetermining childhood. Mankind's unhesitating rootedness in the world as well as in an intersubjective life is insufficiently explained by the concept of progressive development.

In Merleau-Ponty's account, intersubjectivity clearly doesn't signify two subjectivities engaged in some type of communication or mutual recognition. On the contrary, intersubjectivity's nature involves a mode of being where subjectivity is either not yet formed (as in the case of infant intersubjectivity) or not primary (as in adult intersubjective experience). To begin to describe infantile intersubjective experience, one must turn toward how an infant responds to internal and external stimuli. Traditionally, classical psychology suggests that we understand our own sensations through kinesthesia—an organizing of a mass of brute sensations that tells one about one's body (*CPP* 246). Merleau-Ponty notes that such a conception makes the discussion of the other practically impossible. Others would be nothing but an amalgamation of sense-perceptions. We would have to argue that at a certain stage children "conclude" that other persons are other subjects through watching the other's behavior. Children's relations to others would be no more emotionally charged than their relations to any other moving object. For Merleau-Ponty, it is true that children, for an extended period in childhood, have an ambiguous understanding of other people as other subjects. But it is not the case that other people are objects for children. Such a description not only presents an argumentative difficulty when explaining intersubjectivity; it also ignores the true manner in which the child, and the adult, experience their bodies and perceptions. Perceptions are not transmissions from the external world into the internal one. The body is not a processor of these perceptions, and, most importantly, intersubjectivity is not a matter of discrete subjects. When I live in the world, it is not similar to watching a movie where things pass in front of me and I passively receive them. Nor do I experience my body like a thing that processes sensations akin to how a money-counter counts bills. For instance, it is impossible for me to separate my physical processing of a visual perception from the sense that perception gives me.

In the *Phenomenology of Perception,* Merleau-Ponty invokes the necessity of the infantile to account for adult interpersonal relations. In contrast to adults, children do not consider "other minds" to be a problematic issue. They undergo no inferential acrobatics in assuming that others are "like" them. For the child, perspectives are not possessions of particular subjects. The world is not a world "for her." The world itself simply is, and all are immersed in it:

> The perception of other people and the intersubjective world is problematical only for adults. The child lives in a world which he unhesitatingly believes accessible to all around him. He has no awareness of himself or of others as private subjectivities, nor does he suspect that all of us, himself included, are limited to one certain point of view of the world. (*PP* 355)

Naturally, children are not concerned with the philosophical issue of "other minds." They are also impartial to the more everyday problems of reconciling their own opinions with the views and lifestyles of others. Children do not differentiate others as having "other" lives; there is only one life. The typical childhood response to difference is frustration, not indignation.

The most complicated, and philosophically relevant, part of Merleau-Ponty's description of the early stages of life is the idea of syncretic sociability. This idea is characterized by experiences that appear to emanate from a *shared* rather than an individuated experience. For instance, a subject responds to the other's emotional state prior to any outward, readable sign that indicates what the other is feeling. Of course, we can easily think of explanations for syncretic sociability that make no speculative leaps about a common, affective experience. We can understand the childhood tendency to confuse her actions with those of others as projection. The idea of "projection" would argue that I might attribute intentions to others that are in fact my own. I might label my partner as being "selfish" when, in fact, I am feeling selfish. A child would seem particularly prone to projection: blaming other children for bad thoughts and behavior to cover up, or justify, her own.

Merleau-Ponty agrees that often children and adults have psychological reasons for "transferring" emotions to others, but he also suggests that syncretic sociability cannot be completely explained by transference. Suggestively, Merleau-Ponty writes that infantile intentional states are not possessed but are generally experienced by more than one subject. Intentionality is not a subjective directedness that emanates from *one* subject toward *one* object; rather it is the sheer movement of life that can be shared among subjects. Adult reflections on intersubjectivity emphasize the cognitive awareness of the other as another person like me. While this is part of our intersubjective life, Merleau-Ponty's work highlights a more primary continuity that precedes our subjective intersubjectivity

Merleau-Ponty thinks this early stage has a continuous and principal place in adult life. Without the transitive stage, interpersonal relations would have to arise from an intellectual inference, namely, "He acts like me, and therefore, he is a subject like me." Such a conception would fail to explain how other-identification occurs *alongside* the genesis of subjectivity. Merleau-Ponty adopts the view that child development shows us how our increasing grasp of ourselves as self-conscious beings with agency develops alongside our increasing sense of the consciousness and agency of others. A reciprocal model of other-awareness, while sensible from our adult perspective, cannot be the original manner of our intersubjective relations. If it were the case that at some point the child infers that the other is "like her," she would need to already have a sense of herself. Somehow, subjectivity would have to develop alone. How could this occur? What would subjectivity mean to the subject when it is not juxtaposed to other subjects?

As described above, others are not in any way "comprehended" given the rudimentary state of the infant's psychological development. Yet, the infant's experience of others is not simply a void; the infant is not a vacant container of sensations. Infants demonstrate unusual kinds of coexistence with other infants and adults that indicates a strong attachment to others, even though one assumes that there is no corresponding set of intentional states toward others. One example Merleau-Ponty mentions several times is how a room full of babies will simultaneously break out into almost uniform crying during the first three months of age (*CPP* 249). After this stage, babies are relatively indifferent to the whines and noises of their nursery mates. The transition is marked by infants' increasing ability to recognize others as distinct from themselves. Prior to the self-other distinction, Merleau-Ponty describes infants as holding pain and other emotive/intentional states as general experiences. Infantile intentional states are transitive, intersubjective states not because they are directed toward other persons, but because they are held in common.

The emotions children display toward others are a reflection of their ignorance of other minds, not self-centered reactions to difference. Typically, such truly childish behavior is viewed as childhood narcissism, and parents are prone to proclaim, "You think the world revolves around you!" For children, however, it isn't that the world revolves around them. The child is expressing frustration at others for not seeing things "for how they are." Children lack an understanding that mother and father, for instance, have the freedom not to feel the way they do. At the same time, the child does not appreciate that her own thoughts, ideas, and opinions could be changed. For that matter, the child does not grasp that she has opinions, thoughts, and ideas and that, as such, they are *her* opinions, thoughts, and ideas. Egocentrism, in this sense, is the absence of the knowledge that humans have interior states that vary from person to person. For children, experience is not something that is had; it is something that is. Merleau-Ponty writes: "He [the child] has no knowledge of points of view. For him, men are empty heads turned towards one single, self-evident world where everything takes place" (*PP* 355). Since the child has visually identified the other's body as a lived body, it has exceeded the early syncretic stage, but it has not yet achieved an appreciation of the otherness of the other, nor of the mineness of the self.

The child's frustration with others would seem to indicate that she fails to appreciate the other's point of view, and hence the other's own subjective states. In "The Question of Method in Child Psychology," Merleau-Ponty writes that children's behavior is characterized by a lack of concern for the other because there is no category of "other" versus a concept of "self." Children are thus both more altruistic and individualistic for this reason:

> Children do not think of themselves, but rather of what interests them, since they are ignorant of the frontiers which separate the self and others and they are indifferent about themselves and others. The self

ignores itself insofar as it is the center of the world. It is imitation that
will bring about self-consciousness. The child is radically altruistic and
individualistic at the same time, because of this lack of differentiation
with regard to others. In fact, it would be better to say that the child is
neither truly altruistic nor truly individualistic for precisely this reason.
(*CPP* 427)

In his discussion of Paul Guillaume's (1971) work on imitation in children, Merleau-Ponty stresses the interpretation above that children confuse themselves with others.

However, does not the above description seem to ultimately uphold the thesis that first we are entrapped within our own subjective states and only as we mature can we truly understand the other? While there is an aspect of childhood egocentrism that highlights the internal preoccupation of children and their disinterest in other people's emotional states, Merleau-Ponty also appeals to an idea of life itself as something that predates and postdates all subjective experience. He encourages us to render "*lived experience* more profoundly" and suggests that the self and other are about certain orientations in lived experience rather than about essential qualities (*CPP* 32, italics original). Merleau-Ponty lectures that life is the ur-Gestalt upon which individual experience takes root. Not only are our philosophical problems with other minds only possible upon such a ground, but so too are our philosophical concerns about death. "When Malraux says, 'One dies alone, therefore one lives alone,' he is making a false deduction. Life in fact radically surpasses individualities, and it is impossible to judge it in relationship to death, which is an individual failure" (32). Later in a discussion of Wallon's notion of "ultra-things," we will see how both the child and adult are most likely to provide fantastical answers to issues that go beyond lived experience.

This concept of syncretic sociability allows us to see our relations with the other as not requiring selfhood or other-awareness. If we have an ability to "pre-communicate," our first experiences are meaningful and also not localized in adult self-conscious subjectivity. Syncretic sociability is a kind of primary intersubjectivity insofar as it is expresses a relationship. Where it differs is the requirement that to have such a relationship one must have self- and other-awareness. Such a conception of intersubjectivity is a bold thesis to advance, since its defense in part relies upon a stage of life that an impenetrable veil has been drawn over. Moreover, Merleau-Ponty writes about a stage of pre-subjective life that is almost totally foreclosed by the limits of sense. Experiences are not typically understood to be "general." Rather, they are *someone's* experiences.

Of course, our own experiences can be more or less clear and we can struggle to find fitting descriptions of them. But language does not easily lend itself to describing what it would mean to suggest that an experience can be held in common and that intentions can be shared.

Since Merleau-Ponty's best-known theme, perception, is absent from his discussions of early infant syncretic sociability, we could conclude that this idea of a general, syncretic life is simply a result of his ill-informed ideas about an early inability to visually organize sensation. Perceptions, insofar as they are perceptions *of* something, are decisive for subject-hood. Since Merleau-Ponty thinks that infants lack the physical capacity to focus upon objects and have yet to identify their bodies as *their own* bodies, he concludes that a large part of early confusion between self and other can be correlated with an early pre-perceptual stage.

One striking difference between child and adult perception is the child's lack of clear distinctions between different senses and between affective and visual divisions. Increasingly in his works, Merleau-Ponty argues that this kind of synesthesia is more than an early mode of experience; it is integral to all perception. Why, then, do we typically view synesthesia as a curiosity, even pathological? Since our intellectual judgments are provided by our cultural and linguistic world, we learn that visual data are something distinct from tactile data. We don't have an everyday way to speak of how seeing a fuzzy kiwi is also a tactile experience even when we don't touch the fruit. Indeed, to speak of a blending of visual and tactile information seems somewhat nonsensical, but upon some reflection it is hard to deny that a bed of nails evokes in us a slight recoil even when there is simply no possibility of our skin being exposed to it. Thus, the child's easy fluidity between various "kinds" of sense experience is not only a description that evokes early modes of structuring experience; it is also a hidden aspect of our own.

The importance of this holistic conception of childhood perception is that it runs against any kind of division of the senses or the idea of an initial, insurmountable division between cognitive and physical capacities. Traditional conceptions about the senses—sight, touch, smell, and other senses—depict the child "as the receiver of different sensations from different sense organs which must be subsequently synthesized" (*CPP* 145). The senses are not distinct functions in immature states that develop independently. On the contrary, argues Merleau-Ponty, the senses originally *lack* distinction. The task of development is not to better synthesize disparate senses, but to *distinguish* them: "Instead, it is a question of a *totality* of given sensations experienced through the intermediary of the *whole* body. The child makes use of his body as a totality and does not distinguish between what is given by the eyes, the ears, and so forth" (145, emphasis original). This original "confusion" of the senses supports the argument that psychology and philosophy have been too oculocentric. Perception's primordial status is not disorganized, although it is intersensorial. "We claimed that *perception* does not commence through multiple, disjointed experiences, but rather through some very nebulous *global structures* that undergo a progressive differentiation. Prior to judgment, a more fundamental unity exists" (*CPP* 146, emphasis original). Judgment overlays the original synesthetic unity of experience.

Merleau-Ponty's discussions of a syncretic sociability underlying adult life suggest that there is something he is trying to capture about our intersubjectivity in general. His *Phenomenology of Perception* summarizes that my sense of self, my personal history, my thoughts and beliefs about my body all take place within this primordial existence. "In order to have some inkling of the nature of that amorphous existence which preceded my own history, and which will bring it to a close, I have only to look within me at that time which pursues its own independent course, and which my personal life utilizes but does not entirely overlay" (*PP* 347). Our primordial existence is not just the earliest days, weeks, and months of our life, but an anonymous, asubjective presence in our current existence. I take this part of my life up at every moment, but in no sense is it mine as I have claimed possession of my constitution of the world. Rather, our primordial existence is the shared, subjectless experience which precedes and postdates us.

In a somewhat similar vein, M. C. Dillon expands upon Merleau-Ponty's ideas and argues that adult emotion, especially love, is grounded in the pre-communicative stage. For Dillon, syncretic sociability and pre-communication are relevant to understand adult interactions. He writes that syncretic sociability indicates "how it is possible for human beings to recognize each other as such and develop at a personal level the pre-personal communication that is our birthright" (Dillon 1997, 129). Dillon discusses intersubjectivity as "intercorporality," emphasizing the lack of a mind-body split within the infant, as well as the fact that children respond to other bodies and not to other "minds." The critique of a mind-body split is extremely important for Merleau-Ponty, but more pressing for this investigation into intersubjectivity is not the lack of a mind/body split, but the lack of *subjectivity* in early infantile experiences. Dillon moves between metaphors where a self-other distinction is present to those where one is not. Obviously, his understanding of love (as being grounded upon pre-communication) is an argument which supports the idea of a transitive intersubjective stage, but his employment in the same pages of the reciprocity thesis suggests something more akin to a traditional notion of reciprocity between two subjective intentional beings. Merleau-Ponty's descriptions of early infant experience argue that subjectivity is not necessary for intersubjective relations.

The Birth of Self- and Other-Awareness

Dillon points out that if one takes Merleau-Ponty's descriptions of childhood experience as accurate, one is left with the puzzle of from where does the adult, subjective experience spring? "The problem is not 'how does the infant begin to recognize others as other consciousnesses?' but rather 'how does the infant learn to differentiate himself and others as separate beings within a sphere of experience that lacks this differentiation?'" (Dillon 1997, 12). Why would we leave this undifferentiated stage? What shapes our intersubjective life after we acquire a sense of self as limited and a sense of our own, and others', possession of emotions, desires, and thoughts?

In the *Phenomenology of Perception*, Merleau-Ponty cites Husserl (1970) as writing, in the unpublished material that later became the *Crisis*, that transcendental subjectivity *is* intersubjectivity. Merleau-Ponty writes, "Transcendental subjectivity is a revealed subjectivity, revealed to itself and to others, and is for that reason an intersubjectivity" (*PP* 361). In fact, Husserl did not declare that transcendental subjectivity is the same thing as intersubjectivity. Instead, he claims that subjectivity is what it is—a constitutively functioning ego—only within an intersubjective framework: "Now everything becomes complicated as soon as we consider that subjectivity is what it is—an ego functioning constitutively—only within an intersubjectivity" (Husserl 1970, 172). It is not the case, for Husserl, that *first* there is intersubjectivity and *then* the ego springs into being. By contrast, Merleau-Ponty argues that the incomplete reduction (another non-Husserlian thesis) leads one to acknowledge the existence of an intractable intersubjective bond between individuals that appears prior to individualization.

For Husserl, the ego is self-evident. With Merleau-Ponty's reinterpretation of intersubjectivity as grounding subjectivity, the subject as ego becomes more problematic. In many ways, the problem at hand for Merleau-Ponty is not "what is the nature of a pre-subjective stage?" but "why subjectivity?" Merleau-Ponty describes infantile conscious life in terms of syncretism or indistinction of perspectives; thus, for him, the problem is not "'how does the infant begin to recognize others as other consciousnesses?' but rather 'how does the infant learn to differentiate himself and others as separate beings within a sphere of experience that lacks this differentiation?'" (Dillon 1997, 121). As Dillon writes, after Merleau-Ponty provides a strong argument for a primitive life where effectively no subject-object distinction operates, the issue is not "how the infant transcends an aboriginal self-centeredness, it is rather a question of how he learns to distinguish his experience of himself from his experience of others, that is, how he transcends syncretism" (121). Merleau-Ponty's characterization of infantile experience argues that a developmental account of the subject demonstrates the existence of a syncretic sociability. Nonetheless, Merleau-Ponty does not want to conclude that adult subjective experience is an illusion.

The mirror stage is necessary to explain this break from an infantile intersubjective life to a conscious subjective life. However, the mirror stage does not herald in total self-consciousness and consciousness of others which overlays infantile transitive existence. Merleau-Ponty takes his understanding of the mirror stage mainly from Wallon (1963) and Lacan (2006) and, in interpreting their theory, offers a unique view of the birth of the self. Although critical of some of Wallon's characterizations, Merleau-Ponty is faithful to the key tenets of Wallon's theory of the mirror stage, in particular his stress upon the role of the parent in the mirror stage. Merleau-Ponty was one of the first to pick up on the importance of what would later become a seminal piece of psychoanalytic literature, Lacan's revision (2006, 75–81) of Wallon's mirror stage. Lacan, a friend and colleague of Merleau-Ponty's, emphasizes the radical nature of the mirror stage and the break it initiates between asubjective and subjective life.

What is the mirror stage? The standard view is that between four to twelve months we begin to recognize our own images in a mirror. We start to engage in play with the mirror and understand some kind of equivalence between our actions and those of the mirror-self. While we will continue to take a lively interest in our mirror images long after this stage, the mirror stage heralds the birth of a structure that will allow us to differentiate between the syncretic nature of our initial lived experience and the requirements of knowing the self has limits for mature intersubjective interactions. Merleau-Ponty stresses that the mirror stage itself is a social event and not an internally motivated instinct toward self-identification.

The mirror stage is tightly connected with the images of the parents in the mirror and the behavior of the parents toward the child's image. The first mirror-images the infant focuses upon and responds to are those of the *parent* in the mirror. Typically, the infant is "introduced" to the mirror by the parent holding the child up and pointing her out—"Hey look, is that you in the mirror? Look, here I am! Is that your nose?"

The first step in the mirror stage is not thus not self-awareness, but the identification of the *other* in the mirror. The child first acquires the ability to recognize and play simple games (peek-a-boo, smiling) with her parents' images in the mirror, but does not play with her own image. "For example, the infant smiles at the specular image of his father. When the father speaks, the infant turns around, surprised. He did not therefore have a precise consciousness of the difference between the image and the model" (*CPP* 250). Prior to recognizing himself in a mirror, the infant begins to learn to acknowledge that the other's mirror image is something distinct from the other's physical presence. "The infant begins to consciously grasp something, even though he does not yet have possession of the image-model relationship, and he does not know that the image is a projection of his father in the mirror" (250–51).

However, mirror recognition of the other is not instantaneous or devoid of confusion between image and reality. When the child turns around to refer to the father holding him from looking at the mirror-father, the mirror-father still retains a "quasi-reality" and "phantom-like" existence. Through the development of understanding the mirror image of the other, the infant will focus on her own image, which originally was not as interesting as the specular image of the other. This process of identification will be more complex since we never acquire a perspective of our own faces without the aid of the mirror. Where the infant can move her gaze back and forth between the parent and the parent-image, she cannot perform this kind of reference with her own image and face. Self-awareness is thus posterior to other-awareness. It will be the mirror-parent compared to the mirror-self that will initiate the development of self-recognition in the child.

Thus, the mirror stage initiates *inter*subjectivity. We must distinguish here between two notions of intersubjectivity. One is the kind of asubjective immersion in a shared life that we witnessed in syncretic sociability as discussed above. Another is a subjective intersubjectivity where distinct subjects participate together in a shared social life where they recognize the fact that each subject has her own perspective. Consciousness of oneself as a bodily thing-in-the-world allows for intersubjective relations as we typically conceive of them. However, we do not live in our bodies as things in the world; in other words, I do not first and foremost experience myself as something that I can observe and form judgments about, like a chair, a cat, or another person; rather, I am the center of my existence. I require something to induce me to take a step back from myself and to think of how I might appear to others. Then I can, conceptually if not experientially, think of myself as one of many visible things in the world. Merleau-Ponty follows Wallon in thinking that the stage of one's life that inaugurates this ability to separate from one's lived situation is the mirror stage. The way that the infant is pushed to unify her sensations as belonging to herself is through being given a visual object with which to identify. Without the mirror as symbol of self, the child would struggle to form a strong self versus other distinction.

Merleau-Ponty is quick to write that the mirror stage is not simply the "adding" of subjectivity to the animalistic, asubjective nature of the infant. The mirror stage does not initiate a stage wherein imitation occurs fluidly and without reservation, where the child can easily take the other as "another being like me." In returning to the child's imitation of facial gestures, Merleau-Ponty argues against any kind of account that supposes imitation to be a kind of comparison made by the infant. For instance, in returning a smile, it is evident that the child is not responding with a conscious intent to signal "I like you too." This would require a kind of comparison that the infant is unlikely to be able to make. "This operation would presume a kind of reasoning by analogy: to understand the significance of the smile of the other after one's own smile" (*CPP* 247). Such a move would require that the infant conceptually be able to move from the very different interoceptive image of her own body to the seen body of the other. To smile is not the same as to see a smile. Merleau-Ponty concludes therefore that *"we must presume that the child has different ways to globally identify the other's body"* (*CPP* 247, italics original). Infants, children, and adults all have parts of their bodies that they cannot see except by means of a mirror. How then could we assume that some kind of comparison of "you are like me" is taking place when it comes to facial responses in particular? Merleau-Ponty argues that there is a global identification, a type of Gestalt that the child uses to associate with others and not a conscious intellectual comparison between self and other.

Certainly, the infant has awareness: the infant displays both delight and pain. Merleau-Ponty never depicts the infant as an automaton motivated solely by instinct. But to understand the nature of this awareness, one must not assume a robust sense of self. The infant's "self-awareness" is based upon an embodied perspective that does not recognize her own body as "one of many." The later egocentrism in children is a residual part of the original relationship one has to one's body; the child does not acknowledge the viewpoints of others because she fails to understand that she has a viewpoint.

A self-awareness that includes the understanding of oneself *as* a subject and others as corresponding subjectivities is a much later acquisition initiated by the mirror stage and, hence, has a less stable ground than the original, indistinct neonate life. The primordial nature of original life is also present in adult experience; one is always immersed within one's body and therefore one can never completely relate to it as a thing. The visual representation of one's own body permits one to make the critical step toward taking oneself as a discrete being for other. Citing Lacan's mirror stage essay, Merleau-Ponty lectures that the child becomes a spectacle—the child "is no longer only a sensing ego, but a spectacle; he is this someone we can see" (*CPP* 254). In psychoanalytic language, the child moves from being entirely an id toward an ego—a sense of self as distinct from others—and a superego—an ability to distance herself from herself which is required in order for the child to master her desires: "The infant constructs a visible ego: a superego that ceases to be overwhelmed by his desires" (254). Merleau-Ponty prefers the psychoanalytic view to Wallon's more intellectual characterization of the mirror image because it better captures the affective and imaginative nature of the mirror stage. In so identifying the joy, the alienation, and the ambivalence of the mirror image, Lacan's characterization also better highlights why we continue to be transfixed by our images. If it were the case that the mirror provided an important cognitive tool to understanding the self as a spectacle, it is hard to explain our continued delight and frustration at our own images long after we have mastered self-awareness.

As in *The Structure of Behavior*, Merleau-Ponty argues that while animal responses vary in front of the mirror, it is only humans that play and engage with the mirror image throughout their lives. The behavior of animals in front of mirrors suggests that either they take the mirror image to be another animal, such as in the case of birds, or, as in the case of primates, they discover that the mirror is not another animal and thereafter cease to find the mirror interesting. Thus, animals have a body schema, but they do not have a body image. They are able to move in the world in a meaningful manner but do not develop attitudes or images, conscious or unconscious, concerning their own bodies. Their bodies are a constant given that never calls for explicit objectification. The mirror is uninteresting for primates because it does not represent the animal's own self; the animal does not live its body as this "animal" it sees. In "The Child's Relations with Others," Merleau-Ponty notes that one must not assume that the child's behavior can be compared to animal behavior (*CPP* 250). In his lecture "The Adult's View of the Child" (1949–50), Merleau-Ponty again stresses that:

> Only the child will attentively contemplate the mirror, recognizing himself and responding with an intense jubilation. This jubilation responds clearly to the correspondence between observed changes in visual appearance and interior intention. For the infant, the event of the mirror image signifies a certain recuperation of his own body. Before this visual

control, there is only a splitting, a bodily dispersion (for instance in castration fantasies, a particular case of this state, and unquestionably in many dreams). (*CPP* 86)

The child is fascinated by her own image in the mirror without demanding to find out from whence it came. The primate is only interested to find out if another animal is indeed there. And, when it discovers that the mirror image is not an animal and that the image will not, on its own accord, do anything, the primate often turns its back to the mirror in an act of apparent irritation.

Nonetheless, Merleau-Ponty does not want to assert that one should return to a focus on intelligence. He strongly critiques developmental theories that use intellectual progress as guidelines, since they overlook the importance of the lived-body's development. In "The Question of Method in Child Psychology," Merleau-Ponty rejects a "psychology of cognition" as espoused by Piaget, and sides with a psychology which gives the body "a central function" (*CPP* 422). Merleau-Ponty calls this a "correlative psychology" and finds that:

> The body is no longer only one of the elements involved in the development of the child's intelligence; it is not simply one object among many. The restructuration of experience becomes a central phenomenon and the development of the body (and concomitantly, that of the personality) are as important as intellectual development. (422)

The child's intellectual progress is critical, but it should be understood as part of "a single developmental dynamism" (422). Wallon correctly depicts the child's developing bodily motility and self-awareness as integral to the emergence of subjectivity.

For the child, images are endowed with a quality that is later suppressed as they increasingly are used as references for "real" things. The image of the father is endowed with a quality similar to the father's real presence. Hence, the child will play with the image, smiling at it, pointing to it, just as she will play with the father. The images have their own reality, and there is no necessary "parceling out" of identity. In other words, the child must not make the mirror image a property of the "father" identity. The mirror image retains more significance than merely being a reference to a real subject. "For the child, there can be in the father's mirror image a phantom that has a certain degree of reality" (*CPP* 423). Critiquing Wallon's conception of "double identification," Merleau-Ponty argues that the child does not have both a "mirror father" and a "real father" which pertain to one father-identity:

> For the child, the visual space (of the image) and the kinesthetic space (where his body resides) are not comparable. There is no true duality for the child; this notion belongs to the adult's thought. Thus, no reduction takes place permitting the convergence of two givens into one via some sort of intellectual effort. (*CPP* 424)

Merleau-Ponty alleges that adults too share this relationship with images, where images retain a quality beyond a simple representation. Among adults, we find that images likewise have a sense of possessing an emotive sense that goes beyond them functioning merely as representations. "Even for adults, the image is not a simple sign of the reality it represents; they are not insensitive to the destruction of photos of themselves. Also, when adults have their pictures stolen, they have the impression that a small piece of themselves has been taken" (*CPP* 423). We can think of how today in a world awash with pictures and videos, we do not tire of these images, but seem to have an endless interest and appetite for them.

As described above, the original world is one of a meaningful background experience devoid of sharp demarcations and representations. The child thus relates through relationships and connections and not through acquiring new judgments about persons, things, or herself. Since the first encounter with mirrors is with the parents, the child learns not just to associate images with the person who creates them, but also to connect the relationship between the images (and, thus, to build on the preexisting relationship with the parent). Instead of comparing and inferring that the two images are the same, the child must develop a sense of herself as taking a certain "role" in the relation between these images: "The child has to learn to see himself as a *role*" (*CPP* 424, emphasis original). It isn't just an intellectual operation of identifying similar visual patterns, but a restructuration of the child's affective relations by virtue of the new status that the child takes up by now seeing himself as also a being observable to others. The role the child learns to play is that of a particular human in a particular world—that is, the child of this mother and father, this brother, and so on. The mirror image provides the visual evidence that the child needs to start a representational map of relationships.

For Merleau-Ponty, the mirror stage revolves around how the infant places her own *body* in relation to others: "The child must come to understand that there are two points of view about himself and that his body which feels is also visible, not just for the child, but also for others" (*CPP* 424). The focus rests upon reconciling embodied experience and the "new" visual givens. The child sees her image as signifying more than "I am the double of this image," because a new organization of her world is demanded where the child takes a place in *relation* to these other images. The most difficult step is "displacing" the image and making a connection between it and one's own embodied experience. The virtual place in the mirror is initially the child's own image coupled with the parent-image "looking in" as well. The child's original asubjective state is transformed into an intersubjective one. This transformation is not a momentary, defining experience that permanently sets down a new paradigm for the child; the mirror stage is "neither instantaneous nor complete" (424). Merleau-Ponty repeats that if the mirror stage signified an intellectual process of self- and other-awareness, we would find children to either have or not have this knowledge, the way I know or do not know the sum of 2 plus 2. Instead the mirror stage is a process and never "completed," hence our fascination and frustration at images of ourselves.

Psychoanalytic theory has returned to reexamine the importance of the parent in the mirror stage. Perhaps influenced by Merleau-Ponty, Lacan later revises his earlier vision of the mirror stage by emphasizing the importance of the images of the parents in the mirror. To form an identification with one's own body image, one must first be prompted by the parents to recognize one's own image. Lacan's earlier mirror stage essay (written in 1936) focused primarily upon the infant identifying herself in the mirror (2006, 75–81). In Seminar VIII (2001), Lacan lectures that the other's mirror image is instrumental in the formation of a sense of self, of an ego. The child's affective relations with the parent are what allow her to be impelled to take interest in her own image, not vice versa. The child undergoes a double identification with the parent (here: *l'Autre*) as well as with the parent-image. It is in the perception of the parent-image's action toward the infant-image that the child forms a sense of self based on the acts of the parent: "À savoir que, déjà dans cette situation spéculaire, se dédouble, et cette fois au niveau de l'Autre, et par l'Autre, le moi desire, j'entends desire par lui" (Knowing this split self, already in this specular situation is at the level of the Other. It is by the Other that the ego desires, and I understand desire through it.) (2001, 415–16). Lacan's own theory develops differently than Merleau-Ponty's. But both Lacan and Merleau-Ponty focus upon the fragility of this ego in its development and the importance of the parent in the child's developing ability to symbolize her experience. Most relevant for this text is the disjunction between the mirror image and primal experience as well as how this difference plays out in intersubjective relations.

Identification of the self and the other in the mirror does not create a robust sense of self. The very experience of doubling is mysterious and focuses the infant to choose between looking at either the mirror-image parent who holds a child in her arms or the real parent. However, when turning to the real parent, the infant-image disappears. Thus, only through the mirror does the child understand (and begin to have anxieties about) the parent's attitudes. Unlike one's own image, the other's body does not change as much from image to perception and thus has a stability that the child does not have with regard to her own image. Both Lacan and Merleau-Ponty highlight how image formation is based upon the experience of the *other*, not upon an innate desire for self-reflection.

For Merleau-Ponty and the later Lacan, the mirror creates a relationship between the infant's body and the parent's. Obviously, a relation existed prior to the mirror stage, but the specular image introduces the child into the world of adult relationships. The child most often turns its head toward the real father or mother in delight when the mirror images are "playing" with one another. The child will continue this "that's you!" play long after we would estimate "recognition" has taken place. Bruce Fink (1999) provides an excellent summary of the importance of Lacan's mirror stage that highlights the intersubjective nature of this stage:

> More important than his early description of the mirror stage, however, is Lacan's 1960 *reformulation* of the mirror stage, currently available only in French. Here Lacan suggests that the mirror image is internalized and invested with libido because of an approving gesture made by the parent who is holding the child before the mirror (or watching the child look at itself in the mirror). In other words, *the mirror image takes on such importance as a result of the parent's recognition, acknowledgment, or approval*—expressed in a nodding gesture that has already taken on a symbolic meaning, or in such expressions as "Yes, baby, that's you!" often uttered by ecstatic, admiring, or simply bemused parents. (88, italics original)

Fink continues by noting that, for humans, the mirror stage is only accomplished with the participation of an important person in the child's life: "In human beings, the mirror image does not become formative of the ego, of a sense of self, unless it is *ratified* by a person of importance to the child" (88). The child's own image in the mirror is not meaningful in itself since it has no necessary affective connection to how the child feels. However, the child has affective relations with the adults in its early environment and, thus, will be immediately interested in *their* images in a mirror. Investment in the mirror "self" comes later.

One of the most significant aspects of the mirror stage is the focus on just how incomplete and fractured the developing body image is for the child. Once the child has, via the other's mirror image, made an affective association with her own mirror image, she will begin to identify her experiences with that reflection. The child's body image will be based upon the unharmonious mixture of lived experience and the distinct image facing the child. Syncretic sociability accepts the nature of experience as ambiguous; the image presents the child with a solid unity which does not accord with the infant's experience. Lacan emphasizes this point in his essay "The Mirror Stage." He writes that the image presents to the child an image, an external Gestalt, that signifies a mastery the child can only *see* in an exterior form since it clashes with the turbulence of the child's immersion in the world:

> For the total form of his [the infant's] body, by which the subject anticipates the maturation of his power in a mirage, is given to him only as a gestalt, that is, by an exteriority in which, to be sure, this form is more constitutive than constituted, but in which, above all, it appears to him as the contour of his stature that freezes it and in a symmetry that reverses it, in opposition to the turbulent movements with which the subject feels he animates it. (2006, 76)

The body image does not nicely complement the preexisting natural body schema of the infant. Instead, the image of one's own body is sharply at odds with the way one experiences one's body and, hence, the child has to struggle to accept that this image is indeed her.*

Merleau-Ponty writes that *"the visual image that the child has of his body is extremely incomplete"* (*CPP* 424, italics original). The new visual data must be integrated into the child's preexisting experience. The child does not have a global picture of her body. This situated aspect of her experiences

---

* A piece Merleau-Ponty was well familiar with, Lacan's "Les complexes familiaux dans la formation de l'individu" [Family Complexes in the Formation of the Individual] (1938), commissioned by Wallon, also articulates this point. Lacan writes: "Mais tandis qu'il subit cette suggestion émotionnelle ou motrice, le sujet ne se distingué pas de l'image elle-même. Bien plus, dans la discordance caractéristique de cette phase, l'image ne fait qu'ajouter l'intrusion temporaire d'une tendance étrangère. Appelons-la intrusion narcissique: l'unité qu'elle introduit dans les tendances contribuera pourtant à la formation du moi. Mais, avant que le moi affirme son identité, il se confond avec cette image qui le forme, mais l'aliène primordialement." [But even while the subject undergoes an emotional or motor influence from the mirror image, he is not able to distinguish the image itself. Moreover, during the characteristic discordance of this phase, the image only adds a temporary alien intrusion. We can call this the narcissistic intrusion: the unity that the mirror image introduces contributes to the formation of the ego. But, before the ego can affirm its identity, it is confused with the image that forms it; it is primordially alienated.] (Lacan 2001, 43)

of the world accounts for the strong egocentric outlook of the child. The child's body is not a part of the world but is, rather, the very invisible nexus of the world. The young infant must integrate the visual givens of her hand with the tactile given of "grasping," but the body image itself requires a new global integration, a new body schema:

> Understanding the mirror image means integrating new givens into its schema. Therefore, the child is going to assume, to take upon himself, the image of the mirror, an operation which is much more concrete than the one described by Wallon. An integration of eccentric givens takes place, givens considered as valuable as those of vision. A restructuration of the corporal schema also occurs. (*CPP* 424)

The pre-mirror stage body schema does not harmoniously blend in with the post-mirror stage body schema. The visual image of one's own body requires a new way of *être au monde* (being in the world).

Lived experience always finds an uncomfortable fit within any representation of it. No picture, movie, mirror image of my body can fully capture my experience. Hence, Merleau-Ponty stresses the dreamlike quality of the image. He does not characterize the image as "unreal," but instead underlines the confusion it raises in real experience. The image appears dreamlike because it asks for an impossible joining together of this visual thing and one's own experiences. The child learns through play that this image is somehow related to her own actions. But her delight at engaging with the mirror image indicates not that she knows it to be her in a straightforward sense. If the infant recognized herself in the mirror in the way I know myself in a mirror, why would she play with her image as if it were a little friend? Adults "play" with their mirror images as well, but not in the same way. We are imagining ourselves with others, how others will see us, how we look with different hairstyles, facial expressions, and clothes. The self-conscious vanity of adults cannot be present in the infant. Yet self-conscious vanity isn't the only motivation of adult investment in mirror images. Even after self-identification occurs, the mirror image retains its special quality and never becomes merely a "tool" we use.

In his Sorbonne lectures, Merleau-Ponty explores the idea that identifying objects as objects through an increasingly sophisticated visual system is a secondary capacity in relation to an intersensorial experience of the world where objects are experienced synesthetically. Originally, one's *être au monde* is not primarily visual, any more than it is primarily auditory. The development of perceptual experience goes hand-in-hand with the insertion into an intersubjective, symbolic human world.

SYNCRETIC SOCIABILITY AND THE BIRTH OF THE SELF

It is language and perception that make possible the secondary, visual mode of being which Merleau-Ponty calls "a new form of existence." It is a "new" form of existence for the child because it rewrites the way in which the child understands herself and others. The child now moves from the "body as lived" to the "body as visible and perceived" (*CPP* 425). The visual image causes the child to inherit a place as a subject among subjects, instead of the way in which the child actually lives: a living being who is the center of the world insofar as she is not individuated from the world. The sense of "capable of being seen" is not founded upon a prior, more infantile, sense of self. Selfhood is a creation out of a nascent, transitive experience; there is no primal subject. Embodied experience, in Merleau-Ponty's account, is often defined as a global, general experience.

Since visual perception is associated with a secondary, subjective stage of life, must we reject Merleau-Ponty's thesis about the primacy of perception? These lectures do help to understand the genesis of experience and how the embodied nature of perception is never fulfilled by a discussion of visual givens. The other side of the analysis is that the linguistic symbols given to explain perception are rarely sufficient to explain how *nonvisual* elements are an integral part of *visual* experience. Language tends to restrict analyses to talking about perception as nothing but the visual givens and the accompanying judgments; it has difficulty accommodating the nonvisual background of perception. Original forms of experience remain the foundation upon which all other experiences are constituted. Because they themselves are rooted in the body's lived being, the subject never outgrows them.

Perception is still primary, but the conception of perception has developed to be more inclusive of nonvisual aspects connected to perception. The sense of "being perceived" and perceiving "oneself" in a mirror are not parts of original perception. Since the identification of one's own body is not demanded from lived experience as being "embodied," it causes a rift between the innate intuitions of the infant and her developing ability to identify herself in the mirror. The visual cues are not sufficient to provide a representation of the affective way in which the subject lives in its body. A "cutting-off" or repressing of the aspects of one's experience that do not accord with a unified self is required for assimilation into the symbolic world of adults. To begin to acquire a symbolic system, the child works between the models of "father" and "self" in the mirror. The experiences of "father" are placed against the more confusing images of the mirror-self.

The compounding element of this experience is the essentially linguistic and intersubjective nature of it—the parents are speaking and pointing, aiding in the transition and compounding the tight connection between visual perception and language. Supporting a Freudian reading, one's own sense of self is inextricably intertwined with one's attitudes toward one's parents. When the child learns to distinguish "self" from "other," she must take the self as an "other." In so doing, the child divorces elements of her transitive experience for the sake of harmony within her new role. The image thus retains an "otherness" which explains its interest even when the "mystery" of the mirror image is solved. The image thus resists becoming nothing but a symbol for the self. It continues to embody a ghostlike quality of reality.

Prior to the mirror stage, the child has only its immersion in the world. Once the body has been objectified, the first kind of *identity* is forged. The child is not merely bettered by leaving its confused infantile world; it is also traumatized by the recognition that it is fundamentally separated from others by the visual body. "At the same time, this image of my own body makes possible a kind of *alienation*, a *harnessing* of the ego by my spatial image. The image prepares me for another alienation, *the other's alienation of me*" (*CPP* 254, italics original). Due to the discord between one's lived experience and the visual images provided to represent the experience, the subjectivity formed in the mirror stage is not a complete overdetermination of the asubjective state. The body image is, to use Lacan's term, an imaginary creation. It is through the acquisition of language that the child is taught to identify this body image with a set of concepts. The mirror image is both an advantage and a disadvantage to the child. It allows the child to integrate its proprioceptive experiences with a visual image, and thereby to take a place among other humans as well as buttressing motor coordination.

But this newfound "specular I" carries with it psychological problems. Merleau-Ponty attributes these findings to Lacan, and notes that Lacan identifies how "the mirror also represents a psychological danger to the child" (*CPP* 87). By taking up the visual representation, the infant begins to invest affect in the imaginary I and to gradually depart from the immediate, lived manner in which she encounters the world. The new symbolic self desires to exclude those relations and experiences that threaten it. Lacan appeals to the myth of Narcissus where self-investment leads to doom. Merleau-Ponty cites Lacan as exposing that this new self can also lead to an inclination for death and the destruction of the self, a desire to be a spectacle, and the rejection of the other.

The new symbolic self allows the child to distance herself from others. "Therefore, the mirror equally permits the subject to isolate himself and to establish a reciprocal system—to facilitate the other's interference" (*CPP* 87). The mirror image permits the child to seal herself off from the world as well as, paradoxically, allowing her to participate in a reciprocal system of exchange of symbols with others. Important differences remain between Merleau-Ponty and Lacan, but both argue for the notion of the self as a *product* of development and not as a preexisting element of any and all human lives. One great distinction between their works is how far they think that psychoanalysis or philosophy can investigate into original experience. Merleau-Ponty argues that all experiences are constituted by original, subjectless experience, and thus all experiences express elements of original syncretic sociability. For Lacan, once the subject has become invested in its image, in the imaginary and symbolic, there is no return to the former state—it becomes consistently "barred" or "foreclosed" (along the lines of primary repression).

There are two general themes in Merleau-Ponty's work that find a certain degree of confirmation within the theory of the birth of the self. First, one finds more support for the idea that the primordial, syncretic stage is never completely overcome by the advent of subjectivity. The mirror stage is precariously built upon a division between visual image and lived experience. As adults we never completely "overcome" the mirror stage because we never can resolve the problems it poses. Merleau-Ponty lectures, "childhood is never fully realized" (*CPP* 254). Merleau-Ponty affirms his previous conclusions about an original, primordial state as well as arguing that this level is never completely effaced. Second, what is most "childlike" in childhood is valued, despite the changes afforded by development, including a more robust understanding of self and other. In the lectures, there is a sense that the child's relations to the world are comparatively less impacted by the damaging effects of cultural imposition and, hence, can be said to reveal our embodied experience more directly. The more determining of a role the new body image has, the less one is living as a *Leib* (lived-body) and the more one lives as a *Körper* (physical, objectified body). In the next chapter, we will examine some contemporary research on early infant experience that has been cited extensively among interdisciplinary researchers in psychology and philosophy. At face value, these studies appear to contradict Merleau-Ponty's theses of a syncretic sociability. We will consider some contemporary phenomenologists as offering us a way to best interpret these important experimental studies.

4

Contemporary Research in Psychology and Phenomenology

The spirit and practice of the Sorbonne lectures is to engage with a wide range of contemporary research. Thus it is fitting not only to summarize Merleau-Ponty's lectures, but also to consider them in the broader context of contemporary discussions about the relevance of child experience for our understanding of the human condition. In the previous chapter, we found that Merleau-Ponty argues that the objectification of the body through the mirror image initiates the distinct sense of self and other. This allows the infant to start to understand that she is observable to others. Prior to this stage, the infant lives in a state of syncretic sociability where she does not yet have the capacity to distinguish self from other or the ability to have a mental representation of herself. However, the large body of contemporary experimental research on neonatal imitation contradicts Merleau-Ponty's depiction of young infants as being unable to imitate or even focus their gaze. This chapter will take up contemporary research in early childhood and a number of interpretations of it, paying particular attention to the arguments surrounding primary intersubjectivity. This experimental research has caused many to challenge ideas about the nature of early infancy. The majority of views argue that neonatal imitation demonstrates that instead of an early syncretic stage, we come to the world with a preliminary understanding of the difference between self and other.

One interpretation that differs greatly from Merleau-Ponty's syncretic sociability is that of the theory of mind. A theory of mind account argues that intersubjectivity is fundamentally cognitive. The degree to which an infant can be said to possess a primary intersubjectivity is the degree to which she has a "theory of mind." A theory of mind is broadly used to describe our understanding of the mental states of others as mental states—that I know you have beliefs, attitudes, desires, and thoughts. My theory of mind will change during my development and my many varied experiences of others, but in order for me to appreciate the other person as another person, theory of mind accounts argue that I must have at least a preliminary "theory" about what mental states are like and that they are subjective. For phenomenologically minded thinkers, such a model appears to overintellectualize the infant and it is difficult to reconcile with other experimental studies. The third section of this chapter will turn to contemporary researchers in phenomenology who take up the same experimental studies but draw different conclusions about the nature of intersubjectivity. They argue that primary intersubjectivity is not a mental operation of comparison or simulation, but an embodied experience. Gallagher's (2005) "interaction theory" presents a view where intersubjectivity is only partially explained by theories of mind. Interactions with others are largely dominated by habit and environmental context. Stawarska's (2009) "dialogical phenomenology" focuses upon the face-to-face communication that occurs between mother and child in infancy. She points out that phenomenology remains unable to explain the genesis of intersubjectivity with its traditional focus on first-person perspectives. Merleau-Ponty would have certainly had to revise his understanding of early infant perception and thus his characterization of early life. He would have likely taken up a similar path to Stawarska and Gallagher in searching for a truly interdisciplinary approach to intersubjectivity.

Neonatal Imitation

The research into our earliest experiences that has taken place in the half century since Merleau-Ponty's death impressively presents us with a growing picture of just how much we are cognizant of ourselves, others, and the world. A baby lying in a crib, wiggling her arms and legs, might look distracted, unable to focus, and dominated by her internal desires, but instead we have found that even moments after birth, infants are capable of fairly complex interpersonal exchanges. This research, while ongoing and subject to significant debate regarding what developmental theory is needed to explain these findings, would seem to contradict many of Merleau-Ponty's statements about the life of the infant.

Studies in neonatal imitation have been used to claim that there is a very precocious, if not innate, ability for infants to understand the difference between self and other. This section will explore contemporary research into our earliest experiences and the theories that conclude the opposite of Merleau-Ponty's thesis. They argue that the infant has not only possession of a primal body schema but also possession of a primal ability to equivocate between self and other. The idea of a primal or innate sense of self and other, whether conceived as a theory of mind or an interactive experience, puts into question Merleau-Ponty's syncretic description of early life.

Human imitation has spawned a wealth of studies and books devoted solely to its explication and the potential ramifications for our understanding of early life and cognition in the last few decades (Meltzoff and Prinz 2002; Nadel and Butterworth 1999). Until the 1970s, models of early infancy tended to depict the young child as internally preoccupied and incapable of processing visual-tactile data from the external world. Greats in the history of psychology such as Piaget, Freud, and Skinner all conceived of infants as being largely incapable of visually processing or responding to their environments. In contrast, recent studies, repeated in various settings and in various countries, have upheld the findings of the psychologists Andrew Meltzoff and M. Keith Moore in their groundbreaking study in 1977 on infant facial imitation. They found that even neonates are capable of coordinating their actions to successfully imitate other humans. Following this and many subsequent studies, the view of many theorists is that the much more sophisticated mechanisms of motor control, self-awareness, and interpersonal interaction are innate capacities, and not largely learned post-birth. Such work has led many to conclude that a primitive kind of self- and other-awareness exists prior to birth. This runs contrary to Merleau-Ponty's assumption that infants are not capable of visually processing their environment as well as his description of a syncretic sociability as our historically primary means of interacting. Instead, it appears that we come into the world self-aware and ready to engage with others and other subjects. In addition, many theorists conclude that the ability to predict and explain the other's beliefs, a theory of mind, is *the* primary mode of intersubjectivity.

What does it mean to be "self-aware"? Some ability to recognize my own subjective experience as *my* subjective experience would lay the foundation for distinguishing self-awareness from awareness in general. A cat is aware, but not necessarily self-aware. Cats communicate, they have intentions, and they socialize; however, do they understand that we have beliefs? I imagine that their seeming frustration at not being able to capture the bird outside the window is not sensed as "owned" by them, just as they don't understand I own my own mental states. In contrast, self-awareness is essential in allowing humans to abstract from the external situation and to comprehend that there exist internal nonvisible worlds in the minds of others.

We need to be careful not to read any sustained kind of communicative or intentional behavior as indicating a sense of self in a primitive or full form. Ascribing a sense of self is often a consequence of our tendency to anthropomorphize: for instance, we ascribe all sorts of mental states and intentions to our pets. Many would object strongly to the notion that their pets do not experience things like emotions and desires.

Animals clearly have unique personalities and idiosyncratic wants. When I observe my cat Abernathy watching a bird outside the window, I know he wants to capture that bird. Describing his desires in such terms seems legitimate only if I am careful not to think that he is aware of his desire as "my desire," in other words, as a subjective state. I have no reason to believe that Abernathy has the kind of second-order reflection that would be constitutive of self-awareness—some kind of ability to reflect upon his desire for the bird as *his*. If observing understandable intelligent behavior were sufficient for self-awareness, then everything from a bee to a human would be self-aware. Rather, self-awareness requires some kind of understanding of ownership. To know I own my emotions and they are not transparent to all, I must know that my mental life is not a shared experience and also that I am the owner of that mental life. I must be able to take a kind of distance from my beliefs, desires, and thoughts and represent them to myself as "mine" in the same way that I can understand Abernathy appears to have a desire for cat food that is his desire. Communication does not appear to require awareness of oneself as a "self." Many animals communicate; around dinnertime Abernathy lets me know where he stands on eating, but not all animals represent their emotional and mental states to themselves. Abernathy does not appear to think about himself; he does not appear to be able to be self-reflective about his inner states, and thus he is unable to be reflective about mine.

In reference to the body, we can draw here the distinction between a "body schema" and a "body image." A body schema is the ability I have to organize my actions, to respond to environmental cues, and to pursue my bodily intentions. Much of my body schema is largely unconscious or unthematic in my everyday awareness. A body image is the ability to know my body as a viewable thing by others. One can speak of body image disorders such as body dysmorphic disorder and anorexia nervosa as examples; the individuals who suffer from these disorders are unable to consider their bodies without extreme distress and a strong compulsion to change their appearance. A body image does not require a mirror (although if one follows the theory of the necessity of the mirror stage, it may require one to develop); after all I have a sense of what my body is like without always needing a reference to a mirror. How I emotively and intellectually relate to my body as body image affects my body schema. If I feel self-conscious about my looks, then I might unreflectively restrain my everyday movements (Young 1990a, 1990b; Bordo 1995). Without a body image, it seems difficult to imagine how imitation could occur. I have to have some sense of what my body is like—not just from my basic embodied awareness—but what its limits in space are, what its possibilities are—to bother imitating another person or thing. Even if I am asked to imitate something that has a very different shape and capacities than myself, say a bird, I map out similarities between my own body and the bird's. Probably I would flap my arms, since I know of the possibilities open to my body, and this is the closest approximation. One can understand here the distinction between a sense of bodily awareness and a sense of bodily ownership. A cat has a body schema, but we assume it does not have a body image. If a baby can imitate, we could conclude that it must have a body image or something that fulfills this same role of being able to provide some kind of bodily representation.

What would I want to see from a nonverbal being to conclude that a sense of self-awareness, and not just awareness, is present in it? It has been proposed that imitation is not only the grounds for much of learning, but also the first indication of a human being's precocious ability to obey the oracle at Delphi. If I truly imitate your gestures, I demonstrate that I understand that you and I are similar beings, capable of similar actions. Unlike the limited mimicry we can obtain from animals, humans imitate in a free, plastic, and spontaneous fashion. Much of human behavior arises from our ability to imitate others, whereas animal behavior seems to be hard-wired. What can account for this remarkable talent? Perhaps our minds are innately imitative and we inherently have a sense of the difference between self and other.

When discussing their findings, Meltzoff and Moore (1977) note that the phenomenon of early imitation could be interpreted in several different ways. One would be to argue that nothing but learning or adaptive behavior is displayed in infant imitation. In other words, "imitation is based on reinforcement administered by either the experimenter or the parents" (77). Obviously infants learn. If early infant imitation is a result of caregiver behavior, no philosophically significant conclusion about an innate sense of self could be drawn from it. Meltzoff and Moore reject this thesis, arguing that their experiments have been specifically designed to avoid unwanted influence. Moreover, the focus upon *neonatal* imitation aims precisely at indicating the existence of imitation prior to any significant interaction with others.

The second possible conclusion would be to argue for a hard-wired releasing mechanism, a type of reflex action. Such a mechanism would likewise minimize the philosophical relevance of such claims since it would suggest that there is no reason to attribute much sense of selfhood or cognition of otherness to the infant. Meltzoff and Moore argue that the range of infant imitation speaks against this conclusion. If it were the case that the infant only performed one act, an innate releasing mechanism would be a likely culprit. Several types of imitation have been documented. In addition, infants show a delayed reaction as well as progressive learning, thereby suggesting the use of memory and representation (Gallagher and Meltzoff 1996, 222).

Therefore, Meltzoff and Moore advance a more philosophically interesting conclusion, namely, that an initial mental structure allows infants to possess an initial equivalence of self and other. "We hypothesize that the imitative responses observed are not innately organized and 'released,' but are accomplished through an active matching process and mediated by an abstract representational system" (1977, 78). Later, Meltzoff and Moore use stronger language clearly tied to the theory of an understanding of mind inherent in the infant:

> We favor an alternative to strong nativism. The notion is that evolution has bequeathed human infants not with adult concepts, but with initial mental structures that serve as "discovery procedures" for developing the more comprehensive and flexible concepts. Imitation is deployed as a discovery procedure in understanding persons. Through interactions with others and the concomitant growth in self-understanding, infants are engaged in an open-ended developmental process. If one adopts this developmental view, it becomes tempting to hypothesize that the foundation for developing an "understanding of mind" may be grounded in the initial equivalence of "self" and "other" manifest in early imitation. (Meltzoff and Moore 2000, 180)

What are the potential philosophical issues at stake here? One is the idea that developmentally speaking, instead of coming into existence as a tabula rasa onto which a later sense of selfhood is grafted, we are, from the very beginning, intersubjective—as self- and other-aware—beings. The self develops concurrently alongside an understanding of the other. If an innate sense of selfhood and otherness is present in the infant, strong claims about the degree to which one is determined by language and culture would have to be reconsidered. In addition, it would support the notion that we are, from the start, not only embodied beings, but also self-aware beings. Thus, adult subjectivity is not something that is "created" out of a quasi-animalistic, subjectless infancy, but a natural development. The study of imitation would be an essential element in any discussion of interpersonal relations and the development of social awareness. Such a conclusion is particularly interesting to psychologists and philosophers who argue for a theory of mind to explain intersubjective life and its development and phenomenologists who assert that the self-awareness accompanies all conscious intentionality.

In their article "The Sense of Self and Others: Merleau-Ponty and Recent Developmental Studies," Shaun Gallagher and Andrew Meltzoff

(1996) discuss the import of neonatal imitation research and claim that "the newborn infant is capable of a rudimentary differentiation between self and non-self" (223). They conclude that a *primitive body image* exists: "Furthermore, although newborns do not have a visual perception of their own faces, or other conceptual and emotional aspects of a developed body image, the possibility is raised by this research that the infant does have the most primitive perceptual element required for the formation of a body image—proprioceptive awareness" (223). A primitive body image suggests that infants understand their bodies as something to be seen and thus similar to other bodies. We will see that Gallagher's interpretation shifts away from being close to a theory of mind in his 2005 book, *How the Body Shapes the Mind*, discussed further below. But this earlier 1996 article provides a philosophical defense of the theory of mind thesis.

Many psychological studies have reevaluated the status of neonascent perception and motor control. Merleau-Ponty held the common view at the time that infants could not visually focus. But we have found that infants, even neonates, are quite perceptually aware. A. L. H. van der Meer, F. R. van der Weel, and D. N. Lee (1996) have shown that early infants, who previously were thought to have no motor control, actually will respond to TV images of their arms. They will continue to keep an arm raised when the corresponding image is shown raised and will drop the arm when the image does so even when they have to "push" against a weight to do so. Such work demonstrates that infants "prefer" to view an image of their own arms when the image is similar to what their bodies are actually doing. Marcela Castillo and George Butterworth (1981) demonstrated coordination between seeing and hearing in neonates. All these studies contribute to the conception that infants are much more aware of themselves as selves.

The conclusion that a body *schema* exists in infants is not necessarily at odds with Merleau-Ponty's work. The thesis that a primitive body *image* exists is contrary to Merleau-Ponty's view of the early infant and his later views on the mirror stage. Certainly, infants display the capacity to control their movements, a requirement for a body schema to be present. "The body schema, in contrast, involves certain motor capacities, abilities, and habits that enable movement and the maintenance of posture" (Gallagher and Meltzoff 1996, 215). But do they display, even in a rudimentary form, "mental representations, beliefs, and attitudes" about their own bodies (215)? A body image, perhaps a uniquely human possession, requires an ability to recognize that one's own body and one's subjective experience of it are equivalent to other people's bodies and their internal, hidden, subjective lives.

To have a body image, I must be able to represent my body to myself. A body image requires a distance from experience that appears difficult if not impossible for our animal cousins. Contrary to the fact that I see only parts of my body and require the use of a device, such as a mirror, to get a "whole" image, I can imagine my body as others see it—as an object to be seen. As embodiment theorists explain, the problem is that any body image will fail to capture how I truly live in my body. I don't encounter myself like I encounter another person in the world; in fact, I don't "encounter" myself at all. I am my embodied life. Why would one assume such a high level of functioning in infants? Precisely because of neonatal *facial* imitation, one is invited to assume that such imitation would require this self-aware ability to represent one's body to oneself in order to mimic the movements of the other's face. Unlike imitating sounds, or hand gestures, neonatal facial imitation would require an ability to possess a basic recognition of similarity. Hence, infant imitation is so compelling since it occurs prior to the infant seeing her own image in a mirror.

One previously dominant thesis about the development of self-awareness is that infants require an image of themselves prior to being able to form any kind of representations regarding their own bodies. As discussed in the previous chapter, a mirror stage, to use Henri Wallon's language later made more famous by Lacan, must occur to have a body image. But researchers in neonatal imitation stress that they do not need to use mirror self-recognition to explain the advent of a sense of self and other. They found that newborn infants without conditioning, extensive interpersonal experience, or self-identification can imitate the adult:

> We do not claim that a newborn is as "good" an imitator as a 1-year-old. We merely suggest that the strong view that infants have no capacity to imitate at birth is contradicted by the data. Evidently the capacity to imitate is available at birth and does not require extensive interactive experience, mirror experience, or reinforcement history. (Meltzoff and Moore 1983, 707)

For Meltzoff, the mirror stage is but a development upon a preexisting self-awareness, not a seismic shift in the child's understanding. Neonatal imitation provides him with sufficient evidence to claim that the ability to imitate demonstrates the primitive ability to understand that one's own body is like another person's body. Thus, there is no conflict created upon seeing one's own body in a mirror at a later stage. Rather, the mirror-perception would help to concretize the proto-body-image already present in the neonate.

Meltzoff finds not only that previous understandings about the lack of motor control in infants were incorrect, but also that the theoretical structure explaining motor behavior was flawed. One issue is "translation." The paradigm of translation, previously the dominant model used to understand the connection between perception and action, is particularly predisposed to rejecting infant imitation. In their introduction to the text *The Imitative Mind*, Andrew Meltzoff and Wolfgang Prinz summarize the two different paradigms—that of translation/sensorimotor views and that of cognitive approaches. Sensorimotor views argue that the language of the sense organs and the language of the motor organs are different. For instance, if I see a cup of coffee, that information travels to my brain vis-à-vis sensory language. If I pick up the coffee cup, motor codes in my brain are activated. There must exist a kind of "translation" between the "seeing" of the cup to cause the "picking up" of the cup. Meltzoff and Prinz write that translation becomes the dominant metaphor and that "this metaphor stresses the incommensurability between sensory codes and motor codes, implying that both belong to separate representational domains and can, hence, only be linked to each other by way of creating arbitrary mappings" (2002, 7). Such an account often argues that, due to the incompatibility between accounts, infant imitation is not a reflection of the fact that the infant has achieved such translating, but, rather, infant "imitation" is simply indicative of the fact that chance imitations were reinforced by others:

> This account proposes that infants learn imitative responses in the same way as all other behaviors, that is, without any functional support by similarity between stimuli and responses. Instead, imitative responses initially occur by chance. They get immediately reinforced by observers (e.g., parents), who are capable of noticing their imitative character. Therefore, functionally speaking, the infant does not copy the parent, and certainly does not intend to copy, but rather the parent reinforces the infant on occasions when s/he happens to behave like him/herself (or some other model). (7)

But such an account cannot explain "the occurrence of newborn imitation or the imitation of novel behavior by adults" (8). By contrast, Prinz and Meltzoff defend *cognitive* paradigms, for they "invoke a common representation domain for perception and action" (8). The cognitive paradigm argues that neonates can apprehend the equivalence between body transformations that they see and body transformations of their own that they feel themselves make. The common paradigm is a "supramodal perceptual system." This system allows for infants to "recognize" the other's body image as parallel to their own body image. Thus, a cognitive theory does not need to assume any kind of "translation," since the same system governs perception and intentional physical movement.

Despite his Piagetian understanding of early infant imitation, that is, it is not possible, Merleau-Ponty does discuss child imitation. In his 1951–1952 lecture "The Question of Method in Child Psychology," he is concerned with Paul Guillaume's (1971) texts on imitation. For Guillaume, imitation is not a matter of the child "mimicking" the adult, but, rather, the child is repeating the objective results of the adult's action upon objects. Thus, if an adult picks up a block and puts it down, the child is interested in the block, not in the adult's movements:

> Guillaume sees the matter this way: when I imitate, it is not others that I imitate, but their behavior in relation to objects. It is the objective results of actions that are imitated, not gestures. For example, when the child imitates someone who writes, it is by accumulation [*par surcroitre*] that the imitation of movements arises. (*CPP* 426)

Merleau-Ponty rejects Guillaume's thesis that imitation is about the child repeating the objective results of the action, that is, the impact upon objects. He poses the same question that is raised with newborn imitation—how is it that children imitate actions that have no purpose, that entail no visible manipulation of objects? Why would a newborn stick her tongue out? What is the "object" in such an imitation? Like Meltzoff and Moore, Merleau-Ponty distinctly rejects any associationalist theory that understands imitation as a matter of conditioning or of some innate reflex. Imitation demonstrates a much more playful and interpersonal connection than a practical desire to manipulate objects.

Based on such studies of infant imitation and infant bodily motility, many have called to revise the theory of *adualism* that appears in earlier authors, including Merleau-Ponty in his theory of syncretic sociability, toward a natural *dualism*. We come to the world with an ability to distinguish self and nonself. George Butterworth (2000) argues against Freud and Piaget's "adualistic confusion" where the infant's lack of body schema development prohibits her sense of self, and he argues for a natural dualism. Following the work of James Gibson (1966) and Ulric Neisser (1988), Butterworth concludes that the ecological perspective better explains development and provides a more convincing theory to explain later development. Paul Bloom's book *Descartes' Baby* (2004) also summarizes research that indicates not only that infants have a sense of ego and nonego, but also that infants treat humans differently than they do objects (14–19).

Contemporary thought thus clearly stands against the thesis of Merleau-Ponty that early infant life is adualist and asubjective. Instead, there is broad consensus that experimental research on neonatal imitation indicates that some kind of primary self and other equivalence is occurring in the infant. The mirror stage, while not necessarily refuted, takes on less significance as the birth of self-awareness and we are required to revisit Merleau-Ponty's thesis of syncretic sociability. The question for contemporary research is: how do we understand this early stage?

Theory of Mind

One popular interpretation that has fueled a significant amount of empirical research and theoretical debate is the "theory of mind." Championed by Andrew Meltzoff himself, theory of mind accounts argue that what neonatal imitation and other studies of early and later childhood tell us is that intersubjectivity is a matter of a developing set of beliefs—a theory—about others and oneself. A theory of mind claim is sympathetic to natural dualism since while it debates the extent of neonatal theories of mind, it does conclude that some primal intersubjectivity must exist to explain neonatal imitation. A theory of mind argues that evolution has provided infants with the ability to detect and map equivalences between their own acts and their bodies as well as the acts of the other and hence to develop a theory of the other's mental states.

Significant debate exists about the nature and extent of this innate ability. Some, such as Josef Perner (1991), argue that we should think of a theory of mind as occurring by four years old in most normal children. Passing false belief tests provides the evidence for this change at around this age. At such an age, children have a *representational theory of mind.* Prior to having a theory of mind, young infants have a model of interpreting the world that is geared toward an increasing ability to faithfully represent the world. Gopnik and Meltzoff (1997) are also, like Perner, "theory theory" theorists of mind because they stress the idea that intersubjectivity is dependent upon a *theory.* Children have actual *theories* about other beings—they attribute intentions and motivations to other things, people, and animals. Development is evidenced by more sophisticated, subtle, and responsive theories. For instance, most of us have seen a young child fall down and instead of immediately bursting into tears, the child looks around for a comforting adult. Upon seeing a possible caregiver, the child bursts into melodramatic sobs. At such a state, the child has gone beyond merely crying when upset to recognizing that if no one is around, no comfort can be given. We can interpret this as a development in the child's theory of other people and a recognition of the other person's perspective. Thus, like Piaget's stages, children are seen to pass through various thresholds in their development—to what degree can they understand the depth of other people's mental states or to what degree are they, such as in the case of autism, unable to theorize about the other? Another theory of mind group is "simulation" theorists who argue for the idea that I use my own mind as a model and then I judge others by imagining or "simulating" myself in that person's position (Davies and Stone 1995).

Gopnik and Meltzoff (1997) prefer interpretations where the infant has the starting capacities for an adult theory of mind but does not yet possess a mature framework. Meltzoff and Prinz (2002) summarize this "starting-state nativism," asserting that *"infants' connection to others emerges from the fact that the bodily movement patterns they see others perform are coded as like the ones they themselves perform"* (10, italics original). Theory of mind accounts explain neonatal imitation and also provide a model to explain future development. Infants increasingly interact with their environment, exploring the reactions of others and building their theories of mind. When a baby stops crying when the caretaker leaves the room, we can conclude that her theory of mind has developed to recognize that others must hear the sounds to respond to them. Starting-state theories of mind also are able to incorporate differences due to brain abnormalities and environmental differences. It is no wonder that the children of Romanian orphanages and the famous studies of the Lebanese crèches are developmentally hindered in interpersonal skills and empathy (Dennis 1973). In these situations, the children were rarely attended to and given minimal human contact. The limited interaction with caregivers did not provide the crèche children with enough experience to develop appropriate connections between their own self-understanding and their understanding of others.

Psychologists and philosophers sympathetic to theory of mind claims often look at the autism spectrum as providing evidence of what happens when one does not have this primary sense of self- and other-awareness. Many people on the autism spectrum who appear to be high-functioning have difficulty with very basic intersubjective interactions. For instance, they have problems with everyday conversations, tending to be too silent or too pedantic. The argument is that people with autism have delays or a lack of ability to form beliefs about the other's mental state, hence they will not respond to obvious verbal and nonverbal cues. Normal development is marked by the acquisition of proper beliefs about the other's mind and should be further evidenced by experimental tests that show children in various stages acquiring more sophisticated styles of intersubjective interactions.

It is difficult to understand how an infant has a "theory" even if it is a very rudimentary one. A theory sounds like something that a psychologist or philosopher has, not a newborn infant. Indeed, even adult experience does not seem to be marked by theorizing about other people's mental states in everyday life. Outside of philosophizing and psychological inquiry, we do not seem to need to refer to a theory to make sense of the other person's behavior. Theory of mind accounts do not argue that the theories of mind we need to have successful intersubjective relations are conscious and deliberative in the way formulating a theory of human development is. Most of the "theory" is unconscious and habitual. Theory of mind theorists argue that to explain neonatal imitation, the child's ability to learn from imitation and play, and our adult complex relationships, we must be referring to some kind of mental theories that allow us to adapt and react to changing situations. In her book *The Philosophical Baby* (2009), Alison Gopnik provides an extensive description of the infant's experience and points out that any theory needs to explain both the baby's natural abilities but also importantly the adaptability and flexibility of human development. Theory of mind accounts can provide a possible understanding of the development of intersubjectivity.

However, some debate in interpreting the empirical research that provides us with evidence of neonatal imitation exists. The most direct attack is the argument that neonatal imitation *as* imitation does not in fact exist at all. Some arguments claim that the data does not call upon us to reject previously held theories that infant imitation is a type of "reflex": an innate releasing mechanism. The basis for such counter-arguments is that only tongue protrusion is reliably demonstrated in neonates. If only one movement is produced with any regularity, it is more likely that this action is a reflex rather than imitation. Or perhaps tongue protrusion is simply a manner of exploring the world—of interacting with the world—and not imitation per se.

Moshe Anisfeld's paper "Only Tongue Protrusion Modeling Is Matched by Neonates" (1996) examines the very experiments that supposedly prove the existence of neonatal imitation. What Anisfeld notes is that although it is true that other movements, such as mouth opening, are demonstrated in the infant, one doesn't find these results strongly correlated with tongue protrusion. He examined nine studies of tongue protrusion and one other facial gesture (such as mouth opening or head movement) and found that:

> In the studies reviewed, there is solid evidence for a modeling effect of tongue protrusion in the neonatal period. But the evidence for a modeling effect of head movement and mouth opening is weak and contradictory within studies. To the extent that there were effects for mouth opening, the effects appear on reanalysis to be carryovers from the tongue protrusion effects. (159)

In a 2001 article, Anisfeld et al. report repeating controlled experiments on neonatal imitation and again fail to find any compelling evidence of imitative behaviors other than tongue protrusion: "The absence of an MO [mouth opening] effect in this study and previous studies undermines the imitation hypothesis. If neonates are capable of imitation, there is no obvious reason why it should be restricted to TP [tongue protrusion]" (119). Anisfeld suggests that the arousal hypothesis or another hypothesis, such as an innate releasing mechanism, are more likely since the repetition and accuracy of imitating tongue protrusion is not correlated strongly with another imitative act. Infants are excited by active faces, but their own physical excitement can be explained as a kind of arousal of motor movement, since, according to Anisfeld, their head movements are not imitative except in the case of tongue protrusion.

Susan Jones (1996) also questions whether or not the matching displayed in tongue protrusion should be called imitation, partially because tongue protrusion and mouth openings are not strongly correlated, but also, more importantly, because tongue protrusion often occurs with regularity when objects, not the human face, are dangled in front of the infant. Such results suggest that it may be the case that tongue protrusion is a neonatal reflex or a manner of "exploring" the world prior to more sophisticated bodily control. Jones's studies reveal not only that nipple-like objects cause the infant to stick out her tongue, but also other objects of interest—in one case, railway signals with blinking lights—cause the infant to stick out her tongue with much more frequency than when the infant is not looking at the object. Thus, Jones concludes that tongue protrusion might be a very early expression of the infant's natural interest in exploring the world, not necessarily a social communication.

If tongue protrusion is a manner of exploring the world and not an act with intersubjective significance, we could easily explain why one does not discover neonatal imitative abilities in all infants. The thesis, proposed by Meltzoff and Moore, that an "initial equivalence of 'self' and 'other'" exists remains problematic when one doesn't find across-the-board imitative abilities in healthy neonates. Do the infants who aren't imitating lack the initial equivalence? Are they mentally less developed? Are their latter imitative abilities also retarded? If it is imitation, does this mean that imitation is innate only in some infants? "On the other hand, if young infants simply move their tongues when their visual interest is engaged, then individual differences may just be differences in infants' immediate interest in specific stimuli" (Jones 1996, 1967). Moreover, the study would explain the disappearance of the imitation of tongue protrusion in older infants. As children age, motor control increases and hence hands would often be the preferred manner in which to explore the world.

In a more theoretically robust version of Jones's hypothesis about neonatal imitation being a kind of exploration, György Gergely (2004) argues that that goal-directed behavior does not necessarily argue for any kind of innate mental states constituting self-awareness (31). He writes that plausible evolutionary functions more likely cause early affective and imitative behaviors. Gergely's "social biofeedback model" of affect mirroring argues that infants register various distinct facial gestures as different from the resting face. Since parents often mimic in an exaggerated fashion the baby's own facial expressions, the baby begins to associate their lively faces with her own internal sensations which originally were nonconscious. Gergely writes that "there is no compelling evidence either for the view that young infants attribute corresponding subjective intentional and feeling states to the other's mind" (32). Primarily, the infant is seeking to reduce its own stress or to show interest.

In a similar vein as Gergely's social biofeedback model, Victoria McGeer (2001) argues that what we witness in infants is *self-regulation*. First and foremost, our reactions to the world are motivated by sensory organization, not by epistemic conjectures about self and other equivalency. Her theory is particularly interesting when she contrasts normal development with that of autistic children. Autistic children may perform well, or even above average, in imitative abilities. However, they show remarkable deficiencies in controlling and integrating some of their bodily movements—as evidenced by the hand flapping and head banging common in autism. Thus, perhaps autistic children do not achieve the same kind of habitual self-regulation based in moving from nonconscious internally motivated sentiments and actions to conscious awareness of internal states. First one needs self-regulation of internal affect and then one can achieve an ability to equivocate between self and other. She writes, "it does suggest that an infant's innate proclivity for imitating others may be driven as much by machinery dedicated to serving a self-regulative goal as it is to machinery dedicated to the epistemic goal of understanding self and others" (128). McGeer complements Gergely's work in suggesting that imitation might be a product of a desire to reduce the infant's own internal discomfort. Autistic individuals lack this self-regulation and thus do not form appropriate behavior habits, including the high-functioning autistics who do acquire an understanding of other minds.

One can also ask if neonatal imitation is the same kind of behavior as the obvious imitation of older infants. Aside from the direct questioning of neonatal imitation by Anisfeld and Jones, many studies point out the problems of saying that what neonates are doing is "imitation" at all. Olga Maratos (1998) discusses the marked differences between neonatal imitation and later (nine-month-old) imitation. Maratos asks the question, "whether neonatal and early attempts at imitation (between birth and six months of age) of certain models is the same phenomenon, governed by the same mechanisms, as later imitation (from the end of the first year onwards)" (146). Noting that neonates imitate after long pauses and continue to make a series of other movements, Maratos asks if this kind of reaction is really an imitative one. For instance, in the case of tongue protrusion and mouth opening, the infant produces a rather mixed behavior: "Once the infant starts protruding her tongue [when she does so can vary in time], or opening her mouth, she tends to go on repeating the movement several times" (149). However, at the age of nine to ten months, the infant behaves quite differently: "The response is given only once and is a much more accurate match of the model—a clear tongue protrusion with the tongue well visible between the lips, wide mouth opening or well controlled head shaking that reproduces correctly even the rhythmical aspect of the model. None of these responses is followed by any accompanying movements as happens with the younger infant" (149). In addition, the older infant seems aware that she is engaged in a kind of communication/imitation which the younger shows no sign of acknowledging. The older infant will spontaneously imitate new movements, whereas the neonate only can, and this in a clumsy interrupted fashion, imitate a few facial gestures.

Maratos concludes that there is good reason to agree that an innate predisposition toward human faces exists, but disagrees that early imitation indicates any kind of an innate representation of the body. In order for a theory of mind account to work, one must have some way one represents not just others in a theory of the other's mind, but also a way to represent oneself. The basic requirement to have a theory about something is to have some kind of working definition of what that something is. To do that, you must be able to refer to it in your mind; you must represent it. Maratos argues that assuming infants have the ability to represent themselves to themselves "is not necessarily a precondition and it is certainly not supported either by data on early imitation or from the course of development of these early imitative responses" (1998, 157).

Thus, it is unclear if early infant imitation provides evidence of a primal ability to provide a representation required to form a belief about oneself and others. Ecological theorists have also argued for the primacy of a sense of self and other. George Butterworth (2000) argues that "neonatal imitation is just the first level of a developing system of inter-personal relatedness which may contribute in important ways to acquiring self-knowledge . . . newborn imitation can be taken as evidence for direct, primary consciousness of an inter-personal self" (27). Often working with ecological perspectives, phenomenology encourages a focus on understanding that the infant's behavior that we observe is embodied and tries to avoid overintellectualizing the baby. Shaun Gallagher's (2005) interaction theory and Beata Stawarska's (2009) dialogical relatedness theory draw attention to primary intersubjectivity as being not about a set of beliefs the infant increasingly has about the other, but rather about the lived experience between the infant and others. Both these contemporary approaches fit well into the spirit, if not the execution, of Merleau-Ponty's child psychology.

Interaction Theory and Dialogical Relatedness

Interdisciplinary work in phenomenology has also found studies in neonatal imitation both fruitful for certain phenomenological claims and for critiques of traditional phenomenology. Francisco Varela (1996), Gallagher (2005), and Stawarska (2009) are a few of the defenders of a phenomenological, integrative approach to empirical, observational sciences. The first-person perspective required by phenomenology and the third-person approach that dominates much of the sciences do appear to present us with two such fundamentally different methodologies that it is hard to know how they could intersect meaningfully. Yet the spirit of Merleau-Ponty's own work indicates that there is no reason why observational research cannot be part of phenomenology's search to best understand the nature of lived experience. On the other side, observational research requires theory to interpret its results. While extreme approaches might argue that only third-person "facts" can be considered scientifically relevant data (Dennett 1991), such an approach loses lived experience. Phenomenology offers a unique set of theoretical tools to the social sciences and in particular to the discussion of human development.

In their 1996 piece, Gallagher and Meltzoff argue that the existence of an original syncretic sociability is not supported by the data derived from contemporary psychological research, and therefore Merleau-Ponty's understanding of infant experience is flawed. They conclude that there is good reason to suppose that the later development of subjectivity is not a radical break with an asubjective stage. In place of Merleau-Ponty's theory that adult experience is always partially constituted by an infantile syncretic state, Gallagher and Meltzoff write that infant experience is never constituted by a complete lack of selfhood. The mirror stage has been traditionally seen as offering a sharp contrast between a selfless stage and an understanding of self and others. Yet, perhaps newborn imitation suggests that a kind of "recognition" of others is a capacity present in the very first hours of life:

> The studies of newborn imitation, however, not only demonstrate that imitation of actions (conducts, gestures) is possible from the very beginning, and that the supramodal system that makes this possible is innate; they also indicate that the original *in*differentiation is never complete. The first exclusively visual notion of the self may be tied to the later mirror stage, or a later form of imitation.... However, self-recognition in the mirror is only one measure, one aspect of a broader concept of self. (13)

Gallagher and Meltzoff conclude that from the fact that newborn infants display a sense of self in neonatal imitation, it is unnecessary to speak of pre-communication or syncretic sociability. Likewise, it would not be necessary to consider that a significant "break" occurs with the onset of subjectivity. "The newborn infant's ability to imitate others, and its ability to correct its movement, which implies a recognition of the difference between its own gesture and the gesture of the other, indicates a rudimentary differentiation between self and non-self" (13).

Gallagher provides a more extensive and less theory of mind-influenced thesis about early intersubjectivity in his 2005 book *How the Body Shapes the Mind*. He remains sympathetic to the general nativist tendency to see roots of our adult intersubjectivity as being discovered in early infancy. Gallagher agrees with his early assessment of Merleau-Ponty's naiveté about early experience and with theory of mind accounts that argue that infants do have a primary intersubjectivity. However, he speaks against the mentalistic and representational requirements of a theory of mind interpretation because intermodal experience does not depend on having an internal copy (226). The idea held by Gopnik and Meltzoff (1997) that infants have a type of cognitive theory where they have made an internal representation of their actions Gallagher finds is contradicted by a more serious examination of the nature of our relationship to our own bodies and our relationships with others.

Gallagher (2005) writes that theory of mind approaches have what he calls a "mentalistic supposition" where the "problem of intersubjectivity is precisely the problem of other *minds*. That is, the problem is to explain how we can access the minds of others" (209). Gallagher shows that in order for our intersubjective life to be defined by cognizing about the mental states of others, it also requires that my own subjective experience is defined by cognizing about my own mental states. To compare or contrast my mental states with those of others, whether this is through an analysis of beliefs or a simulation, I must relate to *myself* through a strongly mentalistic framework.

Gallagher points out that infants are perceiving and directing their behavior toward goals. They are interacting not just with the other face, but with the entire embodied active life of the other. This includes the way in which the other is directed toward not just the infant but the world as well. "In effect, this kind of perception-based understanding is a form of 'body-reading' rather than mind-reading. In seeing the actions and expressive movements of the other person, one already sees their meaning; no inference to a hidden set of mental states (beliefs, desires, etc.) is necessary" (227). Gallagher's interaction theory is pragmatic in that he emphasizes that our primary mode of interacting with the world, others, and ourselves is not theoretical or based in mental judgments but practical and connected to our immediate environment. His assessment is strongly similar to Merleau-Ponty's discussion of imitation. When an infant imitates an adult's facial motions, it is not because she has understood that "I too have a mouth that can open and shut, just like this being who peers into my crib." Rather, she responds to "an intersubjective significance":

> A baby of fifteen months opens its mouth if I playfully take one of its fingers between my teeth and pretend to bite it. And yet it has scarcely looked at its face in a glass, and its teeth are not in any case like mine. The fact is that its own mouth and teeth, as it feels them from the inside, are immediately, for it, an apparatus to bite with, and my jaw, as the baby sees it from the outside, is immediately, for it, capable of the same intentions. 'Biting' has immediately, for it, an intersubjective significance. It perceives its intentions in its body, and my body with its own, and thereby my intentions in its own body. (*PP* 352)

Gallagher expands upon the embodied nature of early infant experience, noting that a wider look at neurological and other experimental data requires a theory more invested in understanding the infant's general body schema and not simply its ability to imitate expressions. Gallagher defends his theory with a critique of theory of mind explanations for false belief tests, a phenomenological examination of adult intersubjectivity, and an examination of the differences between autistic and normal children.

False belief tests are experiments designed to ascertain if the child can understand the other person's perspective. These tests have a number of different permutations. One example would be to show a child a box that looks like an identifiable box of candy. After some excitement, the child is shown, or discovers, that instead of candy a much different object—a stapler—is inside the box. Another person, Sally, enters the room and the child is quizzed, "What does Sally think is inside the box?" Young children will often say "stapler" and thus are seen to "fail" the false belief test because it seems they state what they know, rather than what Sally will obviously think is inside the box—candy.

Gallagher points out that if we consider what false belief experiments are testing, we must remember the larger situation in which they take place (2005, 218). Many children who "fail" the test have no problem understanding the desires of the experimenter. They respond when asked and seem to understand what the experimenter wants. So we see an ability to understand the other's perspective. "Failing" might indicate more about the artificial situation of the test than a true lack of intersubjective awareness on the part of the young child. Perhaps the child wants to please the experimenter more that she understands the point of the test. Thus, it is difficult to know to what degree the problem is the distanced third-person perspective-taking that is required to pass a false belief test. This does not diminish the fact that passing the false belief test obviously presents us with new evidence of a change between children of different ages or abilities. After all, I have to quite deliberatively put myself in another person's shoes to understand that the other person would think it is candy and not, as I know it to be, a stapler. I must both understand the other's perspective and understand that my belief, "it is a stapler," is a belief.

In order for a theory of mind account of early intersubjectivity to work, we have to see some precocious ability in the infant, even the neonate, to be able to equivocate between self and other in terms of a representational system. In a false belief test, this process is explicit and conscious. Although for the adult it might take a fraction of a second, we can understand that I have to pose to myself something like, "what would it be like to have just seen this box of candy?" But infants do not have the same ability to consciously reflect upon their own thought processes, to think about thinking. Gallagher's critique of certain interpretations of false belief tests is to focus on the need for them to explain why theory of mind theorists would think that such processes are unconscious and primitive as well as conscious and explicit. "The science of false-belief tests does not provide any evidence for the claim that theory of mind processes are implicit or subpersonal" (2005, 219). We follow Gallagher's rejection of theory of mind accounts that argue for an unconscious, perhaps innate, representational intellectual system as the primary means by which we interact with others. After all, in false belief *tests* the subject is placing herself in "the other person's shoes" in a very *explicit* manner. The child has to take a moment to realize that most people would think it was candy in a candy box and not a stapler, which normally is not found in such boxes. For primal intersubjectivity to make sense from a theory of mind account, there must preexist some kind of implicit theory. What theory of mind accounts need to prove is that this explicit ability to consider the other's position in an artificial situation, and perhaps indeed to "theorize" consciously about others, is proof that the other manifold interactive experiences we have with others are likewise theoretical.

This is not to debate the rigor of the experiments designed to test false belief tests. Wellman et al. (2001) performed a meta-analysis of false belief findings and concluded that the impressive extent of findings provided a "largely robust, orderly, and consistent" defense of false belief as signifying a serious shift in understanding around three to five years in the child (678). Instead it is to critique the interpretation of them. In phenomenological examinations of psychological empirical research, the focus tends not to be on the research itself, but on the stated and implicit theories behind the analysis of the research. There is additional empirical research to support Gallagher's rejection of the false belief test as indicating the child has achieved a theory of mind "milestone." Criticisms of the relevance of false belief tasks argue that children, and some children with autism, do possess understandings of the other's position prior to this age, but the findings were a result of overly difficult tasks. Another criticism is that false belief tests were a result of Western styles of education and child-rearing (Lillard and Flavell 1992). Kristine Onishi and Renee Baillargeon (2005) find that even infants appear to present some evidence of false belief. A woman is seen by the infants to place a toy watermelon in a box. When the watermelon is moved (invisibly) to another box than the one it was placed in by the woman, the infants pause longer looking at the woman reaching into the box that she "expects" the watermelon to be in. Such studies lead Martin J. Doherty (2009) to conclude that "clearly, something precedes children's success on explicit false belief tasks, and precedes it by a considerable period" (31). But the question remains—what is this something? Is it an early theory of mind?

Gallagher argues that the mentalistic presuppositions of theory of mind accounts focus on the child's understanding of the other's mental states. In order for the child to understand the other, she must be able to represent herself. But even after children engage in meaningful imitative action with the other, they lag behind in successfully identifying themselves in visual representations. Other experiments with older children seem to support the idea that children have difficulty forming representations of themselves. This is surprising if children already were capable of representing themselves and others in a theory of mind. One would expect to find a strong ability in children, once provided with the rudiments of social life and better motor control, to identify themselves in mirrors and to distinguish their acts from others. The mirror self should easily be graphed onto the representation of the self in the theory that by now the child has had for years. Daniel Povinelli et al. (1996) get to the heart of this issue and find that although young children, two to three years of age, are quite capable of identifying themselves in a mirror, they are not able to react meaningfully to a delayed image of themselves, even if the time delay is but a few minutes. The authors write, "we ask at what age do young children come to conceive of the self as possessing explicit temporal dimensions?" (Povinelli et al. 1996, 1541). Older children in the third and fourth year are capable of self-identification over time.

In this series of experiments, Povinelli et al. found a surprisingly extreme turnaround between 35 and 58 months. Extending the "rouge test" to include a temporal dimension, they sought to determine when children could correctly remove a sticker on their heads from a photograph just taken (the sticker was placed without their knowledge) or from a video of the child taped minutes before. The experimenters would narrate for the children, reminding them that a photo was going to be taken or reminding them that they were being videotaped. Only 13 percent of children under 40 months could correctly identify themselves in a photo taken minutes earlier; but 85 percent of these children could correctly identify themselves in a mirror. Between 53 and 58 months, 93 percent correctly identified themselves in a photo and 100 percent correctly identified themselves in a mirror. (Another interesting finding was that younger children were far less likely to say "me" and thus take possession of their mirror image or photo image; instead, they would often take a third-person perspective and reply with their first names.) We can see here that there is something important about the lived, contextual situation of the mirror in real time that is not reproduced in the photograph and the videotaped examples. If something akin to interaction theory is correct, early self-identification would be contextual and not representational. But if a theory of mind account is correct and the young child already has some ability to provide an internal, unconscious representation of her own abilities, it is puzzling to explain the disaccord between recognition in a mirror and the lack of such recognition in a photo or video.

In live feedback (in videotaped examples) the younger children were even less likely to take the sticker off their foreheads, even if they were watching a video taken moments before. The authors of the study speculate that there is a strong relationship between the ability to have autobiographical memory and the ability to identify one's own image over time: "Children younger than 3½ to 4 years may not treat the delayed images of themselves in the same manner as live images because although the events depicted may be recalled, they were not encoded as autobiographical memories and hence the children do not understand that they happened to them" (Povinelli et al. 1996, 1552). Children younger than 3½ are able to remember events, but do not attribute the quality of "me-ness" to those events. Such results again seem curious if we had practically from birth been working with representations of ourselves and others.

Alison Gopnik and Virginia Slaughter (1991) explore in-depth the extreme differences in self-awareness between three- and four-year-olds in another article in *Child Development*. Like Povinelli et al., Gopnik and Slaughter find a significant degree of difference in the representational system that holds together beliefs about the self and the world. Three-year-olds would not, by and large, affirm that they had just previously been surprised by a novel occurrence, once they had processed the unexpected change. This suggests that three-year-olds have a very tenuous hold over their own mental states, and thus it would seem questionable if they possessed a body image and the ability to represent themselves: "It is no easier to understand your own past mental states than it is to understand the mental states of others. Beliefs, desires, and intentions appear to be difficult to understand even when they are your own beliefs, desires, and intentions" (109). They continue to note that the young children obviously are not inspecting their own past mental states to appropriately respond to the situation at hand. If a three-year-old cannot call upon a representational system to accurately recall what happened but a few minutes ago, is it not premature to assume that an infant has the ability to represent an action to herself and then repeat that action via a primitive body image?

The idea that neonatal imitation is essentially a kind of intersubjective communication can also be examined by considering later intersubjective behavior. Asendorpf (2002) writes that another later form of imitation, "synchronic imitation," develops alongside the ability to recognize oneself in a mirror. Synchronic imitation is when two children play with toys in a similar (although perhaps not identical) manner. According to Asendorpf, the importance of synchronic imitation is that it is a benchmark of whether or not secondary representation has occurred:

> The main hypothesis that guided our work was, therefore, that mirror self-recognition and synchronic imitation develop in close synchrony during the second year of life because they require the same crucial cognitive ability: the capacity for secondary representation. Because mirror self-recognition is often interpreted as indexing a capacity for self-awareness, we introduced the parallel term other-awareness for the capacity to spontaneously take the perspective of others. (Asendorpf 2002, 67)

Asendorpf's studies support his thesis: "*sustained* synchronic imitation (synchronic imitation exceeding ten seconds) was strongly associated with the result of the mirror rouge test" (69, emphasis original). Thus, a sustained ability to recognize oneself in a mirror is closely allied with an ability to interact meaningfully with one's peers. This capacity is at the heart of what it means to be self-aware. One finds this to be a much later occurrence than one would suppose if neonatal imitation was a primitive example of self- and other-awareness. Asendorpf also remains skeptical about early studies of infant self-awareness demonstrated by "recognition" in video feedback of the infant's own face: "The recognition of one's face as familiar does not necessarily imply self-awareness, however. Infants may form memory traces about faces, including their own mirror-image, long before they are able to relate these memories to a concept of their self (the critical cognitive capacity for self-awareness)" (Asendorpf 2002, 70).

Infants and young children are able to engage in meaningful interpersonal interactions and imitative abilities prior to passing the false belief test. But they do not seem capable of representing themselves. They have not yet achieved a capacity over time to represent themselves in a hypothetical third-person stance. Why then would we want to say that neonatal imitation is based on a preliminary theory of mind? As described above, children struggle to understand pictures and video images of themselves even when they are able to imitate in a free and plastic fashion. It would seem that processing a representation of oneself would be an easy development if such skills were already present in infants.

When considering how we relate to others as adults, we also do not find necessarily that theories of mind dominate our behavior. To provide a theory for a surprising occurrence, say, my husband shouting randomly from another room, I already must have in place a structure in which I understand certain things to be the relevant bits of information. For instance, it is relevant what he is shouting, but it isn't relevant that the sun is coming in the window or he is wearing jeans. What we find in persons with autism is that they do not share the same organization of relevant/ nonrelevant data and associations that we do. This does not appear to be a problem of representation or even a theory of mind, but rather a problem of sensory and perceptual organization and focus (Gallagher 2005, 253).

While initially theory of mind accounts appeared to find a confirmation in the fact that many children with autism showed an inability or delayed ability to pass false belief tests, recent research has found that many autistic children can pass these tests (Happé 1995). In addition, as Gallagher points out, theory of mind accounts do not explain the variety of symptoms found in persons with autism. Gallagher argues that if one adopts a more phenomenological approach that emphasizes the embodied differences such as the significant sensory-perception differences, one sees that autism tells us not that a theory of mind is needed for normal, adult intersubjectivity, but that a coherent organization of sensory data is needed (2005, 232–33). Thus the pre-theoretical framework that underlies intersubjectivity in interaction theory is the central coherence that organizes a variety of interpersonal and environmental experiences, not just the second-order representation that we witness in some of our intersubjective interactions.

It is also worthwhile to note that in some narratives of persons with autism or Asperger's (Grandin and Scariano 1986), a common theme is an emphasis on the intense and often disturbing nature of sensory data: rooms that are too loud or too bright, sudden movements, certain colors, shapes, or textures that can be either delightful or entirely unbearable. While many persons suffer from being socially isolated or having trouble fitting in the larger social world, narratives from retreats where everyone has autism are striking for their lack of finding sociality a problem. Indeed, it appears that the problem is more fitting in with the norms of social interaction. Thus one sees a clear tie between differences in processing sensory data and radically different styles of intersubjective relations.

Gallagher notes that what a theory of mind account demands is that we consciously or unconsciously produce explanations and predictions about what the other will do (2005, 213). For instance, if my husband calls out "oh no!" from the other room, I will predict that he will come tell me what he is yelling about. And I might also posit an explanation for his curious behavior. But my normal everyday interaction with him is not colored by a constant evaluative and predictive pattern. Gallagher describes our everyday interaction with others as "pragmatic and evaluative" and only when such habitual modes of interaction break down do we adopt a style of predicting and explaining (213). When we cook dinner and my husband reaches for the dishes, I do not have to predict or explain what he is doing. Rather, the situation, not so much any theorizing on my part, has provided the setting for his actions and my reaction to them. It could be the case that when he takes the dishes out of the cabinet, I unconsciously go through a fairly detailed set of analyses about people and desires and beliefs, as a theory of mind account would insist, but this seems difficult to embrace if a more parsimonious approach exists.

This research dovetails nicely into Gallagher's criticism of false belief tests by pointing out that when even young children seem to have difficulty representing themselves, it is difficult to believe that *neonatal* imitation is proof of a theory of mind as the capacity for self-representation. It appears that any kind of stable body image requires that over short periods of time one is able to consistently "know" one's body as something that can be represented. The ability to engage in meaningful communication and to play with one's image in a mirror fits well with the suggested idea of a primitive body image. Why, then, are children at this age unable to recognize themselves after only a few minutes pass? They do not appear to be capable of self-representation and thus do not seem to support theory of mind claims.

Some of the challenges to a theory of mind approach appear when one takes a broader view of child development. Theory of mind interpretations argue that if one does not assume a capacity to theorize or simulate others, one cannot explain the origin and development of self- and other-awareness. But the wide variety of development in not just self- and other-awareness, but bodily motility, manipulation of objects, synchronic imitation, mirror recognition, passing the false belief test, and recognition of oneself in delayed feedback, are behind these various aspects of development. Gallagher argues that instead of calling for a complex, hidden mental apparatus that must be present in infants, we can explain the origin of intersubjectivity without requiring a mental theory to be the necessary background for development (2005, 224). Our contemporary studies that reveal the cleverness of infants (which was unrecognized in the mid-twentieth century) do not necessarily prove a mental capacity, but an *embodied receptivity* to the environment and others.

Gallagher admits that a theory of mind account is a possible explanation for false belief tests, but he notes that interaction theory better fits with the range of data we have to understand intersubjectivity, broadly speaking. For instance, when we turn to autism, the problems are not merely ones about intellectually grasping the other's perspective, but a range of bodily sensitivities and intellectual peculiarities—obsessive interest in certain objects or parts of objects, extreme sensitiveness to light and sound, repetitious or odd movements. Gallagher notes that even interaction theory insofar as it is a theory of intersubjectivity needs to address the connection between the development of interactions with the rest of the world and interactions with other humans:

> To the extent that these non-social symptoms of autism show the limits of theory of mind accounts, they also show the limits of interaction theory, or any theory that focuses on just the social aspects, to explain all there is to explain in autism. We need to face up to this fact by developing an account of the social symptoms that is not inconsistent with a broader account that would explain the non-social symptoms. (2005, 231)

One of the interesting elements of paying attention to studies of verbal, high-functioning people with autism who have acquired the ability to interact socially is how intensely theoretical their awkward and stilted interactions are. For instance, Gallagher cites the famous author and researcher Temple Grandin (1986), who has learned to process sets of rules and behavior norms to approximate normal interaction (2005, 235–36). Her case draws our attention to how perhaps accurate theorizing is not a hallmark of normal human interaction. Something much more primary and less intellectual underlies the natural connections we form with others. It does not appear that an inability to theorize is at the core of oddness in interaction with others any more than it lies at the bottom of oddness in interaction with the rest of one's embodied environment.

Interaction theory draws attention to how the studies reveal an ability to imitate the facial gestures of others, to track the other's gaze, to respond to the other's gestures, and to try to evoke the other's response, are not necessarily theoretical in the infant any more than they are necessarily theoretical in the adult. It is true that sometimes I do need to "mind-read" to understand the other's behavior, such as when the other does something unusual. But most of the time I am engaged with the other in a circular loop of shared discussion, experiences, investments, and activities and I am not theorizing about the other's mental states. Interaction theory thus stresses that what is primary is not theorizing, but the possibly unique human intersubjective face-to-face interactions (Gallagher 2005, 230). Unlike theory of mind that places primacy on the mental workings of self- and other-awareness, interaction theory stresses the actual embodied practice.

Gallagher's interaction theory provides a much more Merleau-Pontian engagement with contemporary research than theory of mind accounts. It avoids the mentalistic language that Merleau-Ponty already dislikes in Piaget and the overemphasizing of intellectual developments as the hallmark of all development. While it is true, as Gallagher notes, that Merleau-Ponty did not acknowledge a primary intersubjectivity as such, and instead remained with a model of adualism, I think Merleau-Ponty would have modified his approach given his interest in examining and discussing contemporary research.

Another account that works from a phenomenological perspective to take up research in child development and child psychology is Beata Stawarska's "dialogical phenomenology." In her book *Between You and I: Dialogical Phenomenology* (2009), Stawarska develops another possible model for understanding the growth of self- and other-awareness. She critiques the mentalistic presuppositions inherent in much of child psychology that try to explain intersubjectivity. But she goes further than Gallagher to provide an alternative phenomenological framework, not just for empirical research in child psychology, but for phenomenology in general.

Stawarska argues that phenomenology has been too deeply limited by its focus on a transcendental ego that exists in solitude from a direct engagement with other egos through ordinary speech. While one can make an argument as Dan Zahavi (1999) does that transcendental subjectivity is intersubjectivity, this isn't a natural, communicating intersubjective interaction such as we would find in basic everyday human conversations. Zahavi's contribution is to argue that when we fully investigate world constitution, we find intersubjectivity therein. The world is given not merely to a solipsistic subject; the subject's very experience of the world requires that others perceive the world as well. The primacy of this intersubjectivity is not a matter of real humans interacting, as would be the case in speech communication, but an a priori structure of subjectivity itself. Thus, while of course I do encounter others throughout my life, indeed without the care of adults I would have never made it past infancy and childhood, Zahavi is not referring to this kind of intersubjective interaction, but actually suggesting that all possible experiences as such are structured by other egos independent of what one's existential, post-birth life has been like.

Stawarska argues that while such moves do integrate intersubjectivity as primary in a phenomenological analysis, they do not provide a path to consider the relevance of face-to-face natural-language interactions. In her discussion, Stawarska highlights the problem that theorists interested in interdisciplinary work face when confronted with phenomenology.

Can one refer to "natural" events, such as the interactions of mother and infant, the social milieu of the child, the development of language, as relevant to a transcendental phenomenology? Obviously how my parents treated me is very relevant to who I am, but is it relevant to how I structurally, as a subject, experience the world? It would appear that the latter is a discussion about the conditions of possibility of experiencing anything whereas the former is the color, shape, and texture that are built upon that structure. All thinking beings thus share certain similarities, but of course their life-experiences will modify how they value and interpret their lifeworld.

Stawarska argues that unless we incorporate a discussion of the face-to-face interactions that are indeed experienced by subjects in differing fashions and thus require an existential analysis, we cannot really free the ego from its solitude. It becomes difficult to explain how face-to-face interactions arise from an intersubjectivity that is isolated from natural experience. More critically, Stawarska points out that the kind of intersubjectivity that Zahavi refers to is a collection of other identical subjects all peering toward the same world. But in speech, I do not refer to another subject looking at the world, but I am engaged with a "you," a person I am speaking with face-to-face. For Stawarska, dialogical phenomenology explores the primacy of the I-you relationship in our experience. Dialogical phenomenology overcomes the traditional prejudice either in favor of an isolated transcendental subjectivity or a transcendental intersubjectivity that is conceived as a community of egos. It argues for a community of face-to-face relations as the basis of intersubjectivity (and subjectivity). Dialogical phenomenology looks outside traditional Husserlian phenomenology, and of particular relevance for this book is its attention to studies of early child relations with others (Stawarska 2009, 89–134).

Stawarska acknowledges that "it may be that dialogical phenomenology does not draw the boundary between factual and necessary claims as sharply as transcendental phenomenology does" (2009, 39). She appeals extensively to studies in early childhood experience as Gallagher does and she argues that these studies, such as "*in utero* existence and the care received in early infancy," are not just illuminating to show the way in which we are embodied and associate with others, but "are factual *as well as* necessary conditions of selfhood and sociality" (39, emphasis original). Stawarska argues that "it is impossible to disentangle these strands within a phenomenologically concrete narrative, since these factual conditions are essential to the very emergence of selfhood and sociality" (39).

In her discussion of infant and child psychological tests, Stawarska is interested in the way the proper acquisition of personal pronouns, and thus the ability to communicate with a first-person–second-person narrative, is based upon pre-linguistic communicative abilities. Piaget indicated that studies showed that children were excessively egocentric, that they could not understand that there were multiple perspectives on the world. As Merleau-Ponty lectured, this egocentrism is not another word for selfish; it is rather an adualism where the child is unaware that perspectives exist, not as in selfishness where one knows that perspectives exist but one still pushes for one's agenda. Stawarska cites a range of studies that indicate that Piaget was incorrect in his theory of childish egocentrism since even very young children can distinguish themselves from others (2009, 92–103). For instance, she cites Grace Martin and Russell Clark's work (1982) where the cogitation of cries is not revelatory of a lack of self-other distinction in a nursery but actually reveals the existence of a self-other distinction. They found that babies cried less if they heard a recording of themselves than if they heard a recording of others crying, suggesting that they on some level "recognize" their own voices.

However, such studies do not demonstrate that a kind of pre-linguistic communication is at work; they merely suggest that some sense of difference between self-produced sounds and other-produced sounds exists. Stawarska spends more time on the way in which mothers and infants communicate. She notes that mothers and infants have patterns of communication, each responding in rhythm to the other's coos, smiles, and sounds. Thus, language has a pre-linguistic foundation that is very much a practice, like adult speech, and not merely an intellectual capacity or skill-set acquisition:

> A dialogic or conversational competence of a nonsymbolic type, which precedes language-based dialogue, is therefore at work from the earliest moments of human life. Furthermore, some elements of the earliest nonsymbolic dialogic rhythms, such as gaze patterns, remain operative within adult dialogue. Infants are therefore partially skilled in areas of communication that belong to adult dialogic repertoire. (2009, 103)

A mother-infant dialogue bolsters the view that at the heart of intersubjectivity's birth is not the acknowledgment that there are other subjects, but rather the lived experience of communicating with another person.

Contemporary psychologists like Philippe Rochat (2001) argue that observing the importance of face-to-face relations between adults and infants demonstrates the unique human predisposition toward faces as well as the importance of such interactions for development. Merleau-Ponty not only lacked certain experimental data about early infant perception and interaction, but also lacked sufficient theoretical frameworks in developmental theory that permitted an idea of development not based in studying the individual. His interest in broad psychoanalysis, the more existential interpretations of phenomenology, anthropology, and sociology indicate he was looking for an alternative to subject-centered theories of development.

Merleau-Ponty's interest in the Sorbonne lectures in anthropology and sociology demonstrate that he found great appeal in culturalist sociology where one studies the society at large and the mode of upbringing as better exposing how deeply what we experience shapes our intersubjective and subjective experience of the world. I think it is possible that the somewhat curious formations of Merleau-Ponty's language surrounding infantile syncretic sociability demonstrate that he was searching for a means not to expand upon the kind of egocentric adualism of Piaget, but rather a communicative, engaged intersubjectivity that was not based in subjective self-awareness. I do not think he would have struggled with the emphasis on communication between infants and adults, but embraced such studies.

Both Stawarska and Gallagher's work thus indicate how empirical research in child psychology is relevant for understanding intersubjectivity. They also incorporate new studies in child psychology that reveal how aware infants are of their own bodies as different, but as similar to others' bodies. They convincingly indicate that such studies do not require that we adopt an intellectualist perspective such as displayed in theory of mind accounts to explain the precociousness of intersubjectivity.

Dialogical phenomenology and interaction theory are viable means to extend our knowledge of the history of intersubjectivity's development as well as its form in adults or children from a phenomenological perspective. They also offer contemporary examples of how interdisciplinary theorizing enriches both the interpretation of experimental research as well as philosophy. I agree with Stawarska that a strong division between "natural" and "transcendental" areas of research should not be maintained since in the case of intersubjectivity, one cannot understand its formation or actuality without addressing natural face-to-face human interactions. Merleau-Ponty would likely approach contemporary research in a similar fashion, and I believe his lecturing that focuses on adualism so strongly is not just influenced by the state of knowledge of infants in the mid-twentieth-century, but is a search to find a language that acknowledges human communication and connectivity without a mental, intellectualist bias. He is not unaware of the almost mystical claims that seem to be involved in syncretic sociability. He rejects a "telepathic" ideal of interaction in his last lecture, "The Experience of Others." Therein he notes that it appears that when we interact with another, "we do not always know what this gestalt is, and we risk supposing a certain mystical intuition of the other or a sort of telepathy" (*CPP* 442). Rejecting this, he argues that we must accept that something special, even what we might call magical, is occurring but avoid substantializing that experience into another object (that is, some kind of telepathic power): "We must reject the idea of a telepathic perception of the other. But how is it possible to not see something magical in the relationship between consciousness and body? To eliminate this contradiction, we must make clearer the difference between invoked magic as a real force and "magic" that is given to us in the perception of expressions" (448).

Merleau-Ponty is looking for how to capture that magic without adopting an extra-experiential force to explain it. I think interaction theory and dialogical relatedness present contemporary possible means to investigate the development of intersubjectivity without erring on the side of obscurantist powers and forces or isolated subjective development.

Gallagher and Stawarska's work dovetails with Merleau-Ponty's understanding of our "orientation" in intersubjectivity. In his critique of the limits of Guillaume's understanding of imitation, Merleau-Ponty stresses that our relations with the other are not about an intellectual synthesis of self and other. In fact, the very ability to pose intersubjectivity as a problem is based in our experience as being always-already social. Already in the *Phenomenology of Perception*, Merleau-Ponty writes that "the perception of other people and the intersubjective world is problematical only for adults" (*PP* 355). For children, the other is not a problem but part of the coherent structure of their pre-theoretical world. Only post-theory can one find the other to be a philosophical difficulty.

Merleau-Ponty points to two tendencies in Husserl's thoughts on intersubjectivity. One is the tendency to want to depart from self-consciousness, from a cogito that reaches toward others. The other is to start with intersubjectivity and with a consciousness that "is neither self nor other":

> The difference between my point of view and others' point of view only exists after we have experienced other people: it is a consequence. We must not, Husserl says, pose this distinction from the beginning and then oppose all thought of an experience of others. But with this remark, Husserl seems to want to renounce the idea that one attains the experience of others starting with self-consciousness. He seems to bring us in another direction. Thus, there are two tendencies in his work. One is the attempt to gain access to others from the "cogito," from the "sphere of ownness" [*sphère de appatenance*]. The other is to refuse the

problem and have an orientation toward intersubjectivity, that is to say, the possibility of starting without posing the primordial "cogito," starting with the consciousness that is neither self nor other. (*CPP* 29)

What is this consciousness that is "neither self nor other"? It would be the primary intersubjectivity, or dialogical relatedness, that must precede the ability to refer to oneself or others in isolation. In order, for instance, for the false belief test to make sense, one must already be ready to understand the experiment or interaction at all. Solving it is merely the ability to take one's position as changeable; it is an intellectual achievement, but it is not evidence of the birth of intersubjectivity.

As Gallagher notes with his underlining of how bodily difference in sensory perception is connected to intersubjective awareness, Merleau-Ponty argues that identifying others and objects must not be understood as distinct processes. Instead, the identification of another's actions and the objectification of objects occur parallel to one another. The child develops a sense of body-world difference alongside a mine-other distinction. Similar to interaction theory where one is encouraged to not see our relations with the world and with others as separate questions but as connected, Merleau-Ponty argues that others do not "set us on the path" toward things or things set us on the path toward others:

> Is it others [*autrui*] who set us on the path toward things and not vice versa? Is it "the other" [*l'autre*] who enables us to have a truly objective vision of a world which does not exist for me alone? Actually, these two circuits are not alternatives: relations with others and relations with the world are correlatives, and Guillaume's attempt is futile to the extent that he believes one arrives at "the other" solely via things. (*CPP* 427)

Merleau-Ponty upholds the Piagetian thesis that imitation is related to self-consciousness and that the ability to objectify others and objects. However, he does not agree that early imitation can only be the result of a fully self-conscious subject. But this alone does not contradict a primary intersubjectivity; contemporary phenomenologists emphasize that the primal sense of self-awareness is not based in self-representation, but rather in actual living interactions.

Citing Guillaume (1971), in his discussion of imitation, Merleau-Ponty lectures: "A profound and fertile idea: we are not first conscious of our own bodies, we are first conscious of things" (*CPP* 22). He continues to note that when the child first imitates the *actions* of others on the world, he uses the other as an intermediary to accessing the world. He supports Gallagher's idea that there is a type of central coherence, or in Merleau-Ponty's words, a structured experience of the interaction between child and other in imitation: "This is to say that imitation presupposes the apprehension of the other's behavior and, from my own side, realizes a noncontemplative subject, but a motor subject: an '*I can*' (Husserl)" (*CPP* 24). Thus, we are not first connected by a theory of other minds, but by embodied interaction. From this reading, there appears to be little fundamental conflict between contemporary phenomenological assessments of imitation and Merleau-Ponty's work.

What I think remains in question is whether or not we should blend a Merleau-Pontian analysis within a larger framework of developing self- and other-awareness or retain his sense that syncretic sociability is something unique and thus should not too quickly be assumed into the fold of a precursor to normal, adult awareness. Stawarska and Gallagher present views that highlight the sense that we have misunderstood the importance of how experimental and empirical research can inform and strengthen phenomenology and also how phenomenology can shed illuminative light on interpreting experimental studies. The value that is retained in Merleau-Ponty's lectures, despite their ignorance about the progress of the psychological sciences, is the appreciation of child experience as not just precursor to adult experience, but possessing its own rhythm and styles of interaction.

5

Exploration and Learning

When trying to understand the child's intersubjective life, we must be careful to not overvalue intellectual, representational abilities in childhood since this highlights immaturity and reduces the child to a former adult state. Instead, we must approach childhood development with an open mind and be willing to find forms and styles of engagement that are not always found in a more developed sense in the adult. Earlier in this book we have found ways in which to meaningfully discuss intersubjectivity without assuming that it is first and foremost a mental operation. Perception is another example of how we must be careful to not assign to the child a reduced form of adult perception. Merleau-Ponty lectures that we should not assume that the child has a uniform, permanent visual field wherein things are laid out as stable, unchanging parts. Children organize the perceptual field according to their own logic:

> In general, it is not a question of attributing to the child an *absolutely* permanent conception of the thing (such as the physicist's concept of nature which is, in fact, not even found in the adult's perceptual world). It is simply a question of acknowledging that the child's *logical operations* have already established perceptual organization. The child's perceptual organization is able to function according to its own logic. (*CPP* 149, emphasis original)

The child's own logic will be best exposed not in interviewing the child directly, since children do not necessarily form abstract theories about their world, but in seeing how the child interprets "magical" phenomena. In addition, we can learn much from children's own creations, such as their drawings. In this chapter, we will look at two examples—the child's interpretation of magic tricks and the child's artistic depictions. We will discover that while children produce childlike explanations and creations, they are actively engaged with their experience and far less inclined toward fantastical creations than often supposed. This underlines the argument that our early life is best marked by engagement and not withdrawal.

Magic and Scientific Thinking

Due to the linguistic limitations of children, psychologists use objects the child creates or interacts with as diagnostic tools. For instance, some cases involving abuse will call upon the child's drawings as forensic evidence (Katz and Hershkowitz 2010). If a child is being abused, her graphical depictions of the abuser might indicate her disturbed state of mind. The pictorial depiction of the abuser may appear in a threatening position compared to the child's drawing of herself. Or the child might refuse to depict the abuser, afraid he will surface through the very two-dimensional image itself. Indeed, many a popular television drama will have the abused child drawing such pictures, which stands in for a clear indication to the audience that something heinous has happened.

Such a conception leads one to think of children's drawings as largely expressive of internal states: fear, happiness, boredom, and so on, and not as representative of the external world. Thus, children draw what they *feel* rather than what they *see*. In the case of unexplainable events, such as magic tricks, the child is expected to rely upon beliefs in magic and fantasy. For instance, when a rabbit is pulled out of a hat, a child is expected to easily accept, if not even prefer, the "magical" explanation. What one might call the "scientific" or "philosophical" understanding would have to be provided to the child. Naturally the child tends toward an internal, affective, superstitious worldview. As a result, we understand children as not seriously engaged with the world around them.

Merleau-Ponty's lectures reject this view. Instead, he finds that children's comprehension of surprising, "magical" events, albeit different than those of adults, arises from an engaged relationship with the world. Merleau-Ponty argues that we need to find a neutral language when considering our early interpretations and expressions of the world. Otherwise, our investment in scientific and philosophical concepts will cause us to misunderstand the uniqueness of the child's experience.

For Merleau-Ponty, the child is a natural phenomenologist. In adult experience, our cultural and social lives have become so ingrained in our sense of self, others, and the world that we are deeply guided by certain metaphysical assumptions that are themselves an expression of an ideological indoctrination instead of the result of a sustained philosophical reflection. One assumption is that experience is a kind of filter through which the "real self," be it the mind, the soul, or the brain, explores the "real world"—the status of empirical objects, including the human body. While this filter might distort experience by being diseased, as in the case of hallucinations, or by being inappropriately formed by a bad childhood or a fascist culture, it is seen as distinct from the object of the subject's reflection. Subsequently we often fail to question our interpretations of the world—we see possible problems as arising from a faulty science—that is, the status of the objects in the world, or a faulty psychology—that is, the nature of the mind. The child neither employs philosophical distinctions about a mind judging the world nor has she any investment in a scientific worldview. Both theoretical approaches tend to view experience as something distinct from real things and real subjects. For the child, her experiences are not something she has "about reality;" they *are* real.

Such a conception of the child's experience leads Merleau-Ponty to reject the theory, suggested by Piaget, that children have a natural tendency to retreat from the world when pressed to explain it. Piaget (1999) writes that children are drawn to magical explanations when they encounter inexplicable phenomena. Merleau-Ponty sharply criticizes a view that assumes the child is prone to fantasy in her relations with the world. He objects to the theory that children readily create magical, unreal explanations for their experiences. Using the work of I. Huang (1943), Merleau-Ponty observes that children give reasonable explanations of magic tricks when one does not force their conclusions. Huang was a contemporary of Piaget and often a critic of Piaget's thought. Contrary to Piaget, Huang does not ask at what age the child is capable of giving a "correct" response. Merleau-Ponty writes that "Huang does not want to show a separation between the child's thought and that of the adult. His goal is a positive one; he asks what happens within the mind of the child. The responses of children, despite their naiveté, can be 'rational'" (*CPP* 409–10). Huang draws attention to the child's economic and social circumstances, allowing him to understand when "magical explanations" are the result of class traditions. Children from the middle and upper classes are more likely to suggest fantastical explanations given their larger exposure to fairy tales and children's stories, whereas working-class children tend to provide grounded responses. Piaget, on the contrary, fails to take into account the child's socioeconomic situation. One benefit of Huang's analysis is that he allows the child's explanation to come forth without asking leading questions. He focuses on the child's natural responses and not on her linguistic immaturity:

> Huang's *goal* is a descriptive and normative model. Since Huang allows the child to speak, his *method* is very different from Piaget's. He tries to capture the child's implicit view of the world . . . to catch them "dealing with things," rather than "dealing with thoughts." Huang places the child before "a real event involving concrete and tangible objects (as opposed to a situation created by language), an event capable of evoking responses similar to those that child presents in his everyday life."

Piaget, on the other hand, interrogates the child with regard to subjects with which the child has never been confronted. The result of Piaget's interrogations is that the child responds in reaction to a verbal situation. (*CPP* 410, emphasis original)

Because Piaget's interview method restricts the child to certain responses, it is no wonder that the child is incapable of expressing a scientific view of the world. We have to call into question the interview situation itself. Is it possible that the result we are receiving is due to our formulation of the interview questions? Are our questions overdetermined by our own investments and thus constrict and even deform the child's natural responses?

Several of the magic tricks Huang shows children were ones where an adult would either have knowledge of the scientific theory that explained the surprising phenomenon or would understand there must be a logical explanation. Since children have no scientific knowledge or understanding of sleights of hand, we expect them to interpret the trick with appeal to magic. In one demonstration, a researcher had sewn a hidden toothpick into a handkerchief. Placing another toothpick on the handkerchief, the researcher lets the child break the toothpick, moves his hand quickly, and reveals the formerly hidden unbroken toothpick. When asked to explain what they saw, children initially search for a rational explanation. "Very few of the children think that it could actually be the same toothpick. They think it may have been only partially broken (in this case one then has them recommence the experiment) or that a substitution has occurred. They *never* spontaneously suggest a magical explanation" (*CPP* 118, emphasis original). Children first try to find an explanation that is comprehensible to them and to how they understand the world to work. Only when pressed will they resort to an appeal to magic. They know that the toothpick cannot have been "remade" and, thus, try to find an explanation that justifies what they see.

In another demonstration, children are presented with the surface tension of water. A needle is placed, point-down, in a glass of water. It falls to the bottom. The same needle is taken out, dried off, and placed horizontally on the water and it floats. Children offer different explanations—the needle floats because it is very dry, the air in the eye of the needle makes it float, and so on—but they do not resort to imaginary forces to explain what they see. In this account, spontaneous childhood ways of understanding the world are not different from adult approaches to anomalous phenomena. Merleau-Ponty writes that children search for a "spontaneous explanation" and try to "reduce the unknown to a notion that is known, and while this is done in a *naïve manner, it is by no means absurd*" (*CPP* 189, italics original). What is striking is that "in no case do we observe a difference in kind between the reasoning of the child and that of the adult (i.e., a prelogical or mystical-rational form of thought); just like the adult, the child tries to take account of the phenomenon in a 'natural' fashion" (189–90). Children offer sensible accounts of their experiences and do their best to work surprising phenomena into their preexisting structures. While we find their accounts naive, we do not find a lack of engagement with the world or a desire to return to an internal, superstitious worldview.

Piaget's suggestion that children are natural metaphysicians suggests that they are quick to fabricate narratives that provide a kind of intellectual consistency even if these require departing from a connection to experience. Merleau-Ponty's view is that children are natural phenomenologists in that they remain connected to experience and do not require a resolution in a theory. Such a perspective is limiting when one is considering ideal and not natural objects, but it is less likely to sacrifice experience on the altar of consistency. Children explore the world rather than analyze the world. Unlike adults, children do not tend to take objects out of their context, or take themselves out of context. I can imagine myself somewhere else than where I sit at this moment. I'm driving to my house; I'm sitting with my friend on the porch. Moreover, I can with a bit more effort imagine that I had an entirely different life. I can speculate on what it would be like, for instance, to grow up at the turn of the century on a farm. Yet, it is difficult to really "erase" myself, my context, my knowledge, my affections, and my desires and imagine being this other person in an entirely different situation. But telling such a tale to a child: "Imagine you were born on a farm before electricity!" can at most make the child imagine being in a farmhouse but remaining, otherwise, the same. The child's reality has a solidity that while not static, can appear to be rigid to adults who are indoctrinated in certain philosophical and scientific interpretations.

The adult is more likely to provide an explanation of reality that leaves one's lived experience. Stories of aliens, ghosts, wizards, and divine beings come easily to adults. Even when we do not believe in them, we can quickly grasp the sense of what roles they would play in story. You could attribute the surprising hole in your roof to an alien, and although I would doubt the existence of the alien, I can quickly imagine what kind of worldview you have. Children tend to work with what they personally have experienced. Thus, they might accept a supernatural story when provided, but they rarely invent their own unless they've been indoctrinated in a particular worldview. Unless pressed, they typically do not offer ideas that go beyond the lived world. Magical explanations thus are naturally rare in children, according to Merleau-Ponty.

If it were the case that children were naturally given to belief in magic, their extreme delight and frustration at it would be surprising. Why wouldn't they encounter the magician's miraculous rabbit or bird as something ho-hum, a part of an everyday, normal world? Children have a natural tendency to be *surprised* by the anomalous; they do not explain it away with quick recourse to fantasy. One has only to watch a child who has just had a coin "pulled" from behind her ear. The eyes widen and a hand flies up behind the ear to check: Where did this coin come from? How did it get there? Did I just not feel it before? Is there another one hiding there? We must turn our typical conception on its head. It is not that children's interest in wizards and fairy tales is due to their ease at retreating to a magical worldview; rather it is their continuity with the world that makes these stories so outrageous, and thus, compelling. Indeed, children are often disinterested in supernatural worldviews precisely because they are so removed from their experience. A magic trick has real effects and is fascinating. A wizard or witch who creates these effects intrigues, whereas a metaphysical doctrine with no distinguishing impact on the child's life fails to capture the young imagination. Complex religious explanations have a degree of remove from reality that is too sophisticated for the child.

Nonetheless, children do repeat and occasionally spontaneously offer fantastical stories to explain the world. Merleau-Ponty uses Henri Wallon's notion of "ultra-things" to explain why children adopt such conjectures. Wallon (1963) suggests that some aspects of the child's experience are present and lived, but not as objects or ideas that the child can easily grasp. In other words, these elements of experience are not fabricated, such as a wizard, nor are they easily objectified. They lie at the limits of our ability to circumscribe objects. I can very easily turn a tree into an object of contemplation, but the universe as a whole exceeds my imagination. These "ultra-things" are notable for being very unlike the child's own relationship to his body; they cannot be moved or seen to be moving. "Such beings are not fully grasped by simply looking at them and children cannot change them by willing or by moving their bodies. . . . The earth and the sky are exemplar 'ultra-things,' and as such are always incompletely determined by the child" (*CPP* 192). Ultra-things possess an absolute and unchanging kind of being for the child. When it comes to a toothpick or a quarter, children will construct very understandable explanations for "magical" phenomena. When it comes to the nature of the sky or death, children will construct fantastical theories if pressed.

They rest outside of the child's comprehension, even if the child can intuit their presence and feels them to be continuous with her experience.

For instance, children will acknowledge that their parents must have existed once as children, and that they themselves must have once not existed before birth, but they give only lip-service to these concepts. Death is not grasped as an event because it is never part of the child's experience. Thus, unless the death is of a person or animal in the child's life, and thereby affects the child's existence, the concept of death itself is not troubling. The child's own existence is also an ultra-thing. What of our adult experience? Isn't it also the case that birth, death, the universe's infiniteness, and our own contingent existence remain qualitatively different from any other kinds of knowledge we accrue?

> On this level, the child is incapable of conceiving of not having always existed. Moreover, even for the adult awareness it is impossible to really conceive of one's own birth and death. As a result, the subject feels coextensive with being, and this belief, Wallon stresses, is inherent in subjectivity. In a sense, it persists in the adult: we are not able to think outside all points of view, we can push the frontiers of "ultra-things" further (e.g., in learning the Copernican system), but we cannot eliminate them completely. (*CPP* 192–93)

Science consequently can never completely overlay and determine adult consciousness; a childhood residue of immersion in the world exists even when the adult understands the operations of the world as independent from her own existence. Children, similar to adults, strive toward harmony in their worldviews and search for reasonable explanations. They differ in how far one can abstract from one's existence. It is only by recognizing the influence not just of childhood in one's experience, but how we too face ultra-things at the limits of our own understanding: "A more human relation could be established between the adult and the child where the child is not imprisoned in a magical world. The adult can comprehend the child's preobjective experience by virtue of the fact that the 'ultra-thing' forms the horizon of his own experience" (*CPP* 193).

Does the above suggest that with our more elaborate systems of knowledge, adults are more disengaged with reality? Because the child is a type of natural phenomenologist, intertwined with her living experience, is she therefore more connected to some kind of truth that has been lost to us? Merleau-Ponty's texts support careful work in the sciences and philosophy. Although his work includes a critique of certain aspects of modern philosophy and science, he does not depart from the tradition in a global critique as we find in the postmodern and poststructuralist traditions. Unlike children, we can reflect upon our philosophical investments and assumptions in a critical fashion. But Merleau-Ponty does call into question the common idea that our adult ability to comprehend the immediate and evident aspects of our experience as well as the hidden operations that underlie the presentations we are given in our sensory field arises from being more "in touch" with reality than children. Simply because we have acquired better tools and methods to understand the world around us does not mean that those who use these tools and methods are perceiving the world more directly. For Merleau-Ponty, scientific thought is not the thought of children since it requires a belief in the methods and tools of science. The child seeks concrete explanations. We should avoid overinvesting these concrete explanations with the idea that the child thus holds these as beliefs or theories:

> An intellectual explanation is the physicist's concern; the child seeks for more concrete explanations . . . However, the child does not have a belief in the sense that the physicist does, that is, in the domain of thetic thought. Rather, the child needs to arrive at a solution. He seeks to confront a situation and to close what is left open. (*CPP* 411)

Children do interpret; they do search for organization in their experiences. But their explanations are not based on judgments as we assume they are for the scientist. The child seeks "natural" explanations, ones that are based in her life and not in her theories about life. "The child does not proceed at all costs toward 'magical' explanations, but toward natural ones (not in the sense in which the physicist understands this word, but in the sense that it is commonly given)" (411). It is our education wherein the high estimation of Western scientific thinking encourages us to mistake a scientific explanation for a complete explanation.

The child's interpretation of magic tricks reveals this natural kind of interpretation where children provide answers that accord with their experience, that are what we might call "possible" explanations devoid of sophisticated scientific and fantastical schemes. Our scientific education affords us tremendous intellectual power to understand what does not appear in our everyday experience and to avoid false conclusions. However, in our enthusiasm for its obvious advantages, we can pass over the lived experience and in particular the lived experience of those that are different from us. No departure from science is called for in the lectures, but rather an acknowledgment of how its interpretative frameworks do not lay bare all the truths of human life. Having a scientific worldview can be as unreflective and blind as any unexamined metaphysical belief system.

Child Drawing and Adult Oculocentrism

This depiction of childhood experience revealed thorough childhood drawing and the comprehension of magic tricks dovetails with Merleau-Ponty's understanding of early childhood experience as engaged and organized. Children's drawings also indicate that children have a multi-sensorial, almost synesthetic, perception. Interestingly, the highly affective nature of children's drawings, as well as their use of flattening and multiple perspectives in one image, continues *after* the child has the motor skills to better coordinate her work. For Merleau-Ponty, this indicates that children are expressing the fluidity of their senses in the structure of their drawings. Children do not necessarily draw in an easily understandable fashion since they do not adhere to cultural standards of expression. Children act selfishly because they do not understand that other people have different desires and wishes. Likewise, children do not understand their perceptions as their own. They perceive and draw distinctions upon various dimensions—affective, visual, auditory, and temporal dimensions—and these distinctions appear in their work in ways that do not accord with the "visual" object itself. Adult drawing and perception also possess an affective charge, but cultural and linguistic limitations often repress this expression in painting as well as in most adults' hesitation to describe synesthetic aspects of their experience.

A phenomenology of perception, the exploration Merleau-Ponty is most famous for, reveals that our perceptual experience is far more critical to our cognition than we had previously assumed. Few psychologists or philosophers deny the obvious foundational role perception serves, but many treat it as a type of physiological collecting of experiential givens. Perception becomes nothing more than another word for the physical operation of processing sense-data and thus should be explored by physiologists, not by theoreticians. The challenging question is how the proper intellectual or cognitive interpretation applies itself to that perception. Thus, a child might have the physical apparatus to collect the givens, but since the child obviously lacks the intellectual and mental skills to process that data, her engagement will be limited. Merleau-Ponty argues strongly against interpreting perception in such a fashion. In the case of the child, he acknowledges that the child is unsophisticated and lacks many cognitive skills. However, since perception precedes intellectual judgments about the objects of perception, the child is not partially, minimally, or limitedly experiencing the world. The child might not judge an object or be able to name it, but she still perceives it. Childhood drawing provides an insight into the nature of childhood perception and, thereby, the basis of adult perception.

The child's experience also provides a counterpoint to aid us in analyzing certain unquestioned assumptions about adult experience. Thus, the study of child perception provides insight into the workings of the adult psyche. Merleau-Ponty affirms the traditional conception that children draw expressively, but does not suggest that this means their drawing is less perceptual. Rather, it is the false premise that perception is only the psychological-physiological collecting of visual sense-data that is then interpreted by intellectual processing that permits one to draw a line between affective, internally motivated drawing and drawing as solely the representation of the perceived world.

Adult and child drawing can be illustrative for understanding perception. Even in attempts to render the world as though through a camera shot, artistic representations are always modified by the artist. Adults have often been trained to associate photographic representations as being more "honest" depictions of the world, but this itself is a cultural assumption. We do not actually encounter the world as a series of moving snapshots, nor is our experience of reality akin to a movie projected before our eyes. Thus, to assume that a photographic representation is more "real" is itself a questionable assumption. Adult ideas about art and perception are overdetermined by "conventional attitudes." The child's artistic representation of the world is more revealing as to our true perceptual experience:

> *The study of the role of drawing leads us back to the capacity which it serves as its ground: perception.* We have seen that drawings express affectivity rather than understanding. Consequently, we must pay close attention to what the child's perception—and even that of the adult when it can be stripped of conventional attitudes—consists of when encountering things not only as objects of understanding, but also as affective stimulants. (*CPP* 171, italics original)

In many passages, Merleau-Ponty argues that childhood drawing possesses unique advantages to understanding the nature of perception in comparison to adult drawing, painting, and discourse. Merleau-Ponty lectures that children express a more sensually integrated experience in their drawings than adults do. Not only do children use their sense of time, hearing, taste, and touch in their depictions, but they also do not draw divisions between what they feel and what they see. The characteristics of childhood drawing arise directly from the child's experience in an unmediated fashion, since children are not as integrated into the system of styles of representation. From longer accumulated experience witnessing paintings, photos, film, and being schooled in what "good" painting consists of, adults tend to be more oculocentric in their representations.

The traditional Western conception of drawing is of representing two-dimensionally a three-dimensional visual object. One should draw a "thing" in a moment of time—the landscape, the chair, the person. Children weave context, time, and their affective lives into their depictions. When diagnosing children's disorders, psychoanalysis and psychology use the fact that children do not separate their affective relations with persons from their depictions of them. While adults latently retain this affective nature in their drawings and certainly artists endeavor to create beyond the concept of representing objects two-dimensionally as "faithfully" as possible, children's drawings reveal much about how adult drawing has become overlaid by sociocultural determinations.

Psychologists often use drawing to measure the development of the child's visual and motor systems. Can the child successfully put a torso on the body, or does the child merely draw a tadpole man? When asked to draw an object, does the child capture the main components of it? Merleau-Ponty considers the overemphasis on such an assessment as a misreading of child perception as a function of adult perception (that is, the child's drawing is only valued as an expression of how far the child is on the path to adulthood). Modeling development based on the child's artistic representations acknowledges that children's drawings possess unique characteristics (contrasted with a more outdated view holding child drawing as psychologically irrelevant), but such attention in child psychology to child drawing still tends to deemphasize the positive aspects of child experience. "However, they [children's drawings] are always studied as a function of adult drawing. One views children's drawing as imperfect sketches of adult drawings which are the 'true' representation of the object" (*CPP* 132). Thus, their interpretative model constrains them to always find within the child what is present in the adult, not considering that the child may possess unique structures that are not merely "miniature" versions of adult ones. Consequently, such a conception of child drawing assumes that what is "wrong" in children's drawings is the lack of attention to the "real" way in which the object appears. In fact, Merleau-Ponty counters, child drawing can often reveal the elements of the object's being that adult representations pass over or repress.

Drawing helps to distinguish how adults and children perceive and interact with objects. If a child is depicting a visual object, she will provide its global attributes, grasping the essential scheme of the item and passing over the details:

> For example, when the child draws a bicycle, he reproduces a more or less coherent picture with some accentuated details, such as the pedals. The adult's depiction of the bicycle is guided by its mechanical relationships (e.g., the connection between the pedals and the rear wheel), but these links escape the child almost entirely. (*CPP* 149)

Merleau-Ponty cites the work of the psychologists Édouard Claparède (1998) and Richard Meili (1931) to better outline the child's holistic perception. Claparède calls children's perception "syncretic," arguing that children fixate on the smallest details, seeing an intricate connection with the whole (although this connection may not exist) or perceiving very global structures. Meili notes that children tend to grasp what he calls the "form," which would be the general nature of the object, but they rarely grasp the direct connections between particular parts—such as in the drawing of the bicycle. Children do not grasp how the gears are related to the wheels, but certainly grasp the general nature of the bicycle as a means of transport:

> Thus, on the one hand, we see that the child's perception is in fact synthetic, but not *articulately synthetic*. On the other hand, the child's perception has some decidedly positive features. For example, the child perceives totalities much more readily than adults (e.g., the thresholds of "stroboscopic movement" are lower in the child). This suggests that the child possesses a larger number of "good forms." In other words, the child organizes wholes more easily than the adult. Only when the whole is too complex is the child forced to fall back on fragmentary aspects. (*CPP* 150, emphasis original)

Childhood perception harmonizes objects insofar as it attempts to integrate all puzzling givens into known structures. We saw above that children's reaction to magic tricks is one of sensible organization, not an immediate flight from reality into a magical world.

To find evocative descriptions of synesthetic experience we must turn to more literary or philosophical writings. Bringing up Sartre's famous example of honey and lemon in *Being and Nothingness* (1956), Merleau-Ponty demonstrates how visual aspects of things are intertwined with their other sensible qualities which give the object its unity (even though our education tells us to separate color from touch, taste from sound, etc.). Honey's sticky feel and sweet taste are not distinct qualities from the perception of honey; rather, the original unity of the experience of honey combines the senses in a unity, a type of Gestalt. I can sense the viscosity of honey without touching it. The child encounters the world in such a manner, where she approaches things as they appear to her, not through a lens that has encouraged us to overvalue our perception and assume that each sense gives us a separate meaning that can only be combined intellectually. If we return to experience, we find that often our senses combine in the perception, taste, sound, smell, or feel of a singular object. When I eat honey, I cannot sharply distinguish its taste from its texture. Merleau-Ponty writes that "a relation exists between this palatable quality and its tactile quality: each quality cannot be taken to be a little, opaque islet. We can only give a dynamic description of the mode of existence: viscosity and sweetness are two honeylike manners of the being that is called 'honey'" (*CPP* 420). This depiction and Sartre's discussion of the same synesthetic affect of lemon introduces a discussion regarding how childhood drawing reveals the way in which childhood perception, in Husserl's words, gets to the things themselves.

Childhood drawings reveal that sensory categorization is rare in our perception. The object's unity, that totality children so easily can grasp and depict in their drawings, includes nonvisual aspects. Merleau-Ponty calls upon the writing of Francis Ponge (1942) to demonstrate this childhood depiction. Ponge takes up everyday objects—shrimp, oranges—and in particular Merleau-Ponty addresses his discussion of the pebble in highlighting how an object is experienced. The background to our perception includes the nonattended parts of our perception, as Gestalt psychology argues. It also includes synesthetic aspects of objects, how our senses are intertwined in our visual perceptions. Ponge draws our attention to the other things that are referring to by an object, here the sea and wind evoked by a pebble and best understood by the child:

> The wind and the sea are, as it were, already referred to by the pebble, and the pebble itself is a complex which must be illuminated. Ponge observes things in the impact they have on him and not as exterior to him. The pebble that he analyzes is the pebble of the child (we ourselves are obliged to return to our childhood impressions of the pebble in order to recover the poetry of it). Therefore, the symbolization in the pebble is of a whole series of behaviors, as well as the evident relation between certain persons and the pebble. We thus understand that a spectator's conception of perception would not permit us to truly comprehend things. (*CPP* 421)

Adult perception often evokes this poetry through artistic creativity. For example, Picasso's use of multiple perspectives in one human figure can be understood as grasping a truth about the perspectival nature of our perception. Likewise, the childhood tendency to flatten perspective illustrates how our eyes do not tend to focus simply on a one-point perspective but wander from place to place within a visual field. Children also distort the comparative sizes of objects and persons depending on their affective relations.

Merleau-Ponty credits psychoanalysis with discovering how childhood drawing demonstrates the manner in which affective associations are depicted, even when these objects are not in the visual field of the child. He cites Sophie Morgenstern's (1937) *Psychanalyse infantile: Symbolisme et valeur clinique des creations imaginatives chez l'enfant* wherein Morgenstern describes how drawing is "sublimation for both the child and the adult" (*CPP* 175). Merleau-Ponty disagrees with drawing too great an emphasis on the catharsis of drawing as being parallel in adults and children. For adults we can envision the creative expression as indicating a latent content deformed by psychic resistances. But children do not have the pasts of adults. "However, in children, it is impossible to imagine that such a censor mechanism exists; rather than discovering a simple duality of manifest content and latent content, one finds a single text of undetermined meaning" (175). For instance, we can understand how adult repression of a taboo subject might appear in a sexually charged representation. However, given the child's nature, there is no sexual content "as sexual" to be repressed. What is sexual is immediately experienced for the child. We can say that for the child there is nothing distinctly sexual; rather, sexuality is one color of the child's entire experience.

Merleau-Ponty returns to Politzer's *Critique des fondements* (1968), citing his critique of Freudian notions of latent content and manifest content; for Politzer this distinction isn't operative in the child or the dreamer (*CPP* 175). As written above, objects do not represent for children what they might for adults: "The child's symbolization does not stem from an understanding separated according to the terms *object* and *symbol*, but rather sexual meaning is immanent in the drawing" (175–76). Thus, affective relations are not behind or beneath children's perceptions (occasionally causing certain kinds of depictions); they are intrinsic to perception itself. The concept that emotional states "cause" the child to draw in a certain manner—a theory of drawing as an expressive function—has a certain truth to it, but an incomplete one. It is true that children are expressive, emotional artists. However, it isn't the case that they have an emotion and subsequently are forced by this emotion to draw in a particular manner. This interpretation argues that the child's affective states are internal, removed from their perceptual experience. We *learn* to create divisions between affects and the senses; we are not born with such distinctions.

We might object that such a position reifies childhood experience as if it were not influenced by the contingencies of the child's situation: her culture, social class, and family. Providing an example from Marxist thinkers, Merleau-Ponty acknowledges that "however, it is impossible to separate cultural influences from what properly speaking belongs to the child. Sociological, even ideological, considerations always intervene in any discussion about drawing" (*CPP* 163). At the same time, Merleau-Ponty considers this kind of objection a false problem. Naturally, children are affected by their situation, others' attitudes toward them, the cultural norms of the society, and so on. What does such an admission entail? For Merleau-Ponty, such a statement is merely a truism and would not affect our ability to investigate the child's structures of perception. "Even a total absence of milieu (if this is conceivable) would affect the child as any particular milieu does" (164). It is a given that environmental conditions shape any being that lives within that environment. The point of Merleau-Ponty's child psychology is to demonstrate to what degree cultural differences demonstrate plasticity in child development and to what degree we find general structures of development. Without such traits no comparison between cultures can be possible, for a comparison requires a framework, or form, that is similar enough in both to afford a comparison. Merleau-Ponty finds that cultural differences reveal structural similarities. Anthropological investigations support the view that processes by which children perceive are similar (although the content of their responses varies widely due to class and culture).

Structural traits are not context-independent. Yet, they do allow for one to leave the description of the cultural, historical situation and consider the theoretical implications of childhood drawing, especially how it uncovers the nature of perception. To understand how childhood drawing is more than just a test or measure of motor development, one must recognize a *positive meaning* within the child's drawing. Pointing out similarities with modern art, Merleau-Ponty writes that child drawing and modern painting challenge the postulate that "the geometrical perspective is truer" (*CPP* 132). He continues by noting that "the efforts of modern painting place this postulate in question and accord a positive significance to other manners of seeing (for example, for Picasso the plurality of profiles is a means of expression)" (132). Modern artists abandon traditional methods of creating the illusion of perspective within a two-dimensional canvas and explore a variety of styles to compose their works. Since traditional Western, perspectival drawing and photography are considered to be more "accurate" visually, modern art is often analyzed in terms unrelated to accuracy or truth (for instance, one can discuss the use of color and line, social commentary, visual effect, etc.). Merleau-Ponty would not claim that modern painting is more accurate about the visual stimuli at a located moment in time. Rather, he argues that, like childhood drawing, modern art better emphasizes the truth of *perception*. We must recognize the idea that photographic representation of an object—its visual stimuli—is itself an intellectual exercise of isolation that always occurs post-perception.

Naturally, adult distinctions cannot be too hard and fast. We are not "trapped" in our own culturally overdetermined views and unable to appreciate different cultures or ways of living. Because the modern artist (or psychologist or philosopher) calls into question unreflective assumptions about perception and representation, she achieves a degree of freedom from cultural norms. Although there is no complete liberty, there are greater and lesser degrees of independence and, thus, creativity with respect to social-cultural standards:

> We can see proof of children's freedom from our cultural postulates in their drawings. We do understand that a perceptual-motor insufficiency does in fact exist; children are not artists. However, the efforts of modern painting grant a new meaning to children's drawings. We can no longer consider perspectival drawings as the only "truth." . . . The child is capable of certain spontaneous actions which are rendered impossible in the adult due to the influence of, and obedience to, cultural schemas. (*CPP* 132)

To explore the world of the child's drawing and perception, one must find a method that integrates both the historical events of the child's life as well as the responses of the child to her environment. Merleau-Ponty takes a stance contrary to any kind of functionalism or strict developmental schema where children are viewed as either possessing or not possessing age-appropriate skills and behaviors: "Positive contents must be incorporated into explorations of the functional aspects of the child's behavior" (133). Childhood drawings represent an expressive grasp of nature that reflects the child's *global* perception of the world. A global perception is the general manner in which one relates to the world and arises from one's vision, history, and emotive nature. Thus, what a child sees and what a child draws "are not exactly the same" because they do not separate their "internal vision of things" from the sight of the object (164).

The expressive nature of children's drawing means that the object-representation and the affective state are not separate categories of intellect and emotion; rather they both exist intimately in perception. Merleau-Ponty lectures that, for children, drawing is as much about self-expression as it is about thing-representation, but, as argued above, this is not to say that the child is motivated by some kind of internal state to express herself. Merleau-Ponty distinguishes himself from the child psychologist G. H. Luquet (1972) by denying the thesis that the child's drawing is a combination of an internal, affective model and a direct representation of the child's vision. Luquet assumes that drawing is about transmitting visual givens. Hence, both the child and the adult "see" the same way; it is a matter of attention that distinguishes their representations. Since he adheres to a notion that the object is constant (the "constancy hypothesis"), Luquet thinks perception is only a matter of paying attention well or poorly (*CPP* 386).

The theory of object-constancy does not explain perception or art. Attention often does reveal more aspects of a particular experience. Yet, this isn't to say that when I consciously and carefully focus my attention on an object that I am thereby physiologically absorbing more visual givens in my perceptual field. We do not experience the world in a type of cloudy fog until we decide to focus on objects. Certainly we cannot imagine that children have such an experience. Attention doesn't make me perceive "better" even though it restructures my perception. Merleau-Ponty uses Gestalt theory to speak of "restructurations" of perception. He lectures that Gestalt theory has shown us that:

> Attention is no longer a form that more or less lights up an immutable field but rather a restructuring power, one that makes the components of the landscape that did not exist reappear phenomenally. Thus, instead of a clarification of preexisting details, a *transformation of the object* occurs. This new interpretation acknowledges, first, the child's drawing is an initial manner of structuring things and, second, the movement from childhood drawing to adult drawing is another structuration. (*CPP* 415, emphasis original)

The object to be drawn is perceived as temporally, spatially, and affectively immersed in its environment. In this sense, children are capturing the thing as it truly exists with shifting profiles, contextual situations, and one's intentions toward the thing meshed inextricably together. At the same time, the child includes her own feelings about the object within a drawing because, as stated previously, children do not take their emotions as belonging to them. Their lives are continuous with the world. Children's drawings are thus "at one and the same time more subjective and more objective than those of adults: more subjective because they are liberated from appearance, and more objective because they attempt to reproduce the thing as it really is, while adults only represent things from one point of view: their own" (*CPP* 170).

Adult perception, tied to judgments received from prior experience, is also intractably tied to social-cultural significations. The child is also influenced by social-cultural conditions, but these conditions do not constitute child experience in the same manner. On this topic, traditional psychologists are right to note the immaturity of the child. The child does not have a complete and functioning grasp of language and cultural norms. The mistake of traditional psychologists is to assume that it also follows that children have a chaotic, incomplete perceptual system because they do not articulate their experience clearly. Merleau-Ponty agrees with Kurt Koffka (1925), among others, who affirm the notion of a *constancy phenomenon* within perception (and not, as in Luquet, an object-constancy). Returning to the field-figure notion of Gestalt psychology, the constancy phenomenon states that perception always occurs in an organized field; there is no "chaotic" perception: "In the child, thanks to the phenomenon of constancy, a non-chaotic and structured vision of the perceptual field exists (though this is not to say that the structuration is the same as, or as perfect as, that of the adult)" (*CPP* 147). What children do not possess, given their immature state of linguistic development, is an interpretive system of judgments with which to symbolize their perceptions. For children, "there is no secondary work of interpretation" (147).

Merleau-Ponty reiterates many times that this thesis doesn't argue that everything one finds in adult perception is entirely nascent within the child. Gestalt psychology's notion of the constancy of perception argues that infantile perception is not identical to adult perception: "But, to say that infantile perception is structured from its first moment is not to declare the infant's perception and adult's the same. Rather, it is a question of a summary structure replete with lacunae and indeterminate regions, and not the precise structuration that characterizes adult perception" (*CPP* 148). As he argues in *The Structure of Behavior*, to declare that the child or the animal has a meaningful way to organize its experiential world is not to say that its mode of structuration is always an immature, less developed style of our own. Adult perception is influenced by intellectual and psychophysical development as well as by a personal wealth of experience. Once I learn that a kiwi fruit holds within its brown furry exterior a bright green sweetness, I don't see future uncut kiwi fruits in the same way. I cannot look at the president, my mother, or even my cat and merely perceive their physical attributes. Rather, what I know about them, what my expectations are, and how they are connected to my world colors my perception of them.

One conception would be to assume that the child sees merely the visual data—the colors of the president's jacket, his face, or the Rose Garden—and is merely lacking in these other intellectual and affective attributes. This idea models the child's perception as a kind of collecting of visual data that has no meaningful relationship to other data about which the child has no knowledge. This conception rejects the essential aspects of Gestalt theory Merleau-Ponty embraces. Children must have an organized meaningful relationship among their various experiences, their past, present, and future; however, this is significantly different in many respects from adult perception. For adults, a thing has a certain intellectual judgment attached to it, even when the judgment is simply "this is an unknown thing I am witnessing." In Gestalt theory, things also have a *preintellectual* unity, indicating that a child can interact meaningfully with a thing without having any comprehension of it "as a thing." Development brings with it significant transformations and restructurations; these intellectual, linguistic developments are integrated into everyday mature experience. Infantile perception does possess a "worldview" insofar as it presents a whole, structured perceptual field: "In the developmental course of the child's perception a number of transformations and reorganizations occur. However, from the beginning certain totalities (which merit the name of things) do exist and together they constitute a 'world'" (*CPP* 148–49).

In the Sorbonne lectures, Merleau-Ponty refers to his most beloved artist, Paul Cézanne, whom he explores most famously in *Eye and Mind* (1964b). Just as a child will depict an object in motion by drawing lines around it, Cézanne captures the elements of water's motion, touch, and appearance:

> Along the same lines, the fluidity, the "lukewarmness," the "bluishness," and the undulating movement of the water in the pool are each given through each other all at once. This totality is what goes by the name "pool water." This is what a painter like Cézanne actually sees, a painter who claimed to be able to paint everything, odors and tastes as well as forms and colors. (*CPP* 172)

Creative expression does not gain its impetus outside of the world or in a world of fantastical invention, but in a return to our primal perception. The artist recaptures childlike perception in calling forth our basic synesthetic experience. The child's art and interpretation of the world show us how we have misunderstood childhood experience. In attending to the child, we discover a greater and subtler understanding of our own.

6

Culture, Development, and Gender

If we take seriously the call to see our existential condition and the human sciences that study it—history, psychology, biology, sociology, anthropology—as relevant for a general philosophical understanding of ourselves, we cannot avoid turning to the question of cultural relativism. The conflict between cultural analyses and scientific ones is particularly trenchant when considering any theory of child development. Does child development reveal that human maturation will proceed upon a determined path? Or does child development differ radically between cultures? Merleau-Ponty has good reason to be concerned with this conflict between "nature" and "nurture." Strongly influenced by existentialist, Marxist, and Freudian theory, Merleau-Ponty agrees not only that we are culturally determined to privilege certain values over others, but also that our very methods of accessing the "truth" are influenced by our situation. The *Phenomenology of Perception* is famous for its critique of the self-assurance of the sciences, and he strongly argues against the concept that phenomenology should see itself as a science. Nonetheless, Merleau-Ponty by no means rejects the findings of those who rest more firmly on the "nature" side of the debate. His focus on perception and on cases of brain damage, such as the patient Schneider, clearly demonstrate that Merleau-Ponty saw empirical research as informative for any study of perception.*

---

* Merleau-Ponty paid particular attention to the case of the brain-damaged patient Schneider in the *Phenomenology of Perception*. His account of Schneider's pathology was secondhand. Schneider was a patient examined by Adhémar Gelb and Kurt Goldstein who had a remarkable number of impairments: agnosia (the loss of ability to recognize objects, persons, or sense-perceptions usually due to a brain injury in the temporal lobe), loss of movement vision, alexia (word blindness), loss of a coherent body schema, loss of body position, and loss of abstract reasoning. The case was not only striking to Merleau-Ponty, but its analysis greatly shaped the nature and focus of Gestalt theory—in particular the discussion of the relationship between perception and bodily motility. See Merleau-Ponty's chapter "The Spatiality of One's Own Body and Motility" in the *Phenomenology of Perception* for his classic interpretation of Schneider (*PP* 98–147). For the original case of Schneider, see Goldstein and Gelb's (1918) "Psychologische Analysen hirnpathologischer Fälle auf Grund von Untersuchungen Hirnverletzer."

In the Sorbonne lectures, the nature-nurture conflict is impossible to ignore given that it dominates any understanding of child development. The great contribution of the two overshadowing figures in child psychology at the time of the Sorbonne lectures—Piaget and Freud—present us with comprehensive theories of child development. Although Merleau-Ponty is deeply indebted to both, he finds that they reduce the individual's freedom and ignore the cultural and historical factors that obviously shape our styles of child rearing. A theory that conceived of child development as a series of "stages," be they cognitive schemas in the case of Piaget or stages of sexual development in Freud's work, tends to overvalue a type of universal innate motor to human maturation and thus minimizes the relevance of significant individual and cultural differences. Merleau-Ponty's challenge is to express a general theory of development that incorporates freedom as well as contingency.

Merleau-Ponty returns to Hegel's nuanced theory of how the present can hold within it the past, while remaining distinct from it to explain his concept of development:

> Development is as little a destiny as it is an unconditioned freedom, for the individual always accomplishes a decisive act of development in a particular corporeal field. We find here once again Hegel's idea of "surpassing while preserving." The individual only moves beyond his first states if he agrees to retain them. Thus, we rejoin our general conceptions of the personal and interpersonal dynamic. (*CPP* 407)

The freedom I possess in the face of development is not the freedom to be anything I wish. After all, if I suffer from an incurable illness, it isn't possible to reject this part of my condition as if one could remove oneself from the mortal coil with only the power of the mind. Instead of thinking of freedom in development as the ability to be something different in the present or future, Merleau-Ponty emphasizes that freedom only occurs when we psychologically incorporate the past and present. The longer we fight our corporeal natures, the more we are determined by them. Such a passage brings to mind his early comments on freedom and embodiment in the *Phenomenology of Perception* where he writes:

> What enables us to centre our existence is also what prevents us from centering it completely, and the anonymity of our body is inseparably both freedom and servitude. Thus, to sum up, the ambiguity of being-in-the-world is translated by that of the body, and this is understood through that of time. (*PP* 85)

While this theory of development might have appeal in that it doesn't fall into radicalism on one side or another, how can we think about development as qualified freedom? What kind of model of development does it provide? To capture a better sense of how Merleau-Ponty's theory functions, we will turn to some examples. This chapter focuses on the issue of gender because it forcefully has required that we explain the connection between the biological and the social. First, we will address menstruation in young women. Then we turn to Merleau-Ponty's discussion of pregnancy. In conclusion, we explore the contemporary feminist assessment of Merleau-Ponty's work on gender and phenomenologies of pregnancy. Pregnant embodiment underlines how the story of development begins, not with a story about a child being born, but about a mother carrying a child.

Development and the Case of Menstruation

For Merleau-Ponty, the course of development is flexible, but this does not therefore entail that no necessary, or for that matter graspable, developmental patterns exist. The difficulty is to understand how a certain amount of freedom is present and to retain a theory that adopts a general theory of human development. Merleau-Ponty outlines a theory of freedom and determination as the individual possessing innate *tendencies* toward certain styles of being and it is these tendencies that anticipate development. When a psychologist finds a general capacity among a statistically significant pool of one-year-olds, she might conclude that she has discovered a capacity that can be claimed as part of human nature, in other words, a general human trait. For Merleau-Ponty, this conclusion must be tempered with a more inclusive analysis of the setting of the study itself, including the psychologist's own beliefs.

Merleau-Ponty provides a discussion of development that acknowledges cultural difference as well as the general nature of our condition. He also works against any radical nativist or social constructivist positions (mainly concerning himself with the former), since such theories impose themselves ex nihilo on structures of development. When explaining how the adult arises from the child, the child is retroactively invested with adult features whether or not they truly exist in the child. Instead, one must consider how the child, at her position in history, her culture, and her own psychological-physical state, *anticipates* the future. Merleau-Ponty lectures that "development follows certain lines all the same; the possibilities of aberration are not infinite. This order, entirely contingent as it may be, must surge forth spontaneously from prior states, from materials that it is going to utilize" (*CPP* 407). We are able to depart only from our previous states, but this does not mean that the past determines the present. If that were the case, then the human, personal experience would be epiphenomenal and any phenomenological description would be superfluous to understanding development. Development would be the product of environmental givens and physiological change. Merleau-Ponty wants to avoid the tendency to ignore the cultural and physical environment in the search for a "scientific" account that assumes that the best account of human development would be the one that is applicable to all persons in all times. But, he does not assume therefore that cultural diversity overwhelms any possibility of a general account.

Where we normally start thinking about development in the human is in the physical changes that transform the infant into the adult. The body's development is determined from birth. Barring extreme measures, how one will look as an adult is given. In addition, we increasingly understand the physiological maturation that occurs in brain development. A theory of development would document the normal body's natural course of change. We could easily say, "Of course the contents of the individual's mind will vary according to culture, but the basic physiological development can be determined." Although only the most extreme would deny the obvious effects of culture, many would side with the "nature" side as the only one that can truly form a coherent view of development. Culture, while not ignored, is a kind of add-on one can insert when needed to explain differences after the basic structure of biological development is exposed.

Merleau-Ponty acknowledges that much of development is the body's own physiological change. However, as will be further explicated below with recourse to the example of menstruation, normal development does not occur until the individual *takes up* that physical change. "The individual must take up again what the present bodily state has rendered possible" (*CPP* 407). We are thus free in the sense that we are, as embodied beings, truly in-between the force of natural physicality and the force of cultural determination. It cannot be the case simply that our "natural" development provides the tools with which to process the "nurture" side of our sociocultural position. Such a conception, while embracing the importance of both sides, remains useful only when analyzing a static world. Certainly I can see how my position at this moment has been molded by my physical capacities and limitations and my historical-cultural situation. When I compare myself to persons in different positions, I can tell a story about how their situation and physiology has determined them. Yet, such an analysis fails to explain how we change, how we adapt in our idiosyncratic ways, or how we learn to process radically new cultural and environmental givens. It doesn't explain how someone's upbringing and situation can actually affect her perceptions, emotions, beliefs, and values at their base, rather than just subsequent judgments about them. We need a theory that can account not just for individual and social difference, but one that understands the genetic, changing, and sometimes free nature of development.

An example to illustrate Merleau-Ponty's understanding of how development is connected to environmental and individual cues that are not necessary products of physical changes is Hélène Deutsch's discussion of female development. Deutsch was a psychoanalyst whose text *The Psychology of Women* (1944–45) is cited by Merleau-Ponty. While not as extensively reviewed in the course notes, Simone de Beauvoir's 1949 masterpiece *The Second Sex* (1989) is clearly also influential. One obvious and much-discussed physical change in women is menstruation. Its onset is considered by some to be the passage into heterosexual adult "womanhood." Merleau-Ponty disagrees: "*Heterosexuality is not directly related to the physiological phenomenon of menstruation*" (*CPP* 404, italics original). While ahead of his time in his attention to non-Western and gendered experiences, Merleau-Ponty does not question the heterosexist assumption that the transformation to "womanhood" is a transformation to "heterosexuality." Instead of seeing menstruation as being the direct cause of sexual maturation, Merleau-Ponty agrees with Deutsch's assessment that it is possible to refuse to psychologically assimilate a physiological event. We do not find that biological development simply causes psychological development. Rather, each biological change has to be incorporated by the embodied subject.

Given that Merleau-Ponty does not consider phenomenology to be a timeless project that uncovers a priori truths which are removed from the contingencies of the human condition and its inevitable location within a place, time, and culture, it would seem that pointing out that he is ignorant of such human contingencies calls into question the validity of his analyses. Some tension is inevitable within an existentialist and empirically grounded phenomenology, as it is in any thought that accepts at least partial relevance for claims of social construction. If how I experience the world is significantly shaped by my history, culture, and the class I am born into, it would appear that I am unable to appreciate any truths that significantly contradict my situation. But if this is the case, then what is the point of embarking upon any project that hopes to have some kind of meta-historical discussion of the human condition? Wouldn't any project simply be uncontrollably a product of its author's situation? Merleau-Ponty is keenly aware of the need to provide more structural analyses instead of content analyses to allow for significant cultural differences. In the lectures, he favors approaches that try to evoke general conflicts or challenges that would be universal for all humans because they are a result of our embodied condition in the world. He shies away from approaches that assume that if one discovers a certain kind of "solution" to a conflict, that must be the same one for all time.

Thus, when a physiological change occurs, such as menstruation, one might not accept it for a number of reasons. The role given to young women is more limiting than that given to children in some societies. The experience of menstruation and how it will determine one's life from the monthly imposition to the possibilities of pregnancy also requires much more than simply intellectually understanding physiological development. Merleau-Ponty argues that much of development is anticipated by the child. This provides a means to distinguish between the way in which we are often able to accept significant physiological transformations that can be much more revolutionary for our sense of self (such as pregnancy and menstruation) than we can a single traumatic, imposed experience. "The child anticipates the adult condition" (*CPP* 408). The model of anticipation replaces a model where physiological change causes psychological development. We have within us the seeds of our possible future selves.

In an example regarding creative work, Merleau-Ponty discusses El Greco's paintings. He notes that we can see how the painter's childhood anticipations come through in his work. But these anticipations are not fated. El Greco's masterfully imaginative and unorthodox paintings can be seen as the epitome of free expression, but at the same time we can retroactively see his youth:

> My freedom is related to what I am going to do. I stake myself on what I do when I act. If living is inventing, it is inventing from certain givens. In El Greco's work, for example, we can say that his past was given to him so he could create the work he did, but we could also say that the givens of his childhood appear to us retrospectively as anticipations of his work. There is a circular relationship from work to life and from life to work. In an individual's life, some fruitful moments exist where the individual is particularly expressive, where the individual adds unexpected meaning. With certain events from his past, the individual uncovers a meaning that favors something that surges within or around him. (*CPP* 455)

When a change occurs before I have anticipated it, I will likely reject it and enter into various styles of denial. When such a response is protracted, the discordance will inevitably cause symptoms.

These problems are compounded by the overwhelming push by society to conform to a certain model of womanhood that often causes great resentment and anxiety in the young girl. How someone adjusts to physical development is individual, but the narrower the "normal" category of development, the more problems the girl will face. Merleau-Ponty discusses how families can aid or hinder a girl in her development by strengthening or loosening the expectation to live up to social norms. Thus, a young woman's freedom is itself influenced by various cultural norms. It is impossible to see her resistance to embracing her "womanhood" as a kind of individual immaturity. Instead, it is connected with a world in which womanhood carries with it a curtailing of possibilities rather than an expanding of them. To be a woman is to be required to fit a relatively narrow set of acceptable behaviors. Naturally, young girls will often resist this change when childhood provided them with greater possibilities.

Merleau-Ponty argues that the psychological series of developments a young girl goes through before and after menstruation are related to the actual commencement of menstruation. She is not free to decide any mode of relating to her body. She cannot happily deny she has undergone a physical change; this would be to remain alienated from her own body. Nor can she fully abstract herself from the cultural norms that, for better or worse, exist in her society. Yet, the particular style in which she takes up her embodiment is itself not fated. For Merleau-Ponty, development is flexible, but it is not, therefore, without necessary structure. Social norms can negatively influence our attitudes toward our bodies. A society that relegates women to a narrow set of possible roles will likely cause ambivalence if not outright rejection on the part of young women. Merleau-Ponty also notes in his discussion how the body's transformations in themselves can be a source of negative energy and resentment. The question remains whether or not the negative transference upon one's physical development is created solely by social norms and thus in an ideal world one's physical development would be without internal conflict (or at least with minimal conflict). This seems difficult to imagine in the case of aging or illness. Below we find that significant physiological transformations can result in conflicts that appear beyond the salve of better social norms or more imaginative styles of embodiment.

Pregnancy and Gender

The pregnant woman, for Merleau-Ponty, possesses this same ambivalence about the body's transformations. However, pregnancy has further-reaching philosophical implications. Merleau-Ponty indicates that the developing body in pregnancy carries with it a tie to a primordial, presubjective existence. This "order of life" isn't so much a developmental tendency as a continuum of being which both undermines a sense of self as well as underpins it.

Pregnancy is clearly a time of great physical change and transformation. However, unlike the case of menstruation, its change is not a progressive maturation to adulthood. Although "womanhood" might be defined inappropriately by society, a menstruating body is indeed a different body and carries with it different demands and a different lifestyle. A girl must "catch up" to her body. In an ideal society, once she grows accustomed to menstruation, she might very well experience a harmonious interaction between her individual embodiment and the social allowances for individual lifestyle choices. It might also be the case that in an unhealthy society, no woman can ever feel entirely at ease with her body.

Pregnancy is entirely different because it does not just concern the nexus of social forces, personal upbringing, physical development, and psychological states—it concerns another being entirely. The physical change is not just an individual's confrontation with her situation—be it the nonconscious biological body or the sociocultural world. When pregnant, the woman becomes part of life in a unique way. The life she gives birth to will, in all likelihood, extend past her own. In addition, although we cannot conceive of the child as originating anywhere but in the womb, the child is not merely the extension of the mother's body.

Merleau-Ponty lectures that the developing presence of another body causes the mother to be *alienated* from her former style of embodiment. While the father of phenomenology, Edmund Husserl, spent little time discussing gendered experiences, much less pregnancy, he did say that I experience pregnancy through the teleology of all monads (Husserl 1981, 337). In this fragment, Husserl acknowledges the difficulty he has as a man understanding birth. However, he concludes that since teleology encompasses all monads, pregnancy would also necessarily be brought into the fold of phenomenology. Merleau-Ponty is not apparently worried about his gender influencing his descriptions of women. Referring to Husserl's comments on pregnancy, Merleau-Ponty lectures that the pregnant woman "feels her own body to be alienated from her; it is no longer the simple extension of her own activity" (*CPP* 78). For each woman, this sense of alienation is naturally different given the context of her pregnancy, her physiology, and her psychical state; however, it is similar in all women given the nature of pregnancy. He adds that this alienation is not just about the physical challenges of pregnancy: the heaviness of pregnancy, the discomfort, and the awkwardness. It is also about a shift to an entirely different way of life. Merleau-Ponty argues that pregnancy goes beyond the nexus of individual experience, biological determinations, and cultural expectations. Pregnancy calls one back to a "primitive" mode of embodiment. "The pregnant woman lives this problem in a primitive manner" (78). Pregnancy's "primitiveness" is a participation in an "anonymous process" that is ambivalent precisely because it is not just about the mother's body, her decisions, her relationship with society, and her desires and complexes. Pregnancy is about an experience that goes beyond the individual body. Thus, the pregnant woman might feel alienated because she seems to have lost control. "Her own pregnancy is not an act like all the others she accomplishes with her body. Pregnancy is more an anonymous process which happens through her and of which she is only the seat" (78).

The example of pregnancy illustrates a more complex understanding of the freedom-determination continuum. Here the pregnant woman cannot be said to be anticipating her future development the way the pre-maturation of menstruation might occur. The anticipation of development appears to come from a source not her own. This is not to say that the mother's experience of being alienated from her body is necessarily a negative experience. It is, rather, a sense of going beyond her personal embodiment to a far greater sensation of life. Merleau-Ponty calls this a "mystery" surrounding "the order of life":

> On the one hand, the infant's body escapes her, but on the other, the infant who will be born is truly an extension of her own body. During the entirety of her pregnancy, she lives this major mystery which is not of the order of matter, nor of the order of spirit, but rather of *the order of life*. (*CPP* 78, emphasis original)

What is this "order of life"? In these comments a tie to the primordial aspect of life itself is found. This discussion is very akin to theories of intersubjectivity and syncretic sociability discussed earlier.

Another nontraditional aspect of Merleau-Ponty's understanding of development is that he thinks one cannot spell out exactly what the proper, right, or just relation should be between the child and the adult. Unlike many developmental models which spell out how the parents should raise the child to produce healthy children, Merleau-Ponty is reluctant to promote or forbid behaviors. As no innate instinct inevitably pushes the child to develop in a certain manner, so too do no innate instincts impel the parents to treat their children in a particular way. Merleau-Ponty argues against the idea that there is a maternal instinct which will inevitably resolve problems that arise in child-rearing. The maternal role is a role in a nexus of relationships and only has sense within that context. Indeed, Merleau-Ponty argues that maternity will only accentuate problems rather than alleviate them.

"The fragile woman," Merleau-Ponty lectures, "is a fact of culture and not of nature" (*CPP* 377). Anthropology reveals to us a diversity of attitudes toward women's strength; our own tendency to view women as physically inferior quickly shows itself to be a prejudice. How, then, do we assess what aspects of sexual difference might be essential? Are all stereotypes false? Are some truer than others? Obviously, men and women have different bodies, and this would seem to play some role in experience. Merleau-Ponty argues that "methodologically, there is no point in denying psychological differences between men and women that arise from biological differences" (*CPP* 377). To approach difference more accurately, we must throw away our own notions of what constitutes appropriate female or male behavior. "The only way to know whether, and to what extent, such differences exist is to get rid of notions of a 'feminine nature' and of a 'masculine nature'" (377). To allow the general structure of our experience to arise, we must bracket our own investments.

Merleau-Ponty outlines how sex roles affect one's entire mode of being. We cannot speak easily of "female" and "male" characteristics as if they were facts of nature waiting to be uncovered: to isolate and objectify one group is to misrepresent the entire social web. In the pursuit of challenging the god's-eye view of scientific or absolute psychology, Merleau-Ponty turns to anthropological studies. The studies of "primitive" peoples draw our attention to the malleability of parent-child relationships. The mother remains central in all studies, but the way children are expected to behave and do behave varies greatly. Likewise, Merleau-Ponty argues that society creates the sense that women are in a category separate from "normal," that is, male. This categorization indicates certain prejudices of the psychologists, and it also naturally affects the possibilities for and expectations of women.

Cultural prejudices about our biological natures do not inevitably constrain everyone in the same manner. Rather, culture tends to limit certain tendencies. Our natural tendency is to live within that first total, primal world we as children experienced. This world is one where a constant openness would naturally tend toward a conditioned freedom in development. Unfortunately, cultural prejudices impose limits upon this total experience. In their development, women are so narrowly defined that they often realize the stereotype. Paraphrasing Stendhal (1957), Merleau-Ponty writes, "Stendhal has shown that the traits of the feminine 'nature' are the result of the history and the style of education under which women have been subjected.... 'All the geniuses who are born women are lost to humanity'" (*CPP* 377). Since women increasingly find their natural explorations in the world curtailed, their freedom diminishes, and their inborn tendency toward openness dissipates. The impact of this inequality between the sexes goes far beyond the negative impact it has upon female development. It affects the entire culture.

Instead of viewing sexual development as determined by physiology, Merleau-Ponty cites Beauvoir, who herself brings up Stendhal's ideas about women. He lectures that Beauvoir argues for a society that reintegrates women. Not only does this benefit women and promote equality, but it also actually benefits all society. To lose half the population's innovative spirit, creativity, and productivity only detracts from our world. Beauvoir argues for a civilization that should "include a reintegration of women in a productive society and should abandon masculine oppression. Society should make use of all the values of the feminine condition which until now have been 'lost to history'" (*CPP* 90).

Merleau-Ponty does think that the male-female difference is a universal dichotomy around which society builds itself, as is the child-adult difference. While different societies will have different styles of understanding, freeing, oppressing, controlling, and monitoring these poles, no society will erase their relevance. They provide the structure where the contingent content of culture and its relationship to the environment, history, and social forces play out. As in his discussion of Goldstein, Merleau-Ponty emphasizes that outlining physiological characteristics of sexual difference is to not understand it. The organism's behavior in its environment will always exceed the facts that compose it. An analysis of the social world the organism lives in is valuable and requires attention toward nonphysical components where we find that sexual identity and sexuality are not direct products of biological elements. However, those biological elements, here sexual difference, are indeed facts that do constitute the organism. The distinction is that they do not provide the final explanation for the organism's nature.

The fact that sex difference will be constitutive for any society's norms is a given. The form of those norms is contingent. When we look at Merleau-Ponty's analysis of Margaret Mead's (1971) anthropological studies, we discover a "multicultural" approach. Each native society has its own ways of explaining sexual difference and justifying gender roles. We find that while all societies react to sexual difference in particular ways, they all maintain a masculine-feminine dichotomy: "As we find in this society, the relations between mother and child, between self and stranger, and in general the inter-human relations are all part of the tissue in which we find the masculine-feminine relation" (*CPP* 308). Stereotypes reflect how particular civilizations take up gender difference: they do not reveal essential traits. "We have no grounds to speak of 'the' masculine and 'the' feminine since each civilization, according to its mode of existence, elaborates a certain type of masculinity in correlation to a certain type of femininity. But within any given society one finds sexual stereotypes" (308). Stereotypes founded in physical differences are the norm, but the particular manifestation of stereotypes is flexible. Thus, a psychological experiment that "discovers" women are afraid of angry gesticulations has not necessarily discovered that women are weaker or more easily threatened. We have to ask, how the stereotype of the role women are expected to play contributed to this behavior?

To discuss healthy embodied development, Merleau-Ponty returns again to Simone de Beauvoir's text *The Second Sex*. He lectures that "development's essential nature is restructuration by which a new bodily situation is assumed when realizing a new type of life" (*CPP* 222). Insofar as we are free to adapt to new types of life, we can hope to find healthy styles of structuring our experiences. What is the role between the unjust stereotyping of "normal" development and "normal" embodiment and the authentic, healthy embodied development? Are the frustrations we experience with our changing bodies due largely to social norms which, in principle, could be changed, or are some of those discordances intrinsic to embodied life? The answer to these questions is not present in any full form in the Sorbonne lectures, although many of the texts appear to support a concept that normal, healthy development is possible given the right situation. In the discussion of menstruation, Merleau-Ponty argues that cultural norms likely influence a young woman's resistance to take up her new physical state. In the discussion of the anonymous, primitive, "order of life" experienced in pregnancy, we find a tension between the self-conscious subject and life broadly construed. Should we conceive of the self-conscious subject as the cultural prejudice to overcome or would certain embodied tensions remain regardless of the conditions of the social world? Is "alienation" or "splitting" something essential to the experience of pregnancy or is this very sensation a product of a narrowly conceived conception of body, self, and integrity? The following section will explore contemporary appraisals of phenomenologies of gender and pregnancy.

Contemporary Feminist Views

Despite Merleau-Ponty's appeal to phenomenologists who wish to address pregnancy as one of the important lacunae in Western philosophy, Merleau-Ponty has been critiqued for having a gender-neutral phenomenology. His account is seen to pass over important differences in embodied experience and thus fails to capture it fully. Linda Fisher (2000) summarizes this critique:

> An account that fails to recognize that its descriptions omit particularities of women's experience, such as pregnant embodiment, betrays the underlying (masculinist) assumption that the generic (male) account sets the standard and encompasses all possibilities, and in this manner functions to diminish and marginalize the experience and perspectives of women. (24)

Feminist works that highlight differences in female embodiment illustrate how Merleau-Ponty's work seems devoid of considering diverse gendered experiences. It is true that his most famous works do not contain careful comparisons of gendered experience. But I have argued above and elsewhere (Welsh 2008) that his lectures in child psychology and pedagogy seriously and carefully do explore the experience of pregnancy.

In a critical vein, Shannon Sullivan (1997) argues that Merleau-Ponty and other phenomenologists fail to accurately portray our true existential condition since they describe the body in gender-neutral terms. Unless Merleau-Ponty is describing a pathological embodied condition, such as Schneider's, the body in the *Phenomenology* has no distinguishing gender traits. This reflects a continuation of the Western philosophical tradition of assuming a universal experience exists and thus eliminates careful discussions of difference. Sullivan claims that Merleau-Ponty's body passes over the determining effects of "gender, sexuality, class, race, age, culture, nationality, individual experiences and upbringing, and more" and hence his body becomes a "solipsistic subject's monologue." Fisher (2000) reviews the same argument:

> As such, it is argued that lived experience, especially bodily lived experience, cannot be treated in a generic analysis: bodies are sexed, and individuals are gendered, to follow the well-known feminist distinction of sex and gender. This points then to the irreducible particularity of women's experience that, it is argued, phenomenology has ignored. (21)

Merleau-Ponty's work in the *Phenomenology of Perception* does concern itself most famously with embodiment rather than the effects of history, class, language, race, and gender. Does a feminist who is concerned with lack of attention to female experience in Merleau-Ponty's most famous works find herself with the task of correcting this problem by continuing the spirit, if not the practice, of Merleau-Ponty's work or is she now required to call into question phenomenology in its entirety?

One conclusion is that there isn't a problem *in principle* with a Merleau-Pontian phenomenology but rather a problem with Merleau-Ponty's *execution*. What Merleau-Ponty outlines in the *Phenomenology of Perception* is a valuable method to explore gendered experience even if he failed to accomplish such an undertaking. Gail Weiss (2002) and Silvia Stoller (2000) additionally point out that Sullivan's critique of Merleau-Ponty is based on a serious misreading. Sullivan equates Merleau-Ponty's discussion of "anonymous" with "neutral" and then critiques Merleau-Ponty as offering a gender-neutral, and hence insensitive, analysis of embodiment. Stoller and Weiss point out that Merleau-Ponty does provide room for considering race, class, and gender. His entire approach is deeply defined by the necessity of taking into account the complexities of the situation and not seeing bodies as "neutral" entities that float above their environmental contexts. "To say that an experience operates anonymously, then, is not equivalent to saying that it is universal or that it is trans-historical" (Weiss 2002, 194).*

The promise of Merleau-Ponty's work has naturally inspired feminist phenomenologists because his approach to lived experience works against the disembodied, universalizing tendencies in Husserl. Johanna Oksala (2006) notes that:

> Most feminist appropriations of phenomenology have opted for the Merleau-Pontian version, which builds upon the premise that complete reduction to transcendental consciousness is impossible. This is generally interpreted to mean that the phenomenological investigation must focus on the lived body as opposed to transcendental consciousness. (231)

Attention toward the lived body in feminist theory has drawn attention toward how a "one size fits all" phenomenology fails to live up to its very promise of truly starting from experience. Indeed, careful attention to our experience would reveal the manner in which our gender, for instance, impacts our cognition, our intersubjective life, and our encounters with the world.

One of the most famous pieces in feminist scholarship that arises from and reacts to Merleau-Ponty is Iris Marion Young's "Throwing Like a Girl" (1990b). Therein, Young notes that due to the ways in which women are raised, valued, and situated in society, feminine embodiment "exhibits an *ambiguous transcendence*, an *inhibited intentionality*, and a *discontinuous unity* with its surroundings" (147, italics original). We have been socialized to not take the world as our theater, to extend our bodies without question into the world, to take up space. Instead, we question

---

* It is especially puzzling to understand how Shannon Sullivan could think that Merleau-Ponty, the author of so many texts on politics, such as *Humanism and Terror* (1947) and *Adventures of Dialectic* (1955), does not seriously consider the historical situation in his analyses.

our actions before we accomplish them; we worry about how we look, if our behavior is acceptable, and thus become stilted and uncomfortable in our very embodied existence. Young's work shows us a way to engage in a culturally, historically, and socially sensitive phenomenological analysis of our embodiment.

One of the most celebrated discussions regarding Merleau-Ponty and pregnancy comes not from his own work, but from Luce Irigaray's discussion in *The Ethics of Sexual Difference*. Therein, Irigaray ties her thought on the history of philosophy to Merleau-Ponty and argues that he didn't realize the real significance of his phenomenology. His oculocentrism can be seen to "blind" Merleau-Ponty to "interuterine life" (1993, 152). What Merleau-Ponty refers to as "the order of life" could be understood in Irigaray's language as the need for philosophy to go back and reconsider its roots in prediscursive experience:

> My reading and my interpretation of the history of philosophy agree with Merleau-Ponty: we must go back to a moment of prediscursive experience, recommence everything, all the categories by which we understand things, the world, subject-object divisions, recommence everything and pause at the "mystery, as familiar as it is unexplained, of a light which, illuminating the rest, remains at its source in obscurity." (1993, 151)

Elizabeth Grosz (1994) discusses how Irigaray presents us with a model where Merleau-Ponty is in debt to femininity and maternity because the tactile underlines the visual. Merleau-Ponty's very conceptual foundations are based in "femininity and maternity, a debt whose symptoms reside in the kind of language of pregnancy he continually invokes to articulate the emergence of that torsion within the flesh that constitutes and unites the seer and the visible" (Grosz 1994, 107). Thus it isn't just that pregnancy is a subject area that can and should be discussed by phenomenology, but that pregnancy is at the heart of the phenomenological project.

By focusing upon prediscursive experience, "maternalizing flesh," Irigaray calls to our imaginations the experience of being in utero. This common ground to all our experiences can be seen as a critical expansion upon phenomenological themes outlined in Merleau-Ponty. Such a psychoanalysis of our lived experience broadens phenomenology since it demands that we take into account not only a discussion of the historical, cultural, social, and political milieu in which the pregnant woman is situated, but also a developmental account of her experience, including conflicts that cannot be exposed by traditional phenomenological methods.

In Irigaray and in other feminist adoptions of Merleau-Ponty's philosophy, we find a common theme that inherent within Merleau-Ponty's work the seeds of a more nuanced philosophy of experience exist. He failed to see or did not live long enough to fulfill the promise of his own ideas. Irigaray addresses Merleau-Ponty's refusal to see how flesh is situated in "a maternal, maternalizing flesh, reproduction, subsistence there of the amniotic, placental tissue, which enveloped subject and things prior to birth, or of tenderness and the milieu that constituted the atmosphere of the nursling, the infant, still of the adult" (1993, 159). Thus, we return to the subject not as an embodied being living with other such beings, but as part of a continuum of existence that is behind the categories of subject, perception, visibility, and invisibility.

A phenomenology of pregnancy exposes how the historical fact of our prenatal life is philosophically significant. Our life in utero is not autonomous or discrete. Any account of the human subject would have to reconsider its designation of human life as an independent monad. Merleau-Ponty's discussion of syncretic sociability has a strong double in contemporary language about pregnancy. Pregnancy brings one back to the early primal experience of a lack of a self-other boundary.

Young's piece "Pregnant Embodiment" (1990a) departs "from the pregnant subject's viewpoint" (160). Therein she finds a split in her subjectivity: her inner movements belong to another being, her bodily boundaries shift during the manifold transformations. What this splitting causes is a disruption in the transparent unity of the self. From this description, Young returns to the theory of Merleau-Ponty in the *Phenomenology of Perception*, where Merleau-Ponty admittedly provides us with an embodied, rather than dualist, vision; however, as Young points out, this embodied self is still a unified self (162). Young stresses how pregnancy disrupts the "integrity of my body" because "in pregnancy I do not have a firm sense of where my body ends and the world begins" (163). When her pregnant belly bumps up against her legs, Young is aware of this body and is aware it isn't all hers anymore. She argues against Merleau-Ponty's suggestions that such objectification of one's body is negative. Instead, she claims that in such a moment it isn't that her body has become an object, but she is rather "conscious of the physicality of my body not as an object, but as the material weight that I am in movement" (165).

Young appeals to the work of Julia Kristeva, Jacques Lacan, and Jacques Derrida as better models to explain the split subject. Importantly, Young's account, while in parts consistent with such deconstructive and psychoanalytic accounts of a split subject, is derived not from a rejection of phenomenology as being able to accept a split subject, but from a phenomenological description itself. Instead of seeing phenomenology as inherently tied to a model of the subject as self-enclosed, self-conscious, and unified, as many post-structuralist and psychoanalytic theorists are likely to do, Young finds within pregnant experience a subject who is not just a subject. She writes that the pregnant woman is both "source and participant in a creative process" (167). Young's work thus draws her to the "order of life" and "syncretic sociability" in Merleau-Ponty's terms, or in Irigaray's "pre-discursive experience." Rosalyn Diprose (1994) argues that Young's work shows that "pregnancy, to return to the body in question, involves profound changes to bodily capacities, shape and texture with attendant shifts in the awareness of the body. Yet, as Iris Young argues, pregnancy can be better understood as an expansion in the borders of the self than a collapse of its structure" (115). This is similar to the idea in Merleau-Ponty that the "order of life" is not something opposed to the self but instead the place in which the self finds itself located.

Other phenomenologies of pregnancy have tended to minimize the language of splitting, seeing it as too reductive and negative, in favor of a positive view of the collapse of the boundaries between self and other as well as self and world. For instance, Gail Weiss (1999) writes of her own pregnancy as an experience that is defined not by ambivalence but rather by expansion: "Fluidity and expansiveness, rather than the myths of wholeness and closure (which I don't believe any of us, male or female, ever truly experience) were the tangible signs of this newly discovered bodily integrity" (53). Likewise, in her discussion of her pregnancy, Carol Bigwood (1998) argues that Merleau-Ponty's phenomenology of the body recovers a "noncultural, nonlinguistic body" (101). She calls for a "world-earth-home" as the site of this nonpersonal body.

Bigwood, like many feminist theorists influenced by Merleau-Ponty, disagrees with Judith Butler's characterization of bodies in *Gender Trouble* (2006) where bodies are cultural signs. Bigwood acknowledges that Butler is right to "argue that there is no 'pure' body or untouched nature prior to culture" (1998, 105). But Bigwood criticizes Butler for making the opposite mistake, for asserting that some kind of "pure" culture is always present. "The female experience of pregnancy, childbirth, and breast-feeding perspicaciously shows up a female bodily wisdom and fleshly openness that intertwines with a mother's personal and cultural life" (110). Turning our attention toward our everyday experience, we find the "nonpersonal perceptual existence that underlies and intertwines with our personal cultural and intellectual lives" (108).

A phenomenology of pregnancy from the pregnant woman's experience indicates that the human subject is not necessarily genderless or unified. Instead, we find a subject that is either characterized as "split," as in Young, or as continuous with a larger continuum of life as in Bigwood and Weiss. These descriptions appear to develop the idea that a characterization of the human subject as autonomous, rational, genderless, unified, and discrete is not philosophically sufficient. Instead our experience is grounded upon a continuous, indeterminate, prediscursive experience that subtends all individual experience. Many see the work in feminist embodiment theory on pregnant phenomenology as fulfilling Merleau-Ponty's late promise of "flesh" and "wild being" in his posthumous book *The Visible and the Invisible* (1968). In explaining the importance of these ideas, Grosz (1994) writes that we can find in Merleau-Ponty "a 'wild being,' and uncultivated or raw sensibility," and that this is found in prediscursive experience "before the overlay of reflection, before the imposition of metaexperiential organization and its codification by reason" (96). I argue that we also see this in his Sorbonne lectures where syncretic early life is considered the primary and primal nature of our intersubjective life.

Even if we start with a more sensitive interpretation of the manifold ways in which our embodiment is constituted by social, political, and historical forces, we still seem to be providing a general theory that would apply to all human experience and thus appear to be returning again to a generic account. Thus gender becomes a kind of additional concern that we add onto our previous philosophical conceptions, such as the idea that the way to overcome dualism is to add the body to our preexisting qualifications of what a subject is. If this is the contribution of gender-sensitive scholarship to phenomenology, it is not a slight contribution. After all, providing complete phenomenological accounts of gendered experience is no small task. However, it appears clearly that the desire of feminist phenomenologists and phenomenologies of pregnancy is to claim the relevance of the specificity of experience *against* the tendency of generic phenomenologists to absorb all criticisms as merely suggestions of additional areas for phenomenology to explore.

While the fact that one common experience is being in utero, pregnancy is a particularly difficult experience to absorb into a universalizing account since the experience is foreclosed for men and not a part of every woman's life. Oksala argues that pregnancy gives us "a need to rethink such fundamental phenomenological questions as the possibility of a purely eidetic phenomenology and the limits of egological sense-constitution" (2004, 17). The provocative idea of an "order of life" was obviously not revealed to Merleau-Ponty through his own pregnant embodiment. When discussing the condition of women, Beauvoir wrote that "the most sympathetic of men never fully comprehend woman's concrete situation" (1989, xxxii). Can a person who has never been pregnant understand the concrete reality of pregnant embodiment?

Many experiences are difficult, if not impossible, to convey to others who have not shared in them. Experiencing the death of a loved one, flying an airplane, hallucinating, having religious conversion, fighting a chronic illness appear to demand having had the experience to be truly understood. A sufficient number of parallels to common experience do not seem available to draw a sketch of what hallucination is "like" to someone who hasn't had one. Pregnancy not only might expand our phenomenological conceptions of the nature of primary awareness, but also might indicate that some experiences lie outside the reach of a phenomenological inquiry. It might call upon us to reject phenomenologies that claim to be general phenomenologies of human experience and adopt the idea that a phenomenology can only be relevant for a limited group—be it a gender group, a cultural group, or a life-experience group.

Merleau-Ponty accepts difference without assuming it is foreclosed to the careful philosopher or psychologist. Instead of thinking pregnancy refutes the scope of phenomenology, the language in phenomenologies of pregnancy themselves call upon us to *revise*, rather than reject, our approach. Weiss (1999) writes that in pregnancy she feels a sense of "fluidity and expansiveness" rather than "wholeness and closure" (53). She also parenthetically comments that she doesn't believe any of us, male or female, experience wholeness and closure. The truth of pregnancy is a deeper, all-too-human truth that is obscured by our linguistic and historical tendency to consider human experience at base a subjective, unified, self-enclosed sphere.

Feminist phenomenology provides us a way to acknowledge the relevance of different experiences, but the question has been raised whether it is sufficient to fully address the social, political, cultural, and linguistic context. Does a focus on embodiment encourage a lack of serious engagement with these issues? There are two possible aspects to this concern. One is to suggest that without phenomenology, one cannot *diagnose* the ways in which women's bodies have become constituted. Without an appeal to how gender and power relations shape our experience, we cannot properly understand our embodiment. The other aspect is to suggest that without phenomenology, we cannot *cure* gender imbalances.

In *Volatile Bodies*, Elizabeth Grosz explores this tension. An exhaustive exploration of embodiment would, at least in part if not in full, reveal political, cultural, and social tensions. It is impossible to discuss female embodiment without considering how women's bodies are modified, disciplined, celebrated, and blamed. As a wealth of literature, including famously Susan Bordo's *Unbearable Weight* (1995), has documented, in the West contemporary women's bodies are objectified and controlled through a micropolicing of size. Grosz also explores the notion that not only are discussions of bodies inevitably discussions of power, politics, and knowledges, but so too is the phenomenological project of working from experience. "But it is clear that experience cannot be taken as an unproblematic given, a position through which one can judge knowledges, for experience is of course implicated in and produced by various knowledges and social practices" (1994, 94). Grosz continues to point out that a phenomenology of experience is needed to provide the point of departure for challenging any given knowledge or institution. "Nevertheless, I would contend that without some acknowledgement of the formative role of experience in the establishment of knowledges, feminism has no grounds from which to dispute patriarchal norms" (94).

We can see a famous and clear example of how we can explore embodiment without ignoring the social, political, and cultural world by reading Iris Marion Young's "Throwing Like a Girl" (1990b) in conjunction with "'Throwing Like a Girl': Twenty Years Later" (1998). "'Throwing Like a Girl': Twenty Years Later" provides examples of how social progress has positively changed female embodiment. Young notes that much has changed in her bodily comportment and that of her daughter born two years after "Throwing Like a Girl" first appeared. "It seems to me that she and her friends move and carry themselves with much more openness, more reach, more active confidence, than many of my generation did" (1998, 286). The hesitation of Young in throwing a ball versus her daughter's active enjoyment of sports illustrates that a phenomenology of embodiment is by no means static. Young comments that her original piece might see women as too oppressed, too objectified, too "inhibited, hesitant, constrained, gazed at, and positioned" (289). Young accepts that her depiction in "Throwing Like a Girl" emphasized the ways in which women are restricted and judged according to a universal masculine standard and she writes that one might "also look for specifically valuable aspects of women's experience" (289). It would be these valuable aspects of women's experience that could provide the political grounds to reject limiting structures. While Young does acknowledge that the exploration of women's experience might aid our political goals, she also emphasizes that "a primary feminist task must continue to be exposing and criticizing the violence, overwork, and sexual exploitation that many women suffer as women" (289). To right repressive regimes and stifling social norms, intellectual understanding of injustice from a disembodied stance will not always suffice. We must understand the impact on embodiment and the ways in which new styles of coexistence would permit greater living possibilities for all.

Many have argued that the focus on embodiment in a more Merleau-Pontian phenomenology better lives up to the promise of phenomenology as a descriptive philosophy. The argument that one needs to account for class, history, gender, and race is not a political principle that is imposed from without on phenomenology; instead, any careful phenomenological discussion shows that phenomenology is ideally disposed toward a more historical, and politically progressive, analysis. The above discussion has illustrated that a feminist embodiment theory is attuned to differences in phenomenological descriptions and seeks to avoid condensing embodied experience into a naturalist, nonpolitical mold. While not executed in full in Merleau-Ponty's own texts or lectures, he certainly can be seen as striving to find a model that accepted development as always occurring within the body's insertion in a sociopolitical world.

While the idea of revising the concept of the subject toward a more embodied, inclusive one fits well within the tradition outlined by Merleau-Ponty in the *Phenomenology of Perception*, it seems to not quite capture the uniqueness of *pregnant* embodiment. After all, it appears that we could come to this conclusion of interconnectedness via a wide array of experiences. We can ask along with Oksala (2004) if from such a perspective feminist phenomenologies of pregnancy and birth just "add some missing descriptions of embodiment to the phenomenological project" but they fail to "change the core of it in any essential way" (17). They fail to live up to the challenges of feminist philosophy to the tradition.

Linda Fisher writes that feminist phenomenology searches to go beyond the "generic human experience." "To the extent that the objective is to provide an account of essences or essential structures, phenomenology tends to the generic description, treating experience generically, as pertaining to a generic human individual" (2000, 20). Fisher goes on to point out that this is often taken as problematic by feminists who want to engage with difference, inequality, and oppression. When pregnancy's specificity is removed and one draws out a general phenomenological conclusion about our connection to the world and others, then it seems we have returned to a generic phenomenology simply through a different source.

Thus, thinkers like Grosz (1994) and Diprose (1994) employ embodiment theory not as a "natural" place outside of the contingencies of social, historical, political, and cultural forces, but as a site wherein we can see how female subordination plays out in female (and male) embodiment. In a similar vein, Oksala (2006) cautions us against the dangers of a certain brand of Merleau-Pontian embodiment theory in feminist theory, what she calls the "corporeal reading," because it reduces phenomenology down to a kind of essentialism. It threatens "to push us back into defending a form of corporeal essentialism that potentially precludes political changes in the situation of women" (232).

In the corporeal reading, the focus on the body removes it from a more complex social-political understanding of gender: "the fact that the focus on the body is simply too limited a framework to support a philosophical understanding of gender" (232). I argue that exploring pregnancy with an eye to human development requires us to extend beyond the body conceived in a static state and would, thus, overcome the objections Oksala raises above.

The phenomenological tradition demonstrates that examining pregnant embodiment expands our understanding of existence. The myths of wholeness and closure could stem from an overinvestment in the separateness or at least the primacy of a disembodied mind. Once dualism is left behind us, attention to our everyday experience will reveal that we are unable to extricate our "mind" as something distinct from the living body. Turning toward our embodied existence, we find a basic experience that is much more continuous with the rest of the world and the rest of other human beings. We can revise a traditional conception of the human subject as being defined through mental characteristics: autonomous, rational, genderless, unified, and discrete, and explore a subject defined through its existential, embodied, and all-too-human experience.

Merleau-Ponty writes that viewing any experience as a combination of a machine-like physical body and a soul-like mind is thoroughly discredited by both our philosophy and science. The argument that substance dualism is wrong is hardly novel or rarely appreciated. Most thinkers willing to consider the relevance of phenomenology would almost surely agree that the mind and body are not two metaphysically distinct substances. Merleau-Ponty's embodiment theory points out that what moving beyond dualism means is returning to existence and not seeing the body as added onto the mental. "The union of soul and body is not an amalgamation between two mutually external terms, subject and object, brought about by arbitrary decree. It is enacted at every instant in the movement of existence" (*PP* 88–89). If the point of overcoming dualism is merely to suggest that we need to say the mind and body are connected, we would need to go no further than Descartes, since he noted the complexity of their connection in the sixth "Meditation." The idea of embodiment theory is not just to add "having a body" onto our list of essential characteristics of the human subject, but to suggest that embodiment is prior to all of the other characteristics. Pregnancy is a clear example with which to bring this truth to the forefront by noting that phenomenologies of pregnancy indicate the primacy of embodiment over a self-enclosed mental experience and also remind us that our first experiences are ones of inseparableness from our mothers in utero.

Conclusion: An Incomparable Childhood

Perhaps the argument that our primal experience is also historically primary is an ill-founded romanticism. Merleau-Ponty's descriptions not only want to evoke this early element of human existence, but also want to "praise" childhood insofar as it reveals our true immersion in the world. What divorces us from our underlying syncretic nature could be nothing else but the social-cultural-linguistic world we become increasingly enmeshed with as we mature. Pregnant women, children, artists, and poets bring us back to our real connection with the world, from where all diversity of culture and history spring. At face value, it appears to be a repetition of the classic themes of the romantic ethos—children, poets, and women are more "in contact" with reality since they are not immersed in civilization. Poets, painters, and musicians will be our salvation from the constraining, unnatural effects of our modern society. We could provide a personal account for Merleau-Ponty's insistence upon the importance of childhood experience. Sartre recounts:

> One day in 1947, Merleau told me that he has never recovered from an incomparable childhood. He has known that private world of happiness from which only age drives us. . . . What was he, if not this paradise lost, a wild and underserved piece of luck, a gratuitous gift transformed, after the fall, into adversity, depopulating the world and disenchanting him in advance? (1965, 228)

Does Merleau-Ponty desire to return to this childhood via his own philosophy? By exaggerating the value of childhood experience, does he desire to affirm his own "incomparable" childhood?

Merleau-Ponty does present us with a holistic and positive account of childhood. But he by no means ignores infantile conflicts, nor does he argue for a return to the infantile. He did not suggest that the subject was but a mere epiphenomenon which should be discarded in favor of a subjectless state of being. Yet, we must be careful to think that the subject and its history is the *only* history in our existence. We must call into question whether the history of the subject is self-grounding, or as argued above, grounded in a more primary experience. Merleau-Ponty in his own fashion carries on the Husserlian legacy of "beginning with the things themselves." To begin and end with experience requires a method which does not take any philosophical assumptions for granted. Primal experience, whether conceived as syncretic sociability in Merleau-Ponty's account or as in Gallagher and Stawarska's as interactive and dialogical, permits a nonspeculative ground for philosophy that remains part of an existential approach to the human condition. We must return to the subject as a psychophysical, historical being to overcome the prejudice of previous philosophies. Part of this investigation would be to ask to what degree the ontogenetic story influences and shapes our philosophy and psychology.

Within such an existential approach where one does not presuppose the ability of philosophy to come up with universal truths, two, possibly dangerous, ideologies present themselves. One is the role of science. If our charge is to begin with the here and the now, with the subject as embodied, shouldn't we turn to a properly conceived science? Wouldn't a scientific child psychology better capture the true conditions of the developing child? Accepting that the problem of philosophy has been its investment in idealist theories, science would seem to be fully and properly existential. The other is relativism. Since the "here and now" varies so widely from situation to situation, is it not the greatest prejudice to force a unifying theory upon this diversity? Why assume that all childhood is more or less structurally the same? Perhaps cultural conditions so shape our experience that we cannot even hope to know what essential features of primal existence are.

Merleau-Ponty's theory of primal and primary experience addresses these criticisms by not denying their significance. Evidently, each individual's social, cultural, and historical situation is not identical to all others, and, yes, science is integral to furthering our understanding of the human condition. However, a scientific approach will never capture the phenomenology of the human condition. It can never grasp the world as experienced, and it is through the world as experienced that even science finds its origin. When we examine how we are thrown-in-the-world, we find not only that the physical conditions are relevant, but also that our birth is the condition of possibility for all experience. The conditions of that birth and the growth that follows are here argued to be more critical for a philosophy than previously assumed.

In addition, cultural relativism, like scientific psychology, depends upon a God's-eye view of existence. I stand disconnected from my own experience and note cultural differences between various groups. I re-

CONCLUSION: AN INCOMPARABLE CHILDHOOD

turn to the world and pronounce it to be impossible to form any coherent theory of experience. For Merleau-Ponty, a child's painting can reveal more about our essential engagement with our embodied selves and the world than a theory where our isolation from any common experience is asserted as a universal truth. Cultural differences do exist, but they arise from the same world. In conclusion, we point to how the themes of Merleau-Ponty's child psychology find a rebirth in his later work in philosophy.

Merleau-Ponty's last text completed in his lifetime, "Eye and Mind" (1964b), explores some of his most suggestive thoughts about painting, creation, and perception. The adult painter returns to the child's experience, to the child's birth, to the birth of existence: "It can be said that a human is born at the instant when something that was only virtually visible, inside the mother's body, becomes at one and the same time visible for itself and for us. The painter's vision is a continued birth" (1964b, 167–68). Painting evokes our intimate contact with the world; it articulates a metaphysics. This metaphysics reveals what underlies the culturally contingent plurality of views, opinions, and arguments we encounter in life:

> The metaphysics we have in mind is not a body of detached ideas [*idées séparées*] for which inductive justification could be sought in the experiential realm. There are, in the flesh of contingency, a structure of event and a virtue peculiar to the scenario. These do not prevent the plurality of interpretations but in fact are the deepest reasons for this plurality. (1964b, 179)

Cézanne is lionized for expressing within his works a truth which cannot be articulated through other means. Artistic creation is not a rejection of the world and an acceptance of a fantasy life, but an inventive engagement with the world.

Returning to the conceptions that fueled his rejection of both scientific psychology and critical philosophy in *The Structure of Behavior* twenty years earlier, Merleau-Ponty writes that "only the painter is entitled to look at everything without being obliged to appraise what he sees" (1964b, 161). Judgments require circumscribing and declaring; they demand that we see ourselves as distinct, local subjectivities. They emphasize that our bodies are objects to be seen and judged, like the images in the mirror, and take us away from our lived experience. Our education trains us to separate ourselves from others and from the world, to break it down into component parts and analyze it. In painting, on the contrary, we see the "undividedness of the sensing and the sensed" (1964b, 163). For Merleau-Ponty, we must struggle to capture this seemingly paradoxical aspect of vision, and of life, where there is an "inside of the outside" and an "outside of the inside" (164).

We might reply that someone like Merleau-Ponty can see this in Cézanne but that that is due to his education and class, which are removed from the common ground of primal life he is exploring. When we think contemporary art is "difficult and runs counter to common sense, this is because it is concerned with truth; experience no longer allows it to settle for the clear and straightforward notions which common sense cherishes because they bring peace of mind" (Merleau-Ponty 2004, 49). It is the indoctrination of common sense that blinds us to modern art, not that modern art is necessarily obscure and inaccessible. Commonsense judgments assume that the world can be divided into measurable parts and, in the case of painting, that our traditional Western paintings are how we see the world. A phenomenology of perception illustrates that I do not perceive the world like a series of "realistic" paintings and thus modern art can be more authentic to vision rather than less. Our attention to the unique structures of childhood experience discussed earlier illustrates how sense-making occurs in other forms than that of "common" sense.

The painter is able to discover the nature of our experience because she finds within herself the continuation of the things painted. The painter unites aspects of existence that are disturbed after the formation of a sense of subjectivity. The childlike experience of refusing to create a distinction between affect and vision, between self and other, comes to light in Cézanne's paintings where "essence and existence, imaginary and real, visible and invisible—a painting mixes up all our categories in laying out its oneiric universe of carnal essences, of effective likenesses, of mute meanings" (1964b, 164). Cézanne's ability to evoke "carnal essences" and "mute meanings" appeals not to an immortal, soul-like substance in mankind, but to the universal conditions of birth, to the original manner one is, to use Heidegger's (1962) term, "thrown" in the world.

Painting as a "continued birth" reminds us to look again into the lack of division between the infant and others. The parent's experience of the child and the child's of the parent do not arise from two separate lives, but from a mutual "order of life" (*CPP* 78). As Merleau-Ponty writes about the syncretic sociable stage, the other's intentions are felt as one's own. Merleau-Ponty expands upon these themes in his posthumous work *The Visible and the Invisible*, declaring that the body and world are not separate, that they run into one another, dissolving the distinction between self and world: "Where are we to put the limit between the body and the world, since the world is flesh? . . . The world seen is not 'in' my body, and my body is not 'in' the visible world ultimately: as flesh applied to a flesh, the world neither surrounds nor is surrounded by it"

CONCLUSION: AN INCOMPARABLE CHILDHOOD

(1968, 138). Flesh, like infantile syncretic sociability, presents us with an element of experience that defies traditional separations between self and other and between body and world.

One way to interpret these complex themes in Merleau-Ponty's post-1952 work is to show commonality within his child psychology. This is not to deny alternative sources of inspiration, but to suggest that, in harmony with his earlier work, Merleau-Ponty's late "ontological" conceptions are as concretely and empirically grounded as the ideas presented in his first writings of the 1940s. Childhood experience is not just historically formative, but also nascent in every experience one has. Subsequent work will help elucidate the connection between the philosopher who is willing to observe concrete experiments in child psychology and the one who argues that at the heart of the visible lies the invisible.

This text has shown that Merleau-Ponty's child psychology is both important to understanding Merleau-Ponty's thought as well as a compelling addition to interdisciplinary work in philosophy and psychology. Contemporary research in primary intersubjectivity and gender theory meaningfully engages with his approach to human development. His emphasis on the child's experience remains a timely discussion, one that bears further investigation. We should continue our engagement with theories of human development to better assess if our primal experience can help answer questions about the subject and our pre-subjective origins.

Works Cited

Anisfeld, Moshe. 1996. "Only Tongue Protrusion Modeling Is Matched by Neonates." *Developmental Review* 16, no. 2: 149–61.

Anisfeld, Moshe, Gerald Turkewitz, Susan Rose, Faigi R. Rosenberg, Faith Sheiber, Joseph Ger, and Iris Sommer. 2001. "No Compelling Evidence That Newborns Imitate Oral Gestures." *Infancy* 2, no. 1: 111–22.

Asendorpf, Jens B. 2002. "Self-Awareness, Other-Awareness, and Secondary Representation." In *The Imitative Mind: Development, Evolution, and Brain Bases*, edited by Andrew N. Meltzoff and Wolfgang Prinz, 63–73. Cambridge, U.K.: Cambridge University Press.

Beauvoir, Simone de. 1989. *The Second Sex*. Translated by H. M. Parshley. New York: Vintage. (Originally published in 1949.)

Bergson, Henri. 1944. *Creative Evolution*. Translated by Arthur Mitchell. New York: Modern Library. (Originally published in 1907.)

Bernet, Rudolf, Iso Kern, and Eduard Marbach. 1999. *An Introduction to Husserlian Phenomenology*. Evanston, Ill.: Northwestern University Press.

Bigwood, Carol. 1998. "Renaturalizing the Body (with the Help of Merleau-Ponty)." In *Body and Flesh: A Philosophical Reader*, edited by Donn Welton, 99–114. London: Blackwell.

Bloom, Paul. 2004. *Descartes' Baby*. New York: Basic Books.

Bordo, Susan. 1995. *Unbearable Weight: Feminism, Western Culture, and the Body*. Berkeley: University of California Press.

Brunschvicg, Léon. 1922. *L'expérience humaine et la causalité physique*. Paris: Alcan.

Butler, Judith. 2006. *Gender Trouble*. New York: Routledge.

Butterworth, George. 2000. "An Ecological Perspective on the Self." In *Exploring the Self: Philosophical and Psychopathological Perspectives on Self-Experience*, edited by Dan Zahavi, 19–38. Amsterdam: John Benjamins.

Castillo, Marcela, and George Butterworth. 1981. "Neonatal Localisation of a Sound in Visual Space." *Perception* 10: 331–38.

Claparède, Édouard. 1998. *Experimental Pedagogy and the Psychology of the Child*. Translated by M. Louch and H. Holman. Bristol, U.K.: Thoemmes. (Originally published in 1909.)

Damasio, Antonio R. 1994. *Descartes' Error: Emotion, Reason, and the Human Brain*. New York: Avon.

Davies, Martin, and Tony Stone. 1995. *Mental Simulation: Evaluations and Applications*. London: Blackwell.

WORKS CITED

Dawkins, Richard. 1976. *The Selfish Gene*. Oxford: Oxford University Press.
Dennett, Daniel. 1991. *Consciousness Explained*. Boston: Back Bay Books.
Dennis, Wayne. 1973. *Children of the Crèche*. Norwalk, Conn.: Appleton-Century-Crofts.
Descartes, René. 1991. *Meditations on First Philosophy*. In *The Philosophical Writings of Descartes, Vol. 2*, translated by J. Cottingham, R. Stoothoff, and D. Murdoch, 1–62. Cambridge: Cambridge University Press. (Originally published in 1641.)
Deutsch, Hélène. 1944–45. *The Psychology of Women: A Psychoanalytic Interpretation*. New York: Grune and Stratton.
Dillon, M. C. 1997. *Merleau-Ponty's Ontology*. Evanston, Ill.: Northwestern University Press.
Diprose, Rosalyn. 1994. *The Bodies of Women: Ethics, Embodiment and Sexual Difference*. London: Routledge.
Doherty, Martin J. 2009. *Theory of Mind: How Children Understand Others' Thoughts and Feelings*. New York: Psychology.
Fink, Bruce. 1999. *A Clinical Introduction to Lacanian Psychoanalysis: Theory and Technique*. Cambridge, Mass.: Harvard University Press.
Fisher, Linda. 2000. "Phenomenology and Feminism: Perspectives of Their Relation." In *Feminist Phenomenology*, edited by Lester Embree, 17–38. Dordrecht, Netherlands: Kluwer.
Freud, Sigmund. 1905. "Three Essays on the Theory of Sexuality." In *The Standard Edition of the Complete Psychological Works of Sigmund Freud, Vol. 7*, edited by James Strachey, 125–245. London: Hogarth and the Institute of Psycho-Analysis, 1953.
———. 1913. "Totem and Taboo." In *The Standard Edition of the Complete Psychological Works of Sigmund Freud, Vol. 13*, edited by James Strachey, 1–162. London: Hogarth and the Institute of Psycho-Analysis, 1953.
———. 1927. "The Future of an Illusion." In *The Standard Edition of the Complete Psychological Works of Sigmund Freud, Vol. 21*, edited by James Strachey, 5–56. London: Hogarth and the Institute of Psycho-Analysis, 1953.
———1930. "Civilization and Its Discontents." In *The Standard Edition of the Complete Psychological Works of Sigmund Freud, Vol. 21*, edited by James Strachey, 59–145. London: Hogarth and the Institute of Psycho-Analysis, 1953.
Gallagher, Shaun. 2005. *How the Body Shapes the Mind*. Oxford: Oxford University Press.
Gallagher, Shaun, and Andrew Meltzoff. 1996. "The Earliest Sense of Self and Others: Merleau-Ponty and Recent Developmental Studies." *Philosophical Psychology* 9: 211–33.
Geraets, Théodore F. 1971. *Vers une nouvelle philosophie transcendentale: La genèse de la philosophie de Maurice Merleau-Ponty jusqu'à la Phénoménologie de la perception*. The Hague, Netherlands: Martinus Nijhoff.
Gergely, György. 2004. "The Development of Understanding Self and Agency." In *Blackwell Handbook of Childhood Cognitive Development*, edited by Usha Goswami, 26–46. London: Blackwell.

WORKS CITED

Gibson, James. 1966. *The Senses Considered as Perceptual Systems*. Boston: Houghton-Mifflin.
Goldstein, Kurt. 1995. *The Organism*. New York: Zone Books. (Originally published in 1934.)
Goldstein, Kurt, and Adhémar Gelb. 1918. "Psychologische Analysen hirnpathologischer Fälle auf Grund von Untersuchungen Hirnverletzer." *Zeitschrift für die gesamte Neurologie und Psychiatrie* 41: 1–142.
Gopnik, Alison. 2009. *The Philosophical Baby*. New York: Farrar, Straus and Giroux.
Gopnik, Alison, and Andrew Meltzoff. 1997. *Words, Thoughts, and Theory*. Cambridge, Mass.: MIT Press.
Gopnik, Alison, and Virginia Slaughter. 1991. "Young Children's Understanding of Changes in Their Mental States." *Child Development* 62: 98–110.
Grandin, Temple, and Margaret M. Scariano. 1986. *Emergence: Labeled Autistic*. New York: Warner Books.
Grosz, Elizabeth. 1994. *Volatile Bodies: Toward a Corporeal Feminism*. Bloomington: Indiana University Press.
Guillaume, Paul. 1971. *Imitation in Children*. Translated by E. P. Halperin. Chicago: University of Chicago Press. (Originally published in 1926.)
Happé, Francesca. 1995. *Autism: An Introduction to Psychological Theory*. Cambridge, Mass.: Harvard University Press.
Hegel, G. W. F. 1953. *Reason in History*. Translated by R. S. Hartman. Indianapolis: Library of Liberal Arts. (Originally presented in 1853.)
Heidegger, Martin. 1962. *Being and Time*. Translated by J. MacQuarrie and E. Robinson. London: SCM. (Originally published in 1927.)
Huang, I. 1943. "Children's Conception of Physical Causality." *Journal of Genetic Psychology* 63: 71–121.
Husserl, Edmund. 1970. *The Crisis of European Sciences and Transcendental Phenomenology*. Translated by David Carr. Evanston, Ill.: Northwestern University Press. (Originally published in 1936.)
———. 1977. *Phenomenological Psychology*. Translated by John Scanlon. The Hague, Netherlands: Martinus Nijhoff. (Original work presented in 1925.)
———. 1981. "Universal Teleology." In *Husserl, Shorter Works*, translated by M. Biemel, 335–37. Notre Dame, Ind.: University of Notre Dame Press. (Original piece written in 1933.)
Irigaray, Luce. 1993. *An Ethics of Sexual Difference*. Translated by C. Burke and G. C. Gill. Ithaca, N.Y.: Cornell University Press.
Jones, Susan. 1996. "Imitation or Exploration? Young Infants' Matching of Adult Oral Gestures." *Child Development* 67, no. 5: 1952–69.
Jung, Carl. 1970. "Freud & Psychoanalysis." In *Collected Works of C. G. Jung, Vol. 4*, edited and translated by G. Adler and R. F. C. Hull. Princeton, N.J.: Princeton University Press.
Katz, Carmit, and Irit Hershkowitz. 2010. "The Effects of Drawing on Children's Accounts of Sexual Abuse." *Child Maltreatment* 15, no. 2: 171–79.
Koffka, Kurt. 1925. *The Growth of the Mind*. New York: Harcourt, Brace.
Köhler, Wolfgang. 1956. *The Mentality of Apes*. New York: Routledge. (Originally published in 1925.)

WORKS CITED

———. 1971. "An Old Pseudoproblem." In *The Selected Papers of Wolfgang Köhler*, edited by M. Henle, 140–45. New York: Liveright. (Originally published in 1929.)
Lacan, Jacques. 2001. *Livre VIII: Le Transfert (1960–1961)*. Edited by Jacques-Alain Miller. Paris: Éditions du Seuil. (Original work presented in 1960–61.)
———. 2006. *Écrits*. Translated by Bruce Fink. New York: W.W. Norton.
Laplanche, Jean. 1989. *New Foundations for Psychoanalysis*. Translated by David Macy. Oxford: Blackwell.
Lillard, Angeline S., and John H. Flavell. 1992. "Children's Understanding of Different Mental States." *Developmental Psychology* 28, no. 4: 626–34.
Luquet, G. H. 1972. *Le dessin enfantin*. Paris: Delachaux et Niestlé.
Maratos, Olga. 1998. "Neonatal, Early and Later Imitation: Same Order Phenomena? In *The Development of Sensory, Motor and Cognitive Capacities in Early Infancy: From Perception to Cognition*, edited by Francesca Simion and George Butterworth, 145–60. Hove, U.K.: Psychology/Erlbaum.
Martin, Grace B., and Russell Clark. 1982. "Distress Crying in Neonates: Species and Peer Specificity." *Developmental Psychology* 18, no. 1: 3–9.
McGeer, Victoria. 2001. "Psycho-Practice, Psycho-Theory and the Contrastive Case of Autism: How Practices of Mind Become Second-Nature." http://www.ingentaconnect.com/content/imp/jcs/2001/00000008/F0030005/1210. *Journal of Consciousness Studies* 8, no. 5–7: 109–32.
Mead, Margaret. 1971. *Sex and Temperament*. New York: Harper Perennial.
Meili, Richard. 1931. "Les perceptions des enfants et la psychologie de la Gestalt." *Archives de Psychologie* 23: 25–44.
Meltzoff, Andrew, and M. Keith Moore. 1977. "Imitation of Facial and Manual Gestures by Human Neonates." *Science* 198, no. 4312: 75–78.
———. 1983. "Newborn Infants Imitate Adult Facial Gestures." *Child Development* 54: 702–9.
———. 2000. "Resolving the Debate About Early Imitation." In *Infant Development: The Essential Readings*, edited by Darwin Muir and Alan Slater, 176–81. London: Blackwell.
Meltzoff, Andrew, and Wolfgang Prinz, eds. 2002. *The Imitative Mind: Development, Evolution, and Brain Bases*. Cambridge: Cambridge University Press.
Merleau-Ponty, Maurice. 1964. *Sense and Non-Sense*. Translated by Herbert Dreyfus and Patricia Dreyfus. Evanston, Ill.: Northwestern University Press. (Originally published in 1948.)
———. 1964a. "The Child's Relations with Others." In *The Primacy of Perception*, edited by James Edie, translated by William Cobb, 96–155. Evanston, Ill.: Northwestern University Press.
———. 1964b. "Eye and Mind." In *The Primacy of Perception*, edited by James Edie, translated by Carleton Dallery, 159–90. Evanston, Ill.: Northwestern University Press. (Originally published in 1961.)
———. 1964c. "Phenomenology and the Sciences of Man." In *The Primacy of Perception*, edited by James Edie, translated by John Wild, 42–95. Evanston, Ill.: Northwestern University Press.

WORKS CITED

———. 1968. *The Visible and the Invisible.* Translated by Alphonso Lingis. Evanston, Ill.: Northwestern University Press. (Originally published in 1960.)
———. 1969. *Humanism and Terror: An Essay on the Communist Problem.* Translated by John O'Neill. Boston: Beacon. (Originally published in 1947.)
———. 1973. *Adventures of the Dialectic.* Translated by Joseph Bien. Evanston, Ill.: Northwestern University Press. (Originally published in 1955.)
———. 1979. *Consciousness and the Acquisition of Language.* Translated by Hugh J. Silverman. Evanston, Ill.: Northwestern University Press.
———. 1982–83. "The Experience of Others." Translated by Fred Evans and Hugh J. Silverman. *Review of Existential Psychology and Psychiatry* 18: 33–63.
———. 1983. *The Structure of Behavior.* Translated by Alden L. Fisher. Pittsburgh: Duquesne University Press. Referenced in text as *SB*. (Originally published in 1942.)
———. 1996a. "The Nature of Perception: Two Proposals." In *Texts and Dialogues: On Philosophy, Politics, and Culture,* edited by Hugh J. Silverman and J. Barry, Jr., translated by Forrest Williams, 74–84. Atlantic Highlands, N.J.: Humanities Press. (Original work written in 1933.)
———. 1996b. *Phenomenology of Perception.* Translated by Colin Smith. London: Routledge. Referenced in text as *PP*. (Originally published in 1945.)
———. 2001. *Psychology et pédagogie de l'enfant.* Paris: Verdier. (Original work presented in 1949–52.)
———. 2003. *Nature: Course Notes from the Collège de France.* Translated by Robert Vallier. Evanston, Ill.: Northwestern University Press. (Original work presented in 1956–60.)
———. 2004. *The World of Perception.* Translated by Oliver Davis. London: Routledge. (Original work presented in 1948.)
———. 2010. *Child Psychology and Pedagogy: The Sorbonne Lectures 1949–1952.* Translated by Talia Welsh. Evanston, Ill.: Northwestern University Press. Referenced in text as *CPP*. (Original work presented in 1949–52.)
Moran, Dermot. 2000. *Introduction to Phenomenology.* New York: Routledge.
Morgenstern, Sophie. 1937. *Psychanalyse infantile: Symbolisme et valeur clinique des créations imaginatives chez l'enfant.* Paris: Les Éditions Denoël.
Nadel, Jacqueline, and George Butterworth, eds. 1999. *Imitation in Infancy.* Cambridge: Cambridge University Press.
Nagel, Thomas. 1974. "What Is It Like to Be a Bat?" *Philosophical Review* 83, no. 4 (October): 435–50.
Neisser, Ulric. 1988. "Five Kinds of Self Knowledge." *Philosophical Psychology* 1, no. 1: 35–59.
O'Connor, Flannery. 1969. *Mystery and Manners.* New York: Farrar, Straus and Giroux.
Oksala, Johanna. 2004. "What Is Feminist Phenomenology? Thinking Birth Philosophically." *Radical Philosophy* 26 (July/August): 16–22.
———. 2006. "A Phenomenology of Gender." *Continental Philosophy Review* 39: 229–44.

WORKS CITED

Onishi, Kristine H., and Renee Baillargeon. 2005. "Do 15-Month-Old Infants Understand False Beliefs?" *Science* 308 (April 8): 255–58.
Perner, Josef. 1991. *Understanding the Representational Mind.* Cambridge, Mass.: MIT Press.
Piaget, Jean. 1962. *Play, Dreams, and Imitation in Childhood.* Translated by C. Gattegno and F. M. Hodgson. New York: Norton.
———. 1999. *Judgment and Reasoning in the Child.* Translated by M. Warden. London: Routledge.
Pinker, Steven. 2002. *The Blank Slate: The Modern Denial of Human Nature.* London: Penguin.
Poincaré, Henri. 1952. *Science and Method.* Translated by Francis Maitland. New York: Dover. (Originally published in 1908.)
Politzer, Georges. 1968. *Critique des fondements de la psychologie: La psychologie et la psychanalyse.* Paris: Presses Universitaires de France. (Originally published in 1928.)
Ponge, Francis. 1942. *Le parti pris des choses.* Paris: Gallimard.
Povinelli, Daniel, Keli Landau, and Helen K. Perilloux. 1996. "Self-Recognition in Young Children Using Delayed Versus Live Feedback: Evidence of a Developmental Asynchrony." *Child Development* 67: 1540–54.
Rochat, Philippe. 2001. *The Infant's World.* Cambridge, Mass.: Harvard University Press.
Rochefoucauld, François de la. 1930. *Moral Maxims and Reflections (1665–1678).* Translated by G. Powell. New York: F. A. Stokes.
Sartre, Jean-Paul. 1956. *Being and Nothingness.* Translated by H. E. Barnes. New York: Philosophical Library. (Originally published in 1943.)
———. 1965. *Situations.* Translated by Benita Eisler. New York: George Braziller.
Shinn, Milicent Washburn. 1893. *Notes on the Development of a Child.* Berkeley: University of California Press.
Silverman, Hugh, and James Barry, Jr. 1996. Introduction to *Texts and Dialogues: On Philosophy, Politics, and Culture,* by Maurice Merleau-Ponty, xiii–xxi. Atlantic Highlands, N.J.: Humanities Press.
Stawarska, Beata. 2009. *Between You and I: Dialogical Phenomenology.* Athens: Ohio University Press.
Stendhal. 1957. "Concerning the Education of Women." In *Love,* translated by Gilbert Sale and Suzanne Sale. London: Merlin. (Originally published in 1822.)
Stoller, Silvia. 2000. "Reflections on Feminist Merleau-Ponty Skepticism." *Hypatia* 15, no. 1: 175–82.
Sullivan, Shannon. 1997. "Domination and Dialogue in Merleau-Ponty's *Phenomenology of Perception.*" *Hypatia* 12, no. 1: 1–19.
Van der Meer, A. L. H., F. R. Van der Weel, and D. N. Lee. 1996. "Lifting Weights in Neonates: Developing Visual Control of Reaching." *Scandinavian Journal of Psychology* 37, no. 4: 424–36.
Varela, Francisco. 1996. "Neurophenomenology: A Methodological Remedy for the Hard Problem." *Journal of Consciousness Studies* 3, no. 4: 330–49.

WORKS CITED

Wallon, Henri. 1963. *Les origines de la pensée chez l'enfant.* Paris: Presses Universitaires de France. (Originally published in 1945.)

Weiss, Gail. 1999. *Body Images: Embodiment as Intercorporeality.* London: Routledge.

———. 2002. "The Anonymous Intentions of Transactional Bodies." *Hypatia* 17, no. 4: 187–200.

Wellman, Henry M., David Cross, and Julanne Watson. 2001. "Meta-Analysis of Theory-of-Mind Development: The Truth About False Belief Child Development." *Child Development* 72, no. 3 (May/June): 655–84.

Welsh, Talia. 2008. "The Developing Body: A Reading of Merleau-Ponty's Conception of Women in the Sorbonne Lectures." In *Intertwinings: Interdisciplinary Encounters with Merleau-Ponty,* edited by Gail Weiss, 45–59. Albany, N.Y.: SUNY Press.

Wertheimer, Max. 1925. "Über Gestalttheorie." *Symposium* 1: 19–20.

Young, Iris. 1990a. "Pregnant Embodiment: Subjectivity and Alienation." In *Throwing Like a Girl and Other Essays in Feminist Philosophy and Social Theory,* 160–74. Bloomington: Indiana University Press.

———. 1990b. "Throwing Like a Girl." In *Throwing Like a Girl and Other Essays in Feminist Philosophy and Social Theory,* 141–59. Bloomington: Indiana University Press.

———. 1998. "'Throwing Like a Girl': Twenty Years Later." In *Body and Flesh: A Philosophical Reader,* edited by Donn Welton, 286–90. London: Blackwell.

Zahavi, Dan. 1999. *Self-Awareness and Alterity: A Phenomenological Investigation.* Evanston, Ill.: Northwestern University Press.

Index

action, 5–6, 7
adualism, 50, 81, 99, 102
adults/adult experience, 7, 14, 24, 61, 105; childhood traumas relived by, 36–37; child's experience continued in, xi, xxii, 12, 19, 50; Gestalt theory and, 35; objectivity of, 10; oculocentrism of, 115; perception compared with that of children, 11
"Adult's View of the Child, The" (Merleau-Ponty lecture), 62–63
Adventures of Dialectic (Merleau-Ponty), 138n
ambivalence, xviii, 37, 38–39, 141
animals, 4, 5, 76, 82; anthropomorphizing views of, 74–75; awareness and self-awareness in, 74–75; children compared to, 23; experience of positive and negative situations, 9; instinct, 12; mirrors and, 62, 63
Anisfeld, Moshe, 84–85, 87
anthropology, xiv, 22, 23, 102, 120; cultural relativism and, 125; on attitudes toward women's strength, 134
aphasia, 32
arousal hypothesis, 85
Asendorpf, Jens B., 94–95
Asperger's syndrome, 96
autism spectrum, 83, 86–87, 91; false belief tests and, 92; interaction theory and, 98; organization of relevant/non-relevant data, 96

Bachelard, Gaston, 36
Baillargeon, Renee, 92
Beauvoir, Simone de, xxi, 129, 135, 136, 142
behavior, 26, 36; delusional, 43; pathological, 14, 16; physiology and, 31; subjective individual experience and, 22–23

behaviorism, 13
Being and Nothingness (Sartre), 117
being-in-the-world, 9, 14, 68, 126
Bergson, Henri, 5–7, 31
Bernet, Rudolf, 29
Between You and I: Dialogical Phenomenology (Stawarska), 99
Bigwood, Carol, 141–42
biology, 3, 125
birth, 20–21, 141
Bloom, Paul, 81
body, the, 3, 41, 64; body image disorders, 75; body schema and infant perception, 46–47; disintegration of boundary with mind, xiii; gender and, 146; imitation behavior and, 75–76, 80–81; mirror stage and, 61–71; objectification of, 49; perceptions and, 52; primitive body image, 78; psychology and, 25; self-awareness and, 61–62, 79; senses and, 56–57; sexuality and body consciousness, 39; vitalism and, 31. *See also* menstruation; pregnancy
Bordo, Susan, 143
Brunschvicg, Léon, 5
Butler, Judith, 141
Butterworth, George, 78, 81, 88

Cassirer, Ernst, 11
Castillo, Marcela, 78
Cézanne, Paul, 124, 149, 150
character, xii
child development, xiii, xiv, 106, 126; anticipation and regression in, 40, 41; cultural differences and, 120; as dynamic process, 35; pathological experience and, 41–42; psychoanalytic theories of, xvi–xvii, 36; scientific psychology and, 36

Child Development (journal), 94
child psychology, xiv, xxi, 3, 4, 9, 88; concrete experiments in, 151; as diverse and specialized field, xi; mentalistic presuppositions in, 99
Child Psychology and Pedagogy: The Sorbonne Lectures 1949–1952 (Merleau-Ponty), xiv, xv, xviii
children: animals compared to, 23; with autism, 83, 86–87, 91, 92, 96; creative expression in, xx–xxi; ignorance of boundary between self and others, 54–55; imitation behavior, 55, 61; interaction and understanding of, xiv; intersubjective bond with others, 48; magical explanations and, 107–13, 117; other people as subjects and, 52; pansexuality of, 39; play behavior of, 40, 41, 49; romantic ethos and, 147; theory of mind and, 82–83; time delay and self-identification, 93–94
children, "egocentrism" of, 10, 11, 18, 19, 54, 55; relationship to one's own body and, 61; situated aspect of experience and, 67–68; as unawareness of other perspectives, 101
child's experience, xi, xviii, 4, 23–24, 105, 147; adult artist and, 149; continuation in adult experience, xii, xxii, 12, 19, 50, 151; embodiment and, 34; as engaged and organized, 114; forces shaping development and, 23; Gestalt theory and, 32–33; psychoanalytic understanding of, 35, 39–40; as rooted and coherent, xx; socially interactive nature of, xiv; traumatic memories and, 16; "ultra-things" notion and, 111–12; as unique, 23, 26. *See also* infant perception
"Child's Relation with Others, The" (Merleau-Ponty lecture), xv, 62
Civilization and Its Discontents (Freud), 36
Claparède, Édouard, 117
Clark, Russell, 101
class, social, 108, 119, 120, 129, 138, 145
Cobb, William, xv
common sense, 30
complexes, psychological, 42–43
consciousness, 27, 49; action of, 7; child versus adult, 11; definition of, 7; in Gestalt theory, 38; "neither self nor other," 103–4; pathological, 43; uniqueness of, 4, 6
Consciousness and the Acquisition of Language (Merleau-Ponty), xv
coordination, 10
coupling, 45–46
Critique des fondements de la psychologie (Politzer), 12–13, 36, 119
culture, xii, 47, 48, 128, 129–130, 137; cultural relativism, 125, 148; romantic ethos and, 147

Darwinian theory, 22
death, child's understanding of, 112
Derrida, Jacques, 140
Descartes, René, 20, 146
Descartes' Baby (Bloom), 81
Deutsch, Hélène, 129
development. *See* child development; human development
dialectic, 6, 8, 9
dialogical phenomenology, 99–101, 102
Dillon, M. C., 57, 58, 59
Diprose, Rosalyn, 141, 145
Doherty, Martin J., 92
double identification, 63, 65
drawings, by children, 114–24
dreams, 18, 19, 20, 37
drive, in Freudian theory, 12
dualism, 27, 81, 82, 142, 146

education, 35
ego, 49, 62; boundaries with others, 50; face-to-face interactions and, 100; intersubjectivity and, 58; mirror stage and, 66, 70; other and, 46; transcendental, 99
Electra complex, 35–36
El Greco, 130
embodiment theory, feminist, 142, 145, 146
emotions, 18, 53, 54, 74, 75, 129
empiricism, 26–27
environment, xii, 97, 98
epistemology, xiii
essentialism, 145
Ethics of Sexual Difference, The (Irigaray), 139

INDEX

evolution, 22, 77
existentialism, xviii, 125
experience, 3, 8, 55–56; animal life and, 4; background experience concept, xvi–xvii, xviii, xix, 64; childhood and adult experience, xi; feminist theory and, 137, 138, 139–40, 142–44, 145; individual subjectivity and, 22–23; instinctual relationship with world and, 5; I-you relationship and, 100; language and, 17; perception and, 9, 19–20; philosophical theories' origin in, 27; prediscursive, 139, 141; primal, 21, 22, 44, 65, 147, 148, 151; psychoanalysis and, 37; sexual difference, 134; synesthesia and, 56, 117–18. *See also* adult experience; child's experience; lived experience
"Experience of Others, The" (Merleau-Ponty lecture), 102–3
"Eye and Mind" (Merleau-Ponty lecture), 124, 149

facial gestures/expressions, xx, 68, 79; imitative behaviors and, 84–85, 87; mirror stage and, 61; parents and, 86; social biofeedback model, 86
false belief tests, 91–92, 95, 97, 104
femininity, 136, 139
feminism, xxi, 127, 136–46
Fink, Bruce, 66
Fisher, Linda, 136–37, 145
form, 10
freedom, xii, 42, 126; of artist, 121, 130; of children, 23; development as, 126–27; of parents, 54; of women, 131, 133, 134
Freud, Sigmund, 34n, 39, 41, 46, 81, 126; Electra complex and, 35–36; on infant's response to environment, 74; instinct (drive) theory of, 12–13
Freudian theory, xviii, 12, 22; on integration of past into present, 14; latent and manifest content, 119; self-awareness in mirror stage, 70. *See also* psychoanalysis
Future of an Illusion, The (Freud), 36

Gallagher, Shaun, xx, 73, 77–78, 88–93, 100, 102, 148; on autism, 96; on bodily difference in sensory perception, 104; false belief tests criticized by, 97; on imitation, 104–5; on Merleau-Ponty's adualism, 99; "orientation" in intersubjectivity and, 103
gaze, of the other, 18
Gelb, Adhémar, 11, 125n
gender, xxi, 127, 138, 142, 145; social-political understanding of, 146; stereotypes associated with, 134, 135–36
Gender Trouble (Butler), 141
generality, 26
genetics, xii
Gergely, György, 86
Gestalt, 8, 67, 117
Gestalt theory, xiii, 3, 7, 9, 22, 31–35, 123; background experience concept, xvi–xvii, xviii, 37, 44, 118; child's experience and, xiv; Goldstein's critique of, 14; integrative approach to, 43–44; perception and, 20, 122; phenomenology united with, 10; pre-intellectual unity of things in, 124
Gibson, James, 81
Goldstein, Kurt, 11, 14, 26, 31–32, 125n, 135
Gopnik, Alison, 82, 83, 84, 89, 94
Grandin, Temple, 98
Grosz, Elizabeth, 139, 142, 143–44, 145
Guillaume, Paul, 55, 81, 103, 104
Gurwitsch, Aron, 11

hallucinations, 19, 43, 107, 143
Hegel, G.W.F., 6, 16n, 126
Heidegger, Martin, 3, 27
heterosexuality, 41, 129
history, 125, 145, 147
horizon, 37
How the Body Shapes the Mind (Gallagher), 78, 89
Huang, I., 108–9
human condition, xi, xiv, 28–29, 129; child's experience and, xxii; as historical and embodied condition, xvi; origin of philosophies in, xviii; primordial experience and, 30; psychology and, 25; science and understanding of, xii, 148; scientific psychology and, 26; social world and, 48

INDEX

human development, xii, 15–21, 26, 32, 126–27, 151; adaptability of, 84; menstruation and, 127–31; overgeneralization of, xvii; phenomenology and, 88; trauma and pathology, 14–15
Humanism and Terror (Merleau-Ponty), xv, 138n
human order, 5, 6, 8
"Human Sciences and Phenomenology" (Merleau-Ponty lecture), 28
Husserl, Edmund, xiii, xviii, 3, 9, 118; "coupling" notion, 45–46; horizon concept, 37; on intersubjectivity, 58, 103–4; phenomenology of, 24, 44; on pregnancy, 132; prescientific experience and, 30; psychology's connection with phenomenology and, 27, 29

idealism, philosophical, 5, 31
identity, 63
imitation, neonatal, 46, 55, 61, 72, 73–82; interaction theory and, 90; later imitation by infants and, 87; primary consciousness of interpersonal self and, 88; self-consciousness and, 104; synchronic imitation, 94–95, 97; tongue protrusion studies and, 84–86
Imitative Mind, The (Meltzoff and Prinz, eds.), 80
individuality, 23, 47, 51
infant perception, xvii, 7–9, 73, 123; body schema and, 46–47; Gestalt theory and, 33; goal direction and, 90; imitation behavior, 73–82; intersubjective behavior and, xix–xx; mind-body split absent from, 57; motor control and, 78; other-awareness, 53–54; self and world not distinguished, 45; self-awareness and, 61, 95; structuration and, 14; theory of mind and, 82–88. *See also* child's experience
instinct, 5, 12–13
intelligence, 5, 33–34, 49, 63
intentionality, 53, 77, 138
interaction theory, xx, 73, 88, 96, 102; contextual self-identification and, 93; false belief tests and, 97–98; pragmatism of, 90
intersubjectivity, xii, xviii, 17, 48, 98, 151; access to minds of others and, 90; adult, 50, 51, 96; false belief tests and, 104; immersion in the world and, 19; in infants, xix–xx, 57, 72, 89; interaction theory and, xx, 73, 88, 96, 97–98; mirror stage and, 60, 65, 69–70; "orientation" in, 103; precociousness of, 102; as shared experience, 46; theory of mind and, 72, 73, 74, 82, 84, 92
introspectionism, 25
Irigaray, Luce, 139, 140, 141

Jones, Susan, 85, 86, 87
Jung, Carl, 36

Kern, Iso, 29
kinesthesia, 51
Klein, Melanie, xvi
Koffka, Kurt, 123
Köhler, Wolfgang, 10, 11
Kristeva, Julia, 140

Lacan, Jacques, xvi, 36, 42, 59, 62, 71; on children's sexuality, 39, 40; mirror stage theory, xix, 45, 65–67, 70; on Narcissus myth, 70; split subject and, 140
language, xii, 8, 69, 70, 122; as bodily, lived experience, 17; experience represented by, 38; pre-linguistic foundation of, 101; social world and, 47
Laplanche, Jean, xvi
Lee, D. N., 78
lived experience, 3, 25, 55; Gestalt theory and, 22, 31; judgments and, 149; mirror stage and, 67, 68, 70; pathology as part of, 37–38; structuration and, 17; syncretic initial nature of, 59; theory and, 27, 28
Luquet, G. H., 121–22

magic, 103, 107–13, 117
Maratos, Olga, 87
Marbach, Eduard, 29
Martin, Grace, 101
Marxism, 22, 119
masculinity, 135–36
materialism, 31, 32
maturity/maturation, xxi, 19, 39, 41, 128, 132

INDEX

McGeer, Victoria, 86–87
Mead, Margaret, 135
meaning, 27, 119, 150
Meditations on First Philosophy (Descartes), 20
Meili, Richard, 117
Meltzoff, Andrew, 74, 76–80, 82, 83, 85, 88–89
memory, 77, 94
menstruation, xxi, 41, 128–31, 132, 136
mental illness, 43
Mentality of Apes (Köhler), 10
Merleau-Ponty, Maurice, xi, 3–4; on Bergson, 6–7; on development, 15–21; feminist perspectives and, 136–46; Freudian theory and, 12, 35–36, 39; Husserl and, xiii, 27, 28, 103–4; on infant perception, 7–9; on mirror stage, 61–71; on origin of pathology, xvii; on Piaget, 33, 108–9; research project of, 9–10; on scientific "objectivity," xii; on sexual difference, 134–35; Sorbonne lectures of, xiv, xv–xvi, 12, 22, 23
metaphysics, 149
Mill, John Stuart, 24
mind, theory of, 72, 73, 77, 82–88; false belief tests and, 91, 92; interaction theory contrasted with, 98–99; intersubjectivity and, 96; mentalistic presuppositions of, 93; time delay and self-identification, 93–94
"Mirror Stage, The" (Lacan), 67
mirror stage theory, xix, 45, 59–70, 89
Moore, M. Keith, 74, 76–77, 81, 85
Moran, Dermot, 11
Morgenstern, Sophie, 119
mother-infant interaction, 8, 9, 100, 101
motivation, xii

Nagel, Thomas, 19
nature–nurture conflict, 125–26
Neisser, Ulric, 81
neurology, xii, 9, 10, 23, 31
Nietzschean thought, 22

objectivity, 13, 19, 25, 35
O'Connor, Flannery, xi
oculocentrism, 57, 115, 139
Oedipus complex, 40

Organism, The [*Der Aufbau des Organismus*] (Goldstein), 14
Oksala, Johanna, 138, 142, 145, 146
Onishi, Kristine, 92
"Only Tongue Protrusion Modeling Is Matched by Neonates" (Anisfeld), 84–85
optical illusions, 32
order of life, 132, 133, 136, 139, 141
organization, perceptual, 10
others/otherness, 45, 54; infants' understanding of self and other, 72, 76, 77; mirror stage and, 60, 70; other-awareness, 97, 98; subjectivities of others, 52

parents: mimicry of facial expressions, 86; mirror stage and, 59–60, 63–64, 65, 66
pathology, 14–15, 16, 32, 37–38, 42–43
perception, 5, 7, 16, 140, 150; adult, 114, 118, 122, 123, 124; body image and, 81; of children and adults, 11; children's logic of, 106; dialectical nature of, 9; drawings by children and, 114, 115, 118, 120–23; Gestalt theory and, 10, 32; hallucinations differentiated from, 43; intelligence and, 33–34; language and, 69, 70; nascent, 7–15; normative nature of, 8, 9; phenomenology and, 28; primal/primordial, 57; "scientific" status of, 19; senses and, 56–57; structure within, 13; synesthetic, xxi; "telepathic," 102–3. *See also* infant perception
Perner, Josef, 82
Phenomenological Psychology (Husserl), 29
phenomenology, 3, 9, 22–30, 150; dialogical, 99–101; existentialism and, xviii, 102; as exploration of child's world, xii; feminist, 143, 145; gender and, 136; gender-neutral, xxi; Gestalt theory united with, 10; integrative approach to, 43–44; lived experience and, 139; neonatal imitation studies and, 88; postmodernism and, xiii; psychology in convergence with, xvii, 27; subject-centered, 50; of subjectivity, xx
"Phenomenology and the Sciences of Man" (Merleau-Ponty lecture), xv

INDEX

Phenomenology of Perception (Merleau-Ponty), xvii, 3, 27, 103, 125, 145; on childhood and adult experiences, 50; on embodied self, 140; on freedom and embodiment, 126; on gendered experience, 137–38; Gestalt theory in, 32; Husserl's influence and, xiii; on others' subjectivities, 52; on perception's grounding role, 16–17; on prescientific experiential world, 29; on scientific methodology, 24–25; on self and primordial existence, 57
Philosophical Baby, The (Gopnik), 84
philosophy, xvii, 7, 71, 148, 151; human sciences and, 28; neo-Kantian, 5, 9, 11; oculocentrism and, 57; psychology integrated with, 11, 24, 29–30; sciences and, 3, 4–5
physiology, 10, 25, 31, 128, 132
Piaget, Jean, xv, 10, 19, 81; on child as natural metaphysician, xx, 110; Gestalt theory and, 33–34; on imitation and infant's body schema, 46; on infant's response to environment, 74; on magical explanations by children, 108–9; psychology of cognition, 63; stage-theory of, 17, 51, 83, 126
Picasso, Pablo, 118, 120
Poincaré, Henri, 5
Politzer, Georges, 12–13, 14, 36, 119
Ponge, Francis, 118
positivism, 24
postmodernism, xiii
poststructuralism, 112, 141
Povinelli, Daniel, 93, 94
pregnancy, xxi, 127, 130, 131–36, 139–146
Primacy of Perception, The (Merleau-Ponty), xv
Prinz, Wolfgang, 80, 83
Psychanalyse infantile (Morgenstern), 119
psychiatry, xii
psychoanalysis, xiii, xvi, 22, 26, 35–44, 71, 102; ambivalence and the unconscious, xviii; causality and, 12; diagnosis of children's disorders, 116; drawings by children and, 118–19; feminist theory and, 141; integrative approach to, 43–44; of lived experience, 139; split subject and, 140. *See also* Freudian theory

psychology, xii, 3, 7, 44, 125, 151; of cognition, 63; cultural overdetermination and, xii–xiii; developmental, xvi; diagnosis of children's disorders, 116; experimental, xvi, 9, 23; objective (scientific), 13, 26, 32, 148; oculocentrism and, 57; phenomenology in convergence with, xvii, 27; philosophy integrated with, 11, 24
Psychology of Women, The (Deutsch), 129
puberty, 41

"Question of Method in Child Psychology, The" (Merleau-Ponty), 54–55, 63, 81

race, 137, 138, 145
reciprocity, 57–58
representation, 77, 93, 95, 96, 115, 121
repression, 15
research, experimental, xiv, 44, 82
Rochat, Philippe, 101
romanticism, 147
rouge test, 93–94

Sartre, Jean-Paul, 36, 117, 147
Scheler, Max, 27
Schneider (brain-damaged patient), 11, 125, 137
Science and Method (Poincaré), 5
sciences, 146, 148; Darwinian revolution in, 22; division with philosophy, 4–5; human sciences, xviii, 28–29; magic and scientific thinking and, 107–13; methodology of, 24; "objectivity" of, xii, 31
scientism, 31, 44
Second Sex, The (Beauvoir), 129, 136
Selected Papers (Köhler), 10
self, birth of, 44, 54, 58–71; innate sense of selfhood, 45; mirror stage and, 60, 82; primordial existence and, 57
Sense and Non-Sense (Merleau-Ponty), xv
"Sense of Self and Others, The" (Gallagher and Meltzoff), 77–78
sexuality, 22, 39, 40–41, 119, 129, 137
Silverman, Hugh J., xv
Skinner, B. F., 74
Slaughter, Virginia, 94
sociology, xiv, 102, 125

INDEX

speech, 6, 17, 23, 99
spiritualism, 5
Stawarska, Beata, xx, 73, 88, 102, 105, 148; dialogical phenomenology of, 99–101; "orientation" in intersubjectivity and, 103
Stendhal, 134, 135
stereotypes, gender, 134, 135–36
Stoller, Silvia, 138
Structure of Behavior, The (Merleau-Ponty), xvii, 3, 9, 17, 123; on artist's vision, 149; on child and adult behavior, 50; on earliest experience of life, 4; Freudian theory and, 12, 13; Gestalt theory in, 32
structure/structuration, 7, 10, 14–15, 16, 123
subjectivity, xx, 47; adult, 77; childhood and formation of, xiii; emergence of, 63; mirror stage and, 70; other-identification alongside, 53; syncretic primordial stage and, 71; transcendental, 58
Sullivan, Shannon, 137, 138
symbolic order, 14
symbolization, 8, 118, 119
synchronic imitation, 94–95, 97
syncretic sociability, xix, xx, xxi, 45, 71, 74; critique of, 88–89; dualism and, 81; as ego living in others, 49–50; feminist theory and, 141; infantile, 47; intersubjectivity and, 102; "pre-communication" and, 55, 89; primal experience as, 148; as shared experience, 52–53; uniqueness of, 105
synesthesia, 56–57, 114, 117–18

Three Essays on the Theory of Sexuality (Freud), 36

"Throwing Like a Girl" (Young), 138–39, 144
"Throwing Like a Girl: Twenty Years Later" (Young), 144
Totem and Taboo (Freud), 36
traumas, childhood, xiii, xvii, 14, 16, 36, 43
truth, 5, 8, 22, 125

"Über Gestalttheorie" (Wertheimer), 11
"ultra-things" notion, 55, 111–12
Unbearable Weight (Bordo), 143
unconscious, Freudian, xviii, 22, 37, 38, 39

van der Meer, A. L. H., 78
van der Weel, F. R., 78
Varela, Francisco, 88
Visible and the Invisible, The (Merleau-Ponty), xiii, 142, 150–51
vitalism, 6, 31
vital order, 5
Volatile Bodies (Grosz), 143

Wallon, Henri, xix, 34n, 45, 59, 62, 67n, 68; on body image, 79; on emergence of subjectivity, 63; on self and mirror stage, 60–61; on syncretic sociability, 49–50; "ultra-things" notion, 55, 111–12
Watson, John, 13
Weiss, Gail, 138, 141, 142, 143
Wellman, Henry M., 92
Wertheimer, Max, 11
Wild, John, xv
Wordsworth, William, 48

Young, Iris Marion, 138–39, 140–41, 144

Zahavi, Dan, 99, 100

About the Author

Talia Welsh is a University of Chattanooga Foundation associate professor of philosophy at the University of Tennessee at Chattanooga.